Glossary of Undisciplined Design

Anja Kaiser
Rebecca Stephany
(eds.)

Spector Books

D for Dear Reader

A glossary traditionally comes at the ry beginning or end of a book or text on a rticular subject. It contains definitions d explanations of words, concepts or ex– essions that are unusual, specialized or wly coined in the main text and might t, therefore, be obvious to the reader. A ossary usually represents a particular main of knowledge or field of study and commonly listed in alphabetical order.

From 'U for Unstable Signs' to 'F for iling Queerly,' 'M for Monster's Tools' 'D for Dysfunctional Workspaces,' this llection of 52 glossary entries is not und to a specific work of writing, rather attaches to many situations and contexts thin / around the sphere of graphic de– gn—texts, books, objects, people, biogra– ies, institutions, canons and histories.

Like a tiny, bloodsucking horn fly bitin into the skin of a cow, catchweed hook–ing its hairs onto animal fur to help dispers its seeds, or chewing gum stuck to the sol of a shoe, the *Glossary of Undisciplined Design* (*GUD*) offers additional definition and concepts for the field of graphic desig and its current state.

Glossary entries are typically in–betwe texts that are read by flipping from the ma text to the glossary. They help the reader to pause and make sense. What you consid the "main body" of this glossary to be with the radius of our discipline—what you put it next to in order to go back and forth—is to you, dear reader.

Not a(nother) Branding Exercise

To us, undisciplinarity is not a(nother) binary branding exercis to oppose supposedly systematic, classical or neat approaches to designing. Neither do we propose to "undo" graphic design altogethe as a field with a specific history, knowledge and set of skills. Rather we work with undisciplinarity as a feminist unpacking of the disci–pline of graphic design itself, from its particularly one–sided canon an marginalizing historiography and lingering modernist residues,*

* Here and throughout our contributions to *GUD*, we use "modernist" to refer to the influence that Modernism has had on the field of design for better or for worse, until today. As a set of different cultural movements in Western societies of the late nineteenth, early twentieth century, in response to the Western modernity project of technologica advancements, industrialization and profound societal transformation, Modernism bore enormous progressive, culturally subversive potential *and* manifested the dominance of a Western, male world conception—this is where our criticism comes in. Especially in graphic design, this perspective, as well as formalist tropes of efficiency, neutrality an objectivity continue to define and legitimize "good" practice (and practitioners) and remain largely unquestioned.

discriminatory structures and biased definitions that continue
reinforce disadvantages in the field.

The project of undisciplinarity and unpacking is ongoing and velops along with the discipline of graphic design. It is as entangled h our field, its problems and developments, as it is responding to Un–" thus describes and puts into practice the interdependent pro-s of understanding, evaluating, questioning and critical self-re-ction, toward imagining alternate futures for design.

The increasingly expanding field of design has brought about a lening of roles and identifications for designers, leading to a variety definitions and purposes for design work.** At the same time, our ign community seems rather fixated on the figure of the reasonable, dworking expert or the singular star-designer and the marginaliz-definitions of success that come with it. Unsurprisingly, these are e archetypes and manifestations of patriarchal, capitalist and Euro-tric imprints that we need to collectively demystify and dismantle.

This Context is Messy: Complicating Authorship

The *Glossary of Undisciplined Design* is a collaborative initiative designers and educators Anja Kaiser and Rebecca Stephany. The e stemmed from what was conceived as a one-time, joint lecture de-red at GfZK (Leipzig Museum of Contemporary Art) in April 2019, er which point the project developed into different formats: a series ectures, various modes of teaching and a symposium at GfZK ich took place February 20–23, 2020).*** These formats ultimately

, The classic definition of graphic design as a "problem solving" fession, or, at least, a clearly demarcated domain of products and vices, has become increasingly blurry in recent decades, if only in cultural hubs of the Global North. Largely due to the creative im-ative and the promise of self-realization in Western capitalist econo-s, a designer's self-understanding and areas of responsibility have ened to include and address questions of authorship, work at the inter-tion of art, design and theory, as well as organizing, writing curating.

As a museum of contemporary art, the programming of GfZK insists on nterdisciplinary approach to the various modes of contemporary cul-al production and, as such, has established a unique relationship with field of design and graphic design in particular. The GfZK awards annual *INFORM* prize for conceptual design for practices at the inter-tion of graphic design and art (Anja was *INFORM* awardee in 2017, ecca in 2009). Initiated in 2007 by Barbara Steiner, then Director of K, the prize (worth 5,000 euros) is associated with an exhibition, ering a unique opportunity to explore new formats for the production presentation of graphic design in collaboration with the GfZK. rdees include: Nathalie du Pasquier, Karl Nawrot, Experimental Jetset, vs and Tatars, James Langdon, Urs Lehni, Zak Kyes, Julia Born and rent Benner.

served as the extended editorial framework for the *GUD* handbook.*

What follows is a detailed description of the genesis of t project, as it was vital for us to not only posit critique on issues of structural inequality in the field of design, but to put the kind of demands that come about from our feminist positionality to practice within the specific framework of *GUD*. The various formats of the *GUD* project were shaped by a rethinking of structures of participation and collaboration, as well as of the redistribution of financial resources.

In 2017, we began an exchange, just between the two of us, about our specific situatedness as educators and practition in the extended field of graphic design *and* as feminists. As we were both feeling increasingly uncomfortable with the stereotypical pr ciples and role models that were perpetuated by most design schools we knew, we had begun to critically examine our respective semina apparatuses independently of each other. With the intention of devising more inclusive and pertinent tools for teachi we had been researching and adding voices and references which we then began to share and disc with each other.

In April of 2019, we presented this collectio of tools, theories, practices and biographies in the form of a public lecture at GfZK and called it *Gloss of Undisciplined Design*. Introducing 25 terms, th first version of *GUD* was a performative live-asse blage of undisciplined methods and strategies for graphic design. We also introduced the practices c peers and designers of an older generation—such as April Greiman and Sheila Levrant de Bretteville—and pointed to references in femi design theory and critical writing on issues of technology, cultural precarity, visibility and solidarity. With the format of a fragmentary gl sary, we were interested in talking about the larger, messier context that our work and educational approaches are situated in and inform by, instead of presenting our practices as a consecutive story of individual success, illustrated with hi-res images of final outcomes and happy endings.

During informal conversations that followed the lecture and, la on, together with Franciska Zólyom, Director of GfZK, the desire gre to more closely involve the people and peers we talked about during our lecture. We decided to translate our approach to the glossary in a handbook as a way to further develop and expand it. This decision

**** We refer to *GUD* as a handbook, as our intention with it is to "be of use," instructive and supportive. With the narrative structure of a glossary, we deliberately refrain from a linear organization of infor mation or specific set of instructions toward a predefined goal.

would also give us the opportunity to literally place a decidedly fragmented, polyphonous body of design knowledge as a physical object between design history books and notorious designer monographs.

In order to manifest the glossary as a publication, it was important to us that we open the project up and invite design practitioners, educators, theorists and students to add their own terms and concepts. As this approach demanded a plurality of voices, complications and contradictions, we decided to organize a symposium in collaboration with GfZK. We conceived of the conference as an experimental editorial engine that would help us make the ok by establishing a working relationship with everyone involved, making actual encounters between our contributors possible l by mapping and representing the discussions and exchanges that uld take place between all participants.

Polyphony in the Classroom: Sticky Pedagogies

The desires we have for the field of graphic design are substantially informed—if not provoked—by our respective roles in design education, especially by our discussions and experiences with students. Their observations and feelings of urgency around graphic design have sharpened the kinds of questions we direct toward our discipline, as well as the responsibilities we feel toward our students and our role as educators. With awareness that, within the structure of school, students and chers are not equal in terms of power, our understanding of design lagogy is one of holding space for participatory equity. Particularly he context of *GUD*, it would have been paradoxical to not include dents and young practitioners, as they play a decisive role in shaping futures of design.

In order to involve students in the organization of the *GUD Symium*, we offered a preparatory seminar that took place between tober 2019—February 2020 at the Karlsruhe University of Arts and sign (HfG Karlsruhe), where Rebecca taught from 2016 to 2021. ing the preliminary glossary terms of our lecture format as a starting nt, the participating students added terms and knowledge, which they felt were missing in the current discourse on design. They then developed individual and collaborative glossary terms as contributions to the symposium. The resulting projects took the form of printed matter, performance, tool speculation, video essay, installation, workshop or participatory intervention. Among other questions, the students asked: How can industrialized printing processes be destabilized with a queer approach to failure? What would a layout tool look like that only provided wobbly grids? How can the wandering eye be nurtured during a day full of lectures?

All of these works have been translated into glossary entries for the *GUD* handbook, as well as the results of two other teaching formats: In December 2019, we workshopped a glossary term titled 'M for Mad-Mad-Mad-PR' with students of Burg Giebichenstein University of Art and Design Halle (BURG). In the course of one week, the participating students developed a fictive parallel program for the *GUD Symposium*, as a slippery intervention to imagine design history differently. Meanwhile, in Leipzig, Prof. Markus Dreßen, together with students of the Book Design/Graphic Design Foundational course at the Academy of Fine Arts Leipzig, set up a temporary studio where students investigated the potential of undisciplinarity over the course of a semester, from quick drawing exercises to prototypical sculptures.

A Many-Bodied Editorial Engine

The *GUD Symposium* was conceived as an experimental editorial meeting for the *GUD* handbook and a testing ground for possible polyphonic extensions to the glossary. With that format, we wanted to experiment with alternate modes of learning, knowledge production and dissemination, as well as feminist networking.

The symposium brought together seven international designers, researchers and educators of different ages and experiences in practice, whose work we had been referring to or introducing in our lecture format: Sheila Levrant de Bretteville, Clara Balaguer, Ece Canlı, Hackers & Designers (Anja Groten and Juliette Lizotte), Jungmyung Lee, Sara Kaaman, as well as students of HfG Karlsruhe and BURG. Exploring different aspects of, for example, intersectional or queer-feminist perspectives on graphic design, the presentations, lectures a workshops ranged from reflections on the decolonization of design and modes for collective design practices, to queering the history of design.

We approached the programming of the symposium as a patchwork. Just like how small pieces of different kinds of fabric are sewn together into a larger design, the three-day conference was an attempt at "horizontal" programming: lectures, workshops, eating together, as well as performative and spatial interventions were all treated with equal importance. The in-between moments became the yarn that connected these different bits of patchwork to a bigger piece of *GUD*.*****

The first day of the symposium was dedicated to a collective effort to compile the vocabulary of *GUD* with a day full of lectures and presentations. The symposium scenography, designed by students of HfG Karlsruhe, offered a playful and non-hierarchical turn on the traditional separation of speaker and audience. The speakers themselves worked with performative scripts and additional voices.

On the second day, we focused on rehearsing the vocabulary of *GUD* with a day of workshops by our contributors, from exploring collective forms of human-computer interactions or embodied ways of designing, to critically assessing the all-pervading dichotomies engrained in language.

Throughout the weekend, students of HfG Karlsruhe and BURG organized and hosted different informal and discursive settings and interventions: guided tours through all exhibited student projects, a baking workshop with talks about work routines, a summer roll bar with edible glossary terms or a large typographical blanket under ich participants could retreat for private conversations. These litional moments of togetherness, exchange and care made it possi- for all symposium participants to become active pieces of the 'D patchwork.

** We are interested in patchwork as a feminist strategy for design: Canlı uses patchwork as a method when writing about design history n a queer-feminist perspective, as an interlinking of history, theory, ctice and criticism in a distinctly messy and non-linear temporality. ila Levrant de Bretteville uses the example of women's patchwork as an thetic practice for organizing different, non-hierarchical visual ities around many centers and she takes up this method by creating struc- es of participation in design that encourage the piecing together lifferent personal experiences.

Feminismsssssssss

Our understanding of feminism is manifold. To us, feminism nee to be thought of and practiced in plurality, in order to do justice to the different kinds of needs for empowerment and urges for emancipati We resonate with bell hooks' definition of feminism as a movement to end sexist oppression and exploitation, as it addresses all members of society without neglecting other forms of oppression, such as racism or classism. Jack Halberstam fueled our visual and textual arguments by introducing us to queer modes of thinking and failing, especially with regards to our disciplinary understanding of success in heteronormative, capitalist societies. We also rest on the shoulders of Simone de Beauvoir, who insisted on the radical nature of freedom and spurred generations of women to seek independence.

The *GUD* project in its entirety—from the lecture series to our teaching formats, the symposium to this very handbook—is dedicate to undisciplined knowledge production for the field of graphic design, supported by a self-consciously feminist backbone and an unapologe emphasis on practice. With *GUD*, we actively acknowledge the diffe ent theories and movements of feminisms—intersectional, Marxist, queer feminist and others—and honor the people and waves of feminisms that have come before us and have carried us to where we are today. In the same vein, the voices of our contributing authors from different generations complement and complicate each other.

As editors, we are aware that we ourselves are endowed with certain privileges and experiences (being white, cis and from middlecl backgrounds, for example) and are therefore implicated in the perpet ation of structural inequalities. The funding we were able to obtain fr various European institutions and foundations in order to finance the *GUD Symposium* and handbook speaks volumes about the kind of a cess we have to educational and cultural institutions, and to the kinds of legitimization and visibility they produce.

Entangling the Main Body

The *Glossary of Undisciplined Design* as a publishing projec subscribes to the power of naming things and to writing as a way to write something into existence. The language and wording of the glo sary entries is, therefore, often imaginative and suggestive, reparative rather than paranoid, with a humorous and emancipatory approp ation of derogatory language.

For us, as initiators, editors and co-authors of the *GUD* handbook, the decision to complicate questions of authorship by committing to the adventure of working in many voices, in both text and design, has been a joyful and, at times, challenging consequence of this feminist undertaking. The steady accumulation of email threads with contributors, lithographers, translators, funding partners, our dear copy editor, project coordinator, publisher and printer aside, the project hardly fits into any predefined structure, from funding criteria to communicating a list of 23 names as "authors of the book."

While the form of a glossary points to a supposedly didactic rpose, the collection of entries in the *Glossary of Undisciplined sign* is decidedly pluralistic, "untidy" and fragmentary, : up for multiple definitions, complications and contrations. Overall, the 52 terms, arranged in no particular ler, reflect the various, often organic ways in which glossary came about: Contributors to the *GUD mposium* developed entries to the glossary based on ir lectures and workshops; students translated their ividual projects and contributions to the symposium o visual essays; we both developed glossary terms that we had been senting in the format of the lecture into versions for print. As many ntributors are designers, everyone was invited to design their contrition, as an acknowledgment of their visual autonomy.

The *GUD* handbook is best understood s self-consciously incomplete: With its xplicitly fragmentary and experimental ditorial strategy, the handbook is capable f attaching to the "main body," which, for s, is the field of graphic design itself. Yet, ur pleas for design's futures are palpable s, behind every glossary entry, there is particular desire or demand: to collectively ethink universalism as rebellious and omething that insists on equity for all, stead of subsuming everyone under ne same definition of equal; to counter the narrative of the solo–designer with a network of solidarity that doesn't gloss over issues of exhaustion or precarity; or to insist on low–threshold participatior in digital tools for design beyond the estab lished software monopoly.

In this light, we are inviting a multitude of readings and hope to foster discussions about the propositions in the *GUD* hand–book. We believe that understanding and recognizing our respective differences and different experiences is prerequisite for more varied forms of participation, cooper-ation and knowledge, as well as tools for teaching, learning and practice.

You, dear reader, are invited to read an use the *Glossary of Undisciplined Design* as you wish. What kind of "main body" you would like to temporarily attach it to is up to you. You could re–read a specific book o design, take a closer look at your design school, re–examine the canon or check in with your current working conditions. Or, simply, read along its visual opulence as a handbook in its own right.

Onward,
Anja and Rebecca

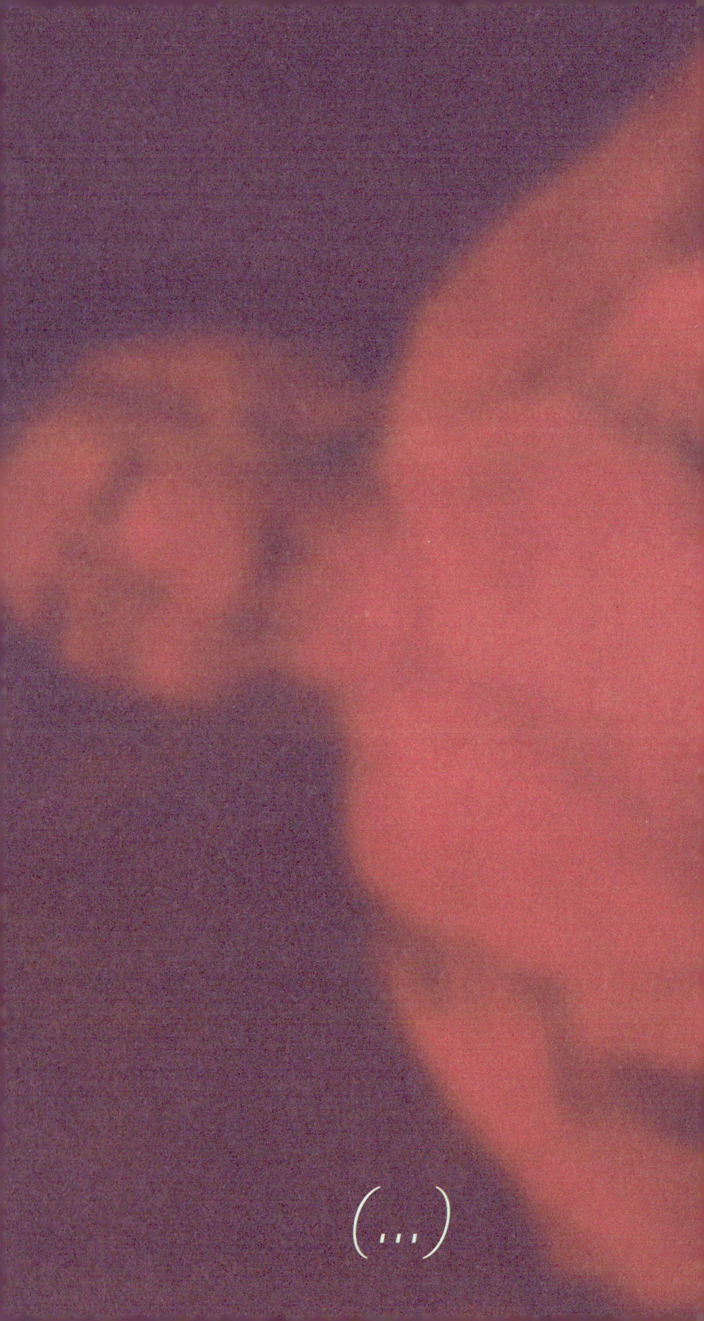

ce upon a time

BODIES, ROOMS, MOVEMENTS, FICTIONS

ome to your present life.
everything that is made can be
e. All history is Unnatural — as
netic — as in Polyester — as in
History can be stretched.

ory is a copy of a copy of a
a copy of a copy of a history
s, from the beginning, a copy of
e's blurry memory.

stories that I will tell you are
and fluid, like the insides of
ies. Language is slippery and
reate worlds. Some words make
more convincing. Some people
ings. Some people are in doubt.

ou do not want to speak as
wer', you talk with a lot
nks and holes and ques-
arks. Perhaps you have no
to fix meaning, which may
mes lead you to a place
sense. But, in language,
hen you work with nonsense,
find meaning. Nonsense,
, holes and gaps could be
stations of confusion but
lso open up to new possi-
es if we don't try to fill
ith the pre-known and the
ar. — Trinh T. Minh-ha[1]

f these — my — words are, by
on, limited. They are subject-
ated in time and space, in this
ar body, with its own particu-
ery history. I speak through a
choir of collaborators, friends (Maryam Fanni, Matilda Flodmark, Robynn McPherson, Jessica Gysel, Katja Mater, Marnie Slater, Nicole Killian, and so many more).

It might have been the artist, writer and poet, Elizam Escobar, who said "The struggle is (also) between one fiction and another."

Welcome to the struggle. Welcome to a soup of past and future fictions.

ONCE UPON A TIME, there was something called

"graphic design."

Graphic design was

optimistic,

complicit,
idealistic, naive, narcissistic, confused.

Graphic design was a kind of

"job."

A job was something you did, often in exchange for money, to be able to pay for

things.

Another word for job is "labor." Labor means "work." Work means an activity involving mental or physical effort done in order to achieve a result. A task to be undertaken. A thing to be done.

The things that graphic designers had to do, in exchange for money, was arranging words and images on surfaces.

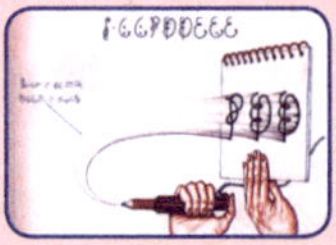

Codex Seraphinianus
Luigi Serafini, 1981

Money was a system of symbo
invented to move objects and no
objects between people. Humans
the money they had earned doing
that had to be done, to have a saf
place to sleep, to cook, eat and w
Sometimes they paid for care, m
or emotional. They paid to acces

life.

ONCE UPON A TIME, man
graphic designers spent much tir
wanting to understand what they
doing in the world, and why, and
whom. They talked to each other
wrote books, they gathered in sy
Some searched for the origin sto
graphic design. The creation myt

Where had graphic design com
and why was it here, and why we
all doing it? They looked into fo
colors and machines, searching f
meaning and answers. What was
for? Sometimes they cried into f
and platforms. They cried into sp
of books and magazines, hiding
despair and confusion behind glo
covers and shiny, foil blocked le

Many graphic designers found
Answer in something called

grids.

d was an arrangement of lines
easurements, drawn onto a paper
r digital sheet. The grid was a
and a safety net. It lent security
iciency to the things

that had to be done.

world leaned back into the grid.
were worshipped, replicated,
uced. Words and letters were
ed onto the grid. Many things
be sprinkled onto grids.

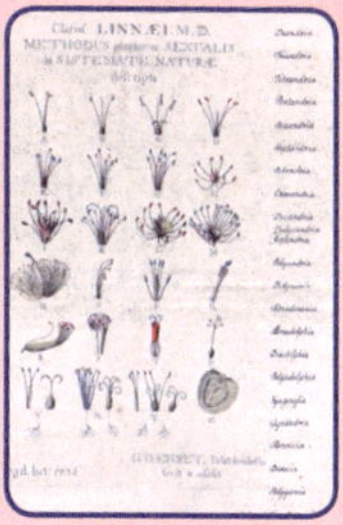

Systema Naturae, Carl von Linné, 1735

Flowers,

'The Country's Races', images presented in the showcase from the Swedish State Institute for Racial Biology at the Stockholm Exhibition, 1930

humans,

nature.

ONCE UPON A TIME, grids were considered useful tools to achieve overview, control, order, structure. The result seemed to be a certain kind of readability. Reliability.

As the legend goes, in the middle of the 20th century, a handsome young white man called

Joe
wrote a big, orange

book.

Joe was from a geographical area formerly known as

in what used to be called "Western Europe." For some reason, much of what was considered the Holy Scriptures of Graphic Design had been composed in the ancient kingdoms of this part of the world. Joe was very convincing. He spoke in tongues,

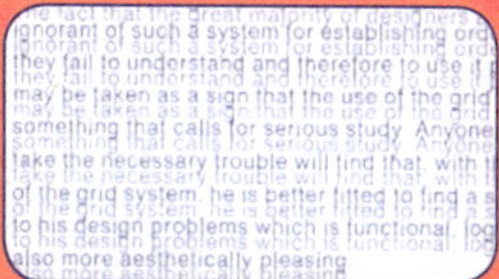
ignorant of such a system for establishing ord
they fail to understand and therefore to use it p
may be taken as a sign that the use of the grid
something that calls for serious study. Anyone
take the necessary trouble will find that, with t
of the grid system, he is better fitted to find a s
to his design problems which is functional, log
also more aesthetically pleasing

preaching and praying, praising the grid as a safe haven, away from the incomprehensible, the distorted, the queer. Where before there might have been a pile of *stuff*—of words and letters and images, an entangled mess of life—grids created surfaces of order and borders.

The Holy Scriptures of Graphic Design told stories of (men) revolutionizing, changing, pushing the field of graphic design, into new forms, new colors, new ways of gridding. The

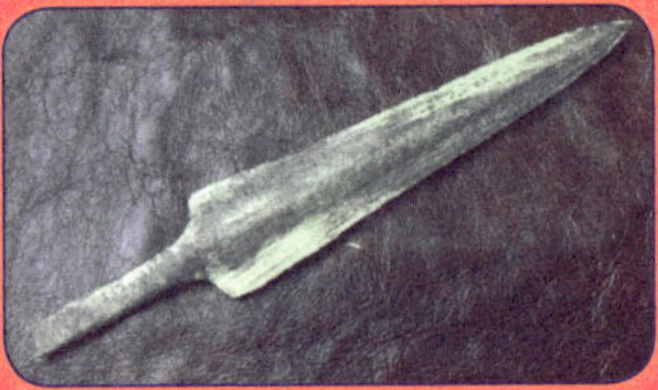

spearheads
of the field.

Spearhead is another word for avant-garde, meaning being on the forefront of, meaning being cutting edge, meaning cutting, meaning being a weapon, meaning being at war. Many of the missionaries who believed in saving humanity from illegibility and dangerous dissonance left Europe for North America, where the Holy Scriptures gathered more strength. They brought the canons and built new

canons.

The Holy Scriptures of Graphic Design, along with the words of Joe & the Grids, gathered masses of devoted followers. The followers were called "graphic designers." Some followers came together to form larger gatherings,

companies or businesses, also kn

"studios."
Some worked on their own

Image by @designershumor

Graphic designers set up their
of worship

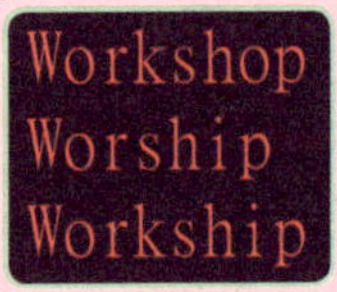

in many urban centers of the w

The natural habitat of the graphi
designer shared some recurring c
teristics. It had what was known
"desktop computer." There was o
window. There was probably a li
of selected Holy Scriptures printe
paper. There were plants and pos
In this "studio," the designer was
at work. Laboring. Doing the thin
that had to be done. To get the m
To be able to pay for the food, co
plants, books, posters, pants, sho
tomatoes, travels, bags, beers.

The desktop computer attached
graphic designer was also known
"laptop." A laptop was a small m
box—a top for the lap—emittin
light and containing the tools for
the things that had to be done. Or
one person at a time could labor
laptop. The work of the designer
tucked away in this small metal b
out of sight, within the warm dar
of the laptop.

CE UPON A TIME, the design-
becoming designer, repeating
oreography of the designer. She
nding designer emails, pushing
er pixels, naming designer files
ders.

eating the work of ~~typing~~
ing, my body comes to feel
ain way. My neck gets sore,
stretch to ease the dis-
t. I pull my shoulders back
now and then as the posture
me (a bad posture I am
is a huddle: I huddle over
ble as I repeat the action
anging of keys with the tips
fingers; the action shapes
d it leaves its impression
h bodily sensations, prickly
gs and the skin surface, and
re intense experience of
fort. I ~~write~~ design, and,
forming this work, I might
come my object and become a
designer, with a ~~writer's~~
er's body and a ~~writer's~~
er's tendencies.
a Ahmed[2]
te edited by Sara Kaaman)

part of her daily practice, the
designer performed many rit-
ritual is *a ceremony consisting*
ries of actions performed accord-
a prescribed order. One of these
was called

"social media."

cial media ritual involved rapid
tion on JPEGs, GIFs and moving
, using your fingers you smeared
cross the surface of your ritual-
vice. The purpose of this ritual
blur the boundaries between
ction and Disconnection and
cy and Privacy and Promotion.

ONCE UPON A TIME, we showed much tenderness and care towards our technological devices and extensions.

ONCE UPON A TIME, we had eyes. We used them to discriminate and divide. We used them to read illuminated squares on a grid. We used them to discern ourselves from others. We used them to determine the value of everything: beautiful from ugly from cool from boring from stunning from nice.

ONCE UPON A TIME, the graphic designer was convinced that she could find community and companionship in competition. Sometimes by actually, literally, competing in competitions where products of her labor would compete against the labor of others.

Design competitions, book competitions, poster competitions, gender design competitions. A competition is: *the activity or condition of striving to gain or win something by defeating or establishing superiority over others.*

ONCE UPON A TIME, the graphic designer was convinced that her individual creativity and success would lead to happiness. Being an individual felt exciting. It felt like

freedom.

Freedom was invented in the early 1400s. It was given away for free to some humans. Others received no freedom.

ONCE UPON A TIME, there were no graphic designers.

This

is a photograph of five women, in 1873, working at a printing office in Stockholm, Sweden. They're wearing black dresses and white aprons, dirty from the lead dust. Their work involves heavy metal. They work with typography.

This

is a photograph from a meeting of the Swedish Association for Typographers, on March 7, 1874. A union is: *a society or association formed by people with a common interest or purpose*.

Around the world, printers and typesetters were among the first professions to create unions. The first workers' association in Sweden was the

Swedish Association for Typographers (formed in 1846). On March 7, 1874, a member of the organization submits a proposal to allow typographers and typesetters of the female gender to join. The proposal is denied by a voting majority, the vote is accompanied by anger and laughter.

This

is a photograph from the next meeting, on April 11, 1874. Another member

insists that nowhere in the regula-
tions is male gender mentioned as
requirement for membership. The
of the organization replies that it
course, not necessary to state the
ous—that, of course, no women
be considered typesetters, even if
worked as such. Several other me
and heated discussions follow wh
men-members worry about typese
jeopardizing the health of the wo
about women dumping the salarie
about women not being fit for the
It takes 14 years of processing the
On March 3, 1888, the first five f
members join the organization.

This

is a photograph of six women aro
a table, another 16 years later, in
They're not working, they're orga
izing. They have formed Typogra
Kvinnoklubben (Women's Typog
Association). Even though they a
welcome as members of the natio
union, they see their specific strug
undermined by their male comrad
the Women's Typographic Assoc
they organize to confront further
allegations of women's lesser val
skill as typographers—within the
as well as in public debates and ir
newspapers.

This

is Beatrice Warde in 1925.

You might have heard about her.
Beatrice Warde was a writer and
researcher on typography. She wo
as a marketing manager for the
Monotype Corporation. She also
about typography. Her most famo

titled 'The Crystal Goblet, or
ng Should Be Invisible.' This
as become a staple in graphic
education worldwide, forcing
a graphic design student to look
word

goblet.

'59, Beatrice Warde is interviewed
her life and practice and says:

ing trade is barred to
. on the craftsman level.
an't be apprenticed to the
ing trade if you're a woman,
t in certain forms like
ng and all that, and that's
true for many centuries.[3]

Warde's position and situated
edge—probably from her read-
the histories that were available
—this was a truth. It gives the
ssion that, according to Warde,
n have been absent from printing
ny centuries.

—

Members of the Women's Typographic Association in 1925

look at the struggles of the many
n in typography during the 20th
y, along with the words of Warde
9. Remember how easy it is to
version of history—a kind of
—that reproduces someone's
pots, and then, through repeti-
ecomes a fact. Remember how
is to listen to the singular voices,
nple stories—one woman's voice.
se this one voice might be clearer,
to make out. It is, most probably,
asily available. Remember how
is to not hear the words of choirs
asses, because they speak over
and through each other. Annoying, too loud, too messy. Remember how easily we all look in the same corners of history, finding the same names, the same narratives.

Often, the stories that we find—or look for—happen to match quite well with a contemporary understanding of what a "graphic designer" looks like. One individual, working alone, "breaking ground," "pushing the field."

All this is to say that a female historiography is not necessarily a feminist historiography. And a feminist historiography is not necessarily an intersectional historiography. And the way we write history today affects the way we imagine the field of graphic design tomorrow.

Some words are less legible, some stories are less legible, some people are less legible. In the words of writer and artist Litia Perta:

unintelligibility is the risk and it is also the promise. Because what does it mean when you're not understood but that somehow the system cannot hear you see you hold you? that the things that have been legible you have somehow exceeded or undone, fallen underneath the radar of the readable or were not written into the laws of legibility to begin with? and so legibility cannot be all there is and so it can't be all there is to work toward, may even be what we need to work against.[4]

Who reads you? Who do you read?
Are you readable?
What are you looking at?
Do you like friction?

ONCE UPON A TIME, in 1937, in San Francisco, there was an elephant called

Jumbo.

Jumbo belonged to Jane Grabhorn. Jumbo was a printing press and Jane Grabhorn was a typesetter, writer and designer. Among many other things, she wrote three tenets—rules—of typography.

Spread from *Bookmaking on the Distaff Side*, 1937

The first one goes like this:

```
Do not hyphenate your words. This
is not because the effect thus
achieved is novel and there-
by striking in appearance, but
because of the beautiful logic of
such procedure.
  Consider these things ladies,
and allow those qualities so
peculiar to the female courage,
imaginativeness, adaptability
& the will to experiment, Oh
give them their head and let the
results be caustic spangled pages
of type shot thru the heavens of
paper and ink.[5]
```

This text, and Jane Grabhorn, is one of about 20 contributions in a book called *Bookmaking on the Distaff Side* that was published in 1937 in San Francisco. "Distaff" is an Old English term denoting "the female sphere" and the work is a potluck in the form of a book, featuring female bookmakers, printers, typographers, illustrators, proofreaders, bibliophiles, type design- ers, et cetera.

In the writing of Jane Grabhorn, the body is present in the way these hyphens, which she proposes we get rid of, are bodies of lead. They are inserted by *hand*. The body is present in how she asks us, readers, to

END OF TENET NUMBER TWO give thanks & take a deep breath

give thanks and take a deep breath.

Jane Grabhorn also wrote:

```
I am not what is commonly kn
as a "designer" and have
always been a little contemp
of people who call themselve
"designers", who seem to thi
this is more artistic and do
want to be thought of as low
labourers.[6]
```

ONCE UPON A TIME, in 19
Macintosh launched a machine ca

"Macintosh Plus."

ONCE UPON A TIME, in 19
the media tycoon Rupert Murdoch fired 6,000 print workers who wo on newspaper production in Lond In secret, he had built a brand-nev printing plant with all the newest technology. Using modern compu technology, journalists would be a input copy directly for printing, ar typesetters were made redundant.

Protest poster by Morning Star Poster, 1986.

By hiring electricians to run the p presses, he was able to bypass the strong unions of typographers and printers. In 1986, 6,000 unionized workers went on a strike that wou over a year.

ℭ𝔈 UPON A TIME, in 1987, st version of the predecessor to e InDesign, called PageMaker, iipped with Macintosh Plus. Gail ail, who worked at a printing at this time, says:

```
e time the technology was
aking the whole industry,
n the union there was a real
gle between conventional
ew technology. We were slow
alise that we would have to
ce unionising and technol-
There is a lesson here for
day with automation. The
isation became much poor-
d the least organised area
 the graphic area, partly
se it became individualised.
 graphic designer I know is a
ancer; it is not a collective
onment. ... When I was in the
try ... Everybody was working
part of a bigger
ny; the minute you are break-
hat up, working for yourself,
ecome vulnerable.[7]
```

ebruary of 1987, the strike, known *Wapping dispute*, collapsed. d the same time restrictive es against unions were introduced government led by Margaret her. Enter "desktop publishing." ktop holds one laptop, one coffee ne lamp, one person.

ℭ𝔈 UPON A TIME, Britney s sang a swan song to the shrink- ength of unionizing:

```
neliness
lling me
 must confess
ll believe (still believe)
I'm not with you
e my mind
ow was I supposed to know?
uldn't have let you go[8]
```

en you are alone, on your couch, r studio, working happily away ur metal box, do you know rooms, historical spaces, bodies, struggles that you are connected to? Do you know where they come from; the physical and mental walls and ceilings of our screens, sheets, interfaces, studios, couches, cafés, offices?

If we would look more closely at how these rooms have morphed and changed through time—from factory-like type-setting workshops to the softly camou-flaged factory of the laptop—can we understand our current rooms, our cur-rent postures? Can we see how spaces and technologies shape our imagination and the ways we work?

And if our rooms are still, *now*, changing, moving, possibly shrinking, is that happening in a way that supports disobedient practices of graphic design?

These stories we tell ourselves about what we do,
and why we do it,
and who did it before,
and why we don't do it,
and how we don't do it,
these stories become truths.
Can we imagine a different professional identity? One built on collectivity and community? Can we try to name and understand our material working con-ditions? What if we can see how we are entangled and dependent, and that we will never be able to find community in competition?

Graphic designer Ramon Tejada writes:

```
DESIGN needs to be more open,
more fluid, have more holes,
literally, and conceptually. ...
```

```
More surreal, magical, absurdist.
Less hierarchical (or at least
single hierarchy and more about
multiple hierarchies).

Leave room    space.

Be more porous, less controlled,
less about organization (organ-
ization for whom? And by whom?).
What does this mean and how do we
```

each individually make it happen? ... PUNCTURE: an act of puncturing a hole, wound or perforation made by puncturing a minute depression. ...

GET OUT OF THE WAY,
MAKE SPACE, STOP HUGGING SO
MUCH OF THE FIELD (THE HISTORY).
MAKE ROOM.

Puncturing as a methodology is about redefining, digging, finding, thinking, ideating, making and probably having to remake and start again. It is about not being afraid, and about getting messy and resisting the reflex of our processes and knowledge. It is about saying, "I don't know it all, and I need to learn more, differently".

Puncturing is about thinking how we design (both the structural, formal, and conceptual form it takes) platforms and spaces that allow for excluded voices to come through. How we cede that spotlight. How we take our personal and DESIGN ego out of the way. ...

LET'S COLLECTIVELY PUNCTURE
AND STIR THE POT.

LET THE FLOODGATES GO.[9]

ONCE UPON A TIME, there was a symposium on graphic design in a town called Leipzig in a country called Germany.

The collective body was awakened.

Individualism was a mistake.

Individualism was a mistake.

Individualism was a mistake.

1) Balsom, E (2018) 'There is No Such Thing as Documentary: An Interview with Trinh T. Minh-ha', *Frieze Magazine* 199.

2) Ahmed, S. (2006) *Queer Phenomenology – Orientations, Objects, Others*, Durham: Duke University Press, 57.

3) de Bondt, S. (2012) 'Beatrice Warde: Manners and Type', *Eye Magazine* 84 (21). Via: http://www.eyemagazine.com/feature/article/beatrice-warde-manners-and-type

4) Perta, L. (2015) 'AGAINST CURATION OR LOSING YOUR GRIP'. Via: http://www.litiaperta.com/writingbodies

5) Grabhorn, J. (1937) 'A Typographic Discourse for The Distaff Side of Printing, a Book by Ladies', *Bookmaking on the Distaff Side*, San Francisco: Distaff Side.

6) Rather, C. & Rather, L. (1975) *Jane Grabhorn, Printer*, Oakland, California: Rather Press, 19–20.

7) Fanni, M. et al (2020) 'Excerpt from a conversation with Gail Cartmail', *Natural Enemies of Books — A Messy History of Women in Printing and Typography*, Fanni, M., Flodmark, M. & Kaaman, S., eds. London: Occasional Papers, 153.

8) Martin, M. (lyrics) & Spears, B. (singer) (1998) 'Baby One More Time'

9) Tejada, R. (2019) 'Decolonizing DESIGN a sermon on the hierarchy of design', *Amalgam Journal* 2, Pouya Ahmadi, ed.

R for
Role Play
Role Play
Role Play
Role Play

As designers,

As female designers in the extended field of design,

As designers-cum-artists,

As conflicted role-models,

we naturally wear many hats and multitask a variety of roles.

we naturally wear many hats and multitask a variety of roles.

one is quickly suspected of lacking "expert knowledge."

for the emotional carnage that is cultural work in late capitalism,

We are content-organizers, image producers, typographers,
We are also mothers, friends, bosses and feminist killjoys,
We design graphics, exhibitions, textiles and CGIs;
we quietly endure being our own conflict managers,

writers, editors, publishers, project coordinators,
because we think about other human beings and their needs
conceive of objects, conversations and installations.
anti-stress squeeze balls or fortune cookies.

secretaries, accountants and so on.
during the day.
Our resumé is complicated. We often work for free.
We are care workers, this is care work.

German journalist and writer Kurt Tucholsky was a prominently outsp
columnist of the Weimar Republic. He also wrote under the pseudor
Kaspar Hauser, Peter Panter, Theobald Tiger and Ignaz Wrobel. Tuch

As women designers,

As non-male cultural workers in a patriarchy,

As creatures working at the intersection of art and design,

... Seriously?

role-playing has become a crucial strategy for us.

we need slippery identities and polyphonous deliveries,

the art of switching hats has become our most special skill.

Who even buys into this "critical surplus role play" shit in 2021?

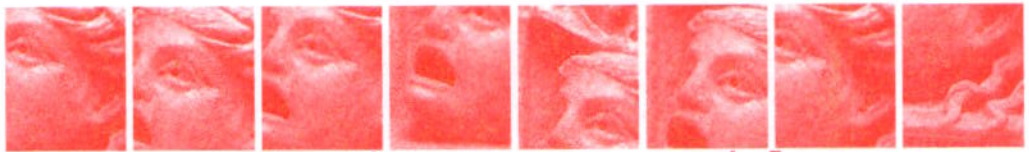

In order to create the agency and leverage we need

to decide when to be visible and when it's better to go unnoticed.

We step in and out of character like it's nobody's business,

We all know any critique is already pre-owned ...

ribed the reasons for his role play: "It was useful to exist five times—
who in Germany believes that a political writer can be humorous, or a
ist can be serious? Who would credit a playful person with knowledge

in regards to the different and, at times, contradictory roles,

Let's be clear, in our society the so-called

putting on vocational seriosity whenever necessary,

so we can also just lalala ...

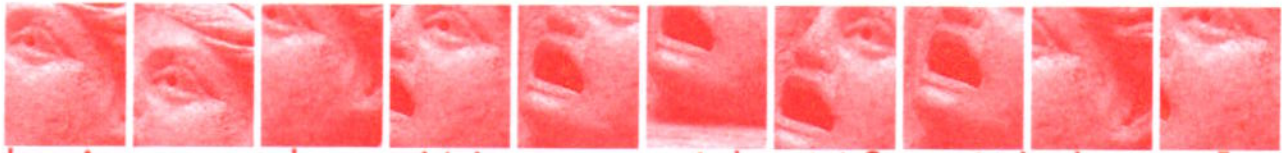

desires and positions we identify with but also

"female perspective" is still rendered as "other"

pushing our post-professional desires whenever possible,

"Breathe in, now breathe out / Hands up, now hands down ...

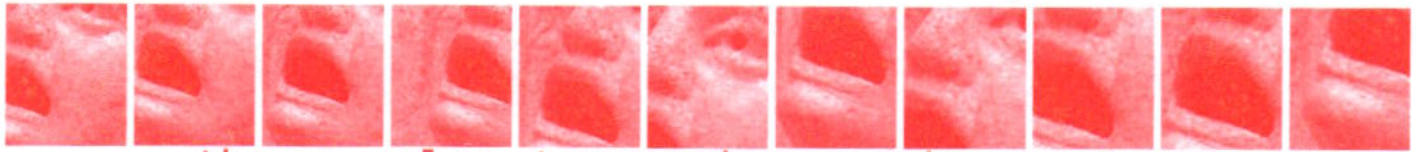

those roles imposed on us by society.

to the presumed "universal" (male) perspective.

forever questioning the pigeonholing of cultural labor.

Keep rollin' rollin' rollin' rollin' (what?) / Keep rollin' ..."

of the penal code, or who would believe that a describer of cities can amusing verse? Humor discredits." Tucholsky, Kurt (1954 [1927]) 'M PS', *Panter, Tiger & Co.*, Hamburg: Rowohlt, 8.

iling Queerly stands for an approach to design which critically
aces failure as part of the production process of design Referring
the book *The Queer Art of Failure* by queer theorist and
r Jack Halberstam, failing, as opposed to winning, can be seen as a
condition, in which normative
and standardized
expectations
or values,
even common
sense, are not

AILING

lled Translated to a design process
ailing Queerly" can mean to opt for inefficient tools, to resist
ery, to oppose the known and learned rules of one's discipline,
emphasize the negative, to accept accidental results,
all it surprises This approach is an
ise in unlearning, in
g on new
nfamiliar
pectives,

QUEERLY

to let go of the
u of surprise and try to think anti capitalist
ebook for unstable minds, stupid thoughts and ideas born to fail'
cuments my own path towards failing queerly In questioning
normative regime of industrial mass print production, I used
ternative, inefficient and time consuming methods of visual
oduction, like linocut, silk screen printing, x y plotter or stencil
techniques Also, I experimented with "weak and unstable"
ng inks made from plants like cabbage, turmeric or algae, which
resulted in a variety of prints that will fade away with time
pages were printed on leftovers and flawed paper, that became
nusable for an industry committed to the highest standards
erfection The text fragments on the prints are quotes from the
ook *The Queer Art of Failure* The prints are folded twice
tapled as handy notebooks The user has to rip open the upper
folded edge of the pages in order to reveal the prints

Memory
is itself
a disciplinary
mechanism
that Foucault calls
a "ritual of power"

t consider the
st over finding
so we should
inian stroller a
an ambulatory
the unplanned,
e improvised,
rprising.

... we have to untr
ourselves so that
can read the strug
and debates back
questions that see
settled and resolv

Failure as a way

capitalist practices,
reproductive
styles, negativity,
critique.

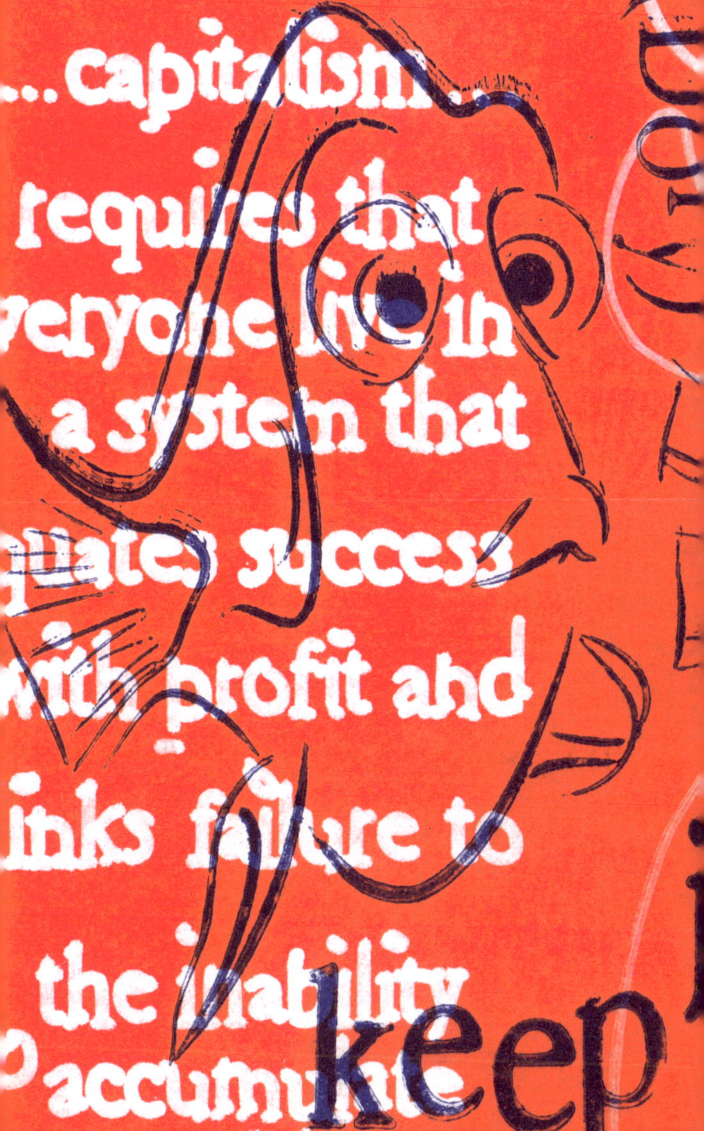

...capitalism...
requires that
veryone live in
a system that
uates success
ith profit and
inks failure to
the inability
o accumulate
wealth.

investing in **counterintuitive** modes of *kno wing* such as failure and stupidity.

Failure can be counted within that set of **oppositional tools** that James C. Scott called “the weapons of the weak”

T FOR
OKEN

).2020 at 2:17 pm
Subject: Writing in Rage + Glossary of Undisciplined Design
@ .

ar Miriam Cahn,
're writing to you about your 1983 correspondence with un Schimmel—who was then a student at the Academy of Arts Munich—which was published in Writing in Rage. In letter, Schimmel draws your attention to a job offer professorship in Painting + Graphic Arts and appeals to sense of solidarity, as there were still no women pro- ›rs at the academy back then.
would like to reprint the correspondence between you he student in a publication that presents and incites sciplined strategies, tools and role models in the field ntemporary graphic design.
..]
the Glossary of Undisciplined Design, we address the ctural inequalities still prevalent in art schools and emies and, as such, we interrogate the genius principle culty and historical analysis.
ur correspondence is still red-hot and inspiring for ow often in recent years have we ourselves received job s that only functioned as a token gesture, intended to ase pre-existing structures with a sprinkling of parity. st 40 years have passed and not much has changed. Beyond l opportunity appointments, there is still much work to ne at German universities. For the Glossary of Undis- ined Design book, we'd like to have different generations and also to highlight emancipatory and disobedient eers. We would therefore very much appreciate it if we l print your correspondence under the glossary entry r Token Women.'
..]
st regards,
becca Stephany and Anja Kaiser

om: @ . 28.10.2020 at 4:10 pm
Writing in Rage + Glossary of Undisciplined Design
@ .

ar Anja Kaiser and Rebecca Stephany,
s, you are welcome to use this correspondence—it's a dal anyway that so little changes in art schools ... glad cts of undisciplined design whenever necessary.
l the best
ur miriam cahn

Munich
February 24, 1983

Academy of Fine Arts Munich,
'Working Group on Aesthetics'

Dear Miriam Cahn,

At the Academy of Fine Arts Munich, half of the students are women, yet in the teaching body there is not a single woman professor to act as an example and role model.

For us, therefore, it is a matter of urgent concern to bring your attention, as a recognized and successful woman painter, to the job advertisement for a Professor in Painting + Graphic Arts—see the attached copy—with the request that you apply for the post, if you are interested in taking up a teaching position.

If this is ultimately not your serious intention, we ask you nevertheless to apply—for tactical reasons, so that, in the extremely patriarchal structure and mind-set of our Academy, emancipation can be further promoted and advanced.

Your solidarity would be a major support for our endeavors, if only because the percentage of applications from women would thereby be increased. In the first instance, all that is required for

19th century and to re-open them with an entirely new system adapted to suit today's technology—and, of course, with a teaching body based on gender parity.

i think that your tactic for moving emancipation forward is wrong: first of all, one must examine whether the quality of such a position is at all worth a committed woman applying for it. the policy of taking one small step after another through the institutions has its limitations, on the one hand it is a question of women and on the other hand it is a question of making art. i think that as far as making art for women is concerned, emancipation can be better advanced with dedicated weeks, or circles or working groups on the subject, such as you run at the academy and such as are being tried out at other academies in germany. guest lectureships, limited in duration and hence more intensive and more independent than fixed positions, could, perhaps, assist the function of unsettling and so break open rigid patriarchal structures—at these ancient academies, a revolutionary atmosphere needs to be created, but from outside, from "day-to-day life," compelling these long-established institutions to abandon their professional demeanor, their "master-pupil" relationships, to define art anew and to open up these temples of the muses. to put it in concrete terms: if i now apply for this professorial post out of wrongly conceived solidar-

Yours faithfully,
Heidrun Schimmel

Basle
March 15, 1983

miriam cahn
mörsbergerstr. 52
4057 basle/CH

dear Heidrun Schimmel,

many thanks for your letter. i will not, however, be applying for this professorial post. and i will give you my reasons—firstly the personal ones: neither do i wish to become a professor with a fixed position, nor are painting and graphic arts my medium.

now, to my reasoning concerning solidarity: it is clear to me that i would not get this post, or have only a very slight chance. that, however, would not be a reason not to apply. for me the reason is rather: is this post worth my solidarity?

your call for solidarity seems to me a little like the call for equal rights for women in the army—not so dire, of course, but similar. the impression i have gained so far of german academies are so bad that the only remedy i see here is to shut down these things that are left over from the professor in it—i am cementing the idea held by men that such a position is so utterly "important," that now even women apply for it. we should boycott it, just as we boycott the military. we should organize campaigns against the fact that art in the academies has been taught in an identical way for almost a hundred years—the nude models should go strike and the wives of these professors; the women should refuse to draw nudes, to assume traditional painters' stances etc....

that's how I see it. your women's week was a small beginning along this path—i would be immediately prepared, again, to do something in this direction, because i am well aware that examples and role models—women examples—are important for us, and precisely in academies.

but—from outside.

well, i could write pages and pages on these problems, but i hope that you understand me—warm regards

your miriam cahn

WOME N

For Unfaithful Contexts

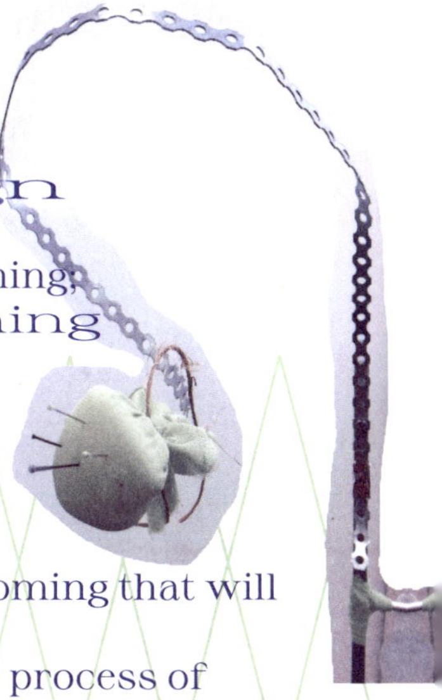

Let us look
at design
as a discipline
of dynamic becoming;
a becoming

that will
never grow into
a predrawn
outline,
but a becoming that will
encounter many things
in its process of
gradually moving into
the proximity
or neighborhood
of an evolving form.

Design
is always
situated;
so are
its designer
and
its recipient.

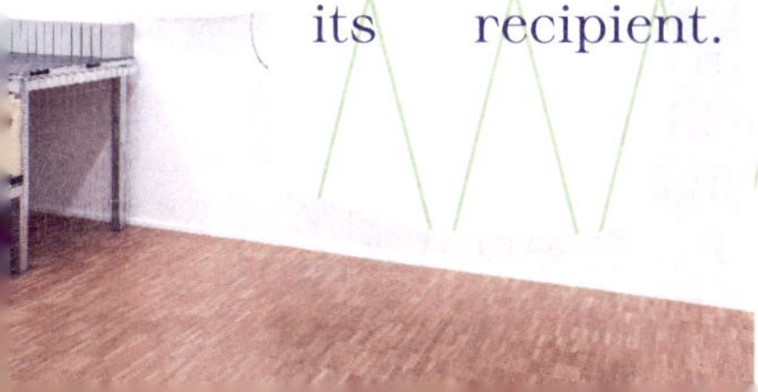

At any point,
at any time,
its becoming
is stimulated and informed
by private influences
feelings
and the physical
and mental
states
of its designers
in the most unpredictable
ways.
In this case,
with the printing
of the publication,
the design
takes a definite form,
from what was previ
a multitude of
possible formalizations.
In spite
of this physical manifestation,
the design
has not stopped
becoming.

I would even
go so far
as to claim

hat its becoming
will never be truly complete,

since the context
n which the design

will spend its further becoming

from now on
is cracked,
(emotionally)
unstable and
unpredictable.

The existence
of a printed form
creates a break
with its context:
the form
will always be detached
from the chain of signifiers
from which it was created,
still it remains
capable of action.

The design
can be inscribed
and received
in new chains
in many unconscious
and conscious ways.

The cracking force
of this unfaithful context
is linked
to the spacing
that constitutes the design:

the act of
spacial manifestation
separates the design
from its
various chains
of reference,
influence
and association.

Nevertheless,
by creating
a yawning gap,
spacing
does not alienate
the design
from its context.

On the contrary,
it is only by spacing
that it truly
becomes
a design.

After its becoming
has taken form,
it can join
all kinds of
different chains of formalization.

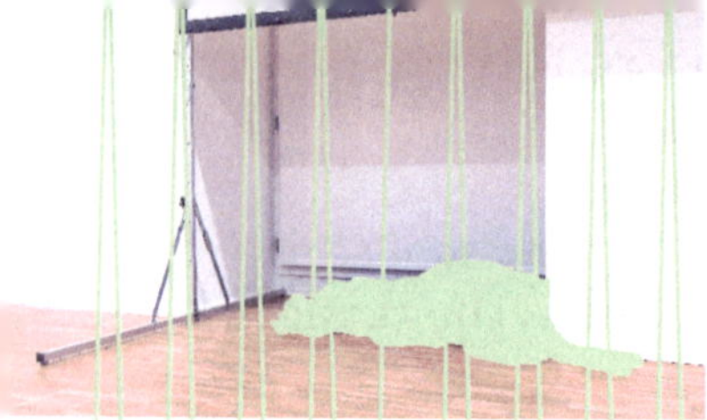

In fact,
the design
was created
by its designer
for the only reason
that the absence
of a recipient
is always possible.

The design,
however,
can continue
to exist and flourish
without either recipient
or designer.

The meaning
that I
as a designer
set out to communicate
on these pages
will always be perceived
differently
than I intended,
just as my own understanding
of this intention
will continue
to shift and blur.

CRUSHING
CRUSHING
CRUSHING
CRUSHING
CRUSHING
CRUSHING
CRUSHING
CRUSHING
CRUSHING
CRUSHING

The Urban Dictionary defines a "crush" as a "burning desire to be with someone you find very attractive and extremely special" and "sometimes it's hard to stop thinking about them."

Crushing describes the peculiar feeling of complete infatuation, strong yet frequently transitory, fueled by an intense and urgent longing to be with someone we often hardly know.

But we also crush on colors, smells, sounds, textures, clothes, artworks, movies, literature, images, metaphors, theatrical plays, music, architecture, nature, gossip, everyday stuff or coincidences that resonate with us, or on people whose works, choices or ideas inspire us.

We quite literally can't stop thinking about the object of our latest obsession, we are fans, we get on our friends' nerves because there is nothing else we can talk about, we want to spend every free second with it, bathe in it, lie awake at night envisioning all the things that we could do with it.

Crushing as a tool for research: Listen to your impulses and intuition while approaching a certain topic. Take thinking-feeling and embracing the not-yet-knowing seriously. Temporarily postpone the search for words. Trust your fascinations. Become a gatherer. Surround yourself with your crushes in material and spirit. Make fan folders for all of your crushes. Feed them. Let the stuff that inspires you talk back to you.

Implicate yourself in your work and your points of critique. Vulnerability is a powerful tool. Allow yourself to crush and crush again.

Unravel the presumed linearity of articulating an idea first, then experimenting, then producing results.

Imagine yourself as part of an organic entity of dynamic directions, movements, associations, expressions and positions. Visualize your process backwards. Work parallel on all ends (reading, writing, designing, making). Let visual material inform your words, let words become strategies for visual gestures.

Crushing is recommended for all areas of research.

is enormous potential in building alliances, particularly so
it comes to creative processes. 'E for Embracing Differences'
:o redirect the focus of collaborative projects ~~to an emphasis~~
~~e shared process~~ away from predefined results and towards
hared process of creating. Rather than seeking the comforts
npromise and middle ground, this set of collaborative meth-
:tively engages with frictions and turns them into a creative
y that appreciates and emphasizes difference. ~~and more cour-~~
~~o give them room in collaborations.~~ ~~It thus rather agrees~~
~~agree,~~ 'E for Embracing Differences' is a field study in how
ee to disagree, openly celebrating the respective quirks and
iarities of two minds thinking in dialogue.
~~acing Differences' is a call for an intimate exchange, for a~~
~~ionship of trust that expresses confidence in~~ The envisioned
of work-partnership requires a much more intimate level
ofessional exchange and has to be based on a relationship of
and confidence, both in ourselves and in our fellow collab-
r. The project was inspired by the practice of Affidamento,
~~d~~ established by the Milan Women's Bookstore Collective
e 1970s. In her book _To Become Two: Propositions for Feminist
ctive Practice_, Alex Martinis Roe describes Affidamento as
hical practice of love, where both women open themselves to
other, and in that act of entrustment, they invent themselves
gh the relation—the commitment is not just to the other,
lso to oneself."

ler to engage with this new form of collaborative work method,
veloped ~~a collaborative method~~ a set of playful frameworks,
ned to ~~raise~~ address personal questions, to share experiences
benefit from each other's skills and knowledge. The publi-
n _I don't know. Are you sure?_ is the record of our six weeks
experiment as two female designers developing and practic-
~~fteen~~ 15 different methods of working and designing together.
ng forces in this ~~kind of~~ three-legged creative race not only
raised practical and methodical questions, but also led
usual exchanges about personal and professional preferences,
s and blindspots. ~~Insights into these examinations are given~~
ur investigations gave rise to a series of short interviews,
~~were~~ conducted in written form ~~over the course of our col-~~
~~ation~~. The complete interviews and methods can be accessed
e via www.bit.ly/idontknow-areyousure. The publication can
lerstood as an open format, created in the spirit of reinter-
tion and adaptation. We, therefore, would like to encourage
s to experiment with and expand on our ~~propositions~~ methods.
ollowing is a ~~sneak preview of our methods and experiences~~
~~flected~~ short preview into our experiment, as documented in
ublication.

Hanna

Goals and values for the collaboration are specified a
discussed through the act of creating an object toge
Manifesting serves to establish familiarity and unde
standing as well as setting up a shared agenda at th
beginning of a shared project.

MA NIFE ST ING

Manifesting is divided into four steps. After each step
exchange your results and continue your work where
other person left off, thus zigzagging your way towarc
a shared manifesto.

1. Vision:
Phrase the values and principles you consider importa
for the project / the collaboration in short, one-senter
statements. Try to break down your ideas to five basi
values or principles. Explain your thoughts, then exch
statements with your partner.

2. Symbols:
Translate each of your partner's statements into abst
symbols or illustrations. Then, hand over each drawing
your partner without revealing which symbol represe
which statement. Talk about the drawings. Try to follo
each other's trains of thought and interpretation.

3. Composition:
Now, combine the symbols created by your partner
into one overall composition. Remember that these s
bols are your partner's translations of the values you
expressed in step 1. Exchange compositions with you
partner and talk about them.

4. Materialization:
Transfer your partner's composition onto a banner o
flag. Sew one composition on each side of the banne
working on opposite sides. Hoist the banner together
at a place that is important to both of you or at your
common workplace.

This method is based on the following proposition: Roe, Alex Martinis (2018) 'A G
from the Future', To Become Two: Propositions for Feminist Collective Practice. B
Archive Books.

the past.

For a long time, I had the feeling that working as a team or in a group slows down a lot of processes. I felt that as every decision has to be discussed, a lot of time and energy has to be spent on communication. There always was a fear of not getting into action fast enough. Although I have had a lot of positive experiences with collaborations, they could not remove my worries entirely. On the other hand, I always thought that cooperation is an asset that enables me to learn on so many levels. By now, I also have the feeling that working together can even accelerate processes, because you can support and push each other whenever you get stuck along the way. I also no longer find it sensible to think so economically about collaboration and communication. There is so much more at stake.

What aspects of the topic interest you the most?

For me, collaboration is mostly about learning processes. I learn something about myself because things are reflected back to me, or because I experience myself in new contexts. I also get to know new people and their abilities, uncertainties and perspectives. I have to see things from another person's point of view just as I learn to communicate my own preferences and opinions. I get to benefit from the experience of others, while I can also pass things on. I find it really exciting when a project gets a certain polyphony and represents different, maybe even contradicting points of view. I think it makes so much more sense to make contradictions and frictions visible and to approach topics dialogically.

And what kind of framework do you need to use ↓

ferences visible, which is the first one that comes to your mind?

Using two font colors in the shared Google Docs. But that is more a visualization of our two voices and emphasizes them on a visual level. Maybe it was, in fact, the decision to communicate via Google Docs in the first place and to establish this method for working in dialogue. The rules for this, which we later formulated as a proposition in the 'No-Delete Policy,' have allowed us to let opposing views stand side by side—both, with regard to differences between the two of us and changes of opinion during the process.

From your point of view, has it often happened that our different opinions or changes of opinion became visible?

I would not describe it so much as different opinions than as different personalities that came to the surface. The colors in the docs show, for example, that many structural inputs came from you, like the set-up for the workshops or to-do lists. For me, textual references were super important, which is why I included so many quotes. I think we both experienced changes of opinion during the process. In my case, this is very obvious in the notes on workshop planning, where I developed entire concepts and then crossed them out again.

Were you aware of these differences before or have they only become clear to you through our sessions?

It depends on what habits we are talking about. To stay with the previous two examples: I've always thought of you as a very organized person and myself ↓

A catalogue of rules to leave traces and visualize polyphony: The No-Delete Policy can be applied in all areas where planning and organization take place. It accompanies a project from an early research pha to the decision-making processes and to-do-lists tha come with the final steps of the project.

NO DELE TE POL ICY

1. Everything should be documented:
   Everything is recorded in text, pictures or sound, anc archived in a way that is accessible to all participants.

   To record conversations, thoughts, plans, exte communication, joint meetings or sources of i tion like Dropbox folders or Google Docs, for ple, can be created to which everyone has acc

2. Nothing must be deleted:
   Files are moved to archives instead of being deleted. Text passages are crossed out or commented on inst of being overwritten.

3. Individual voices should not blur into a single one:
   A method is defined to identify different voices.

   e.g. font in different colors
   different fonts
   handwritings

4. Spontaneous thoughts should be included into the te
   Communal documents are not set in stone, but rathe considered works in progress. The material remains c for changes and new turns, it does not necessarily fit into a linear narrative structure but bears visible trac of the process of creative production. Notes should b kept and expanded in a form of dialogue, i.e. in share documents, and leave room for questions and comm Instead of forcing compromise and consensus, contr dictions should be accepted, even appreciated.

These rules are based on the following propositions: Roe, Alex Martinis (2018) 'Archiving Relations' and 'A Republic of Letters', To Become Two: Propositions for Feminist Collective Practice. Berlin: Archive Books.

---

processes in a comfortable way. Do collaborations have to be pleasant?

I find communication incredibly important for that. Of course, I had to find a language for myself first (and I'm still doing that). That means, I have to learn how I can and want to talk about myself and my work in order to be able to communicate these things to others. This of course requires a basis of trust. I also had to get to know you, learn your references and contexts, in order to understand you properly. In exchange with you, I was able to sharpen my opinions as you asked the right questions or had a convincing counter-argument. Of course, communication can also be unpleasant and lead to conflicts or misunderstandings. But the better you know yourself, the more confident you get and the better you are able to put things in perspective.

Have you (through our project) been able to develop a strategy for future cooperations?

Absolutely! I believe that all of our propositions contain communication strategies, because they offer a certain vocabulary and thus already create a common basis. On top of that, some of our methods also have a list of questions at the end, which also provides a framework and addresses things in a concrete way. In order to communicate expectations and fears, for example, I found it very helpful to be able to refer to our questionnaire.

But the fact that I actually collected more quotes and references than you was a little unexpected—especially since I always had the impression that textual references play an important role in your work and you read more than I do. In hindsight, I would say that the decision to do a series of workshops together was extremely important. It allowed us to experience in a playful way how helpful and productive our different personalities and abilities can be.

Absolutely! I often had the feeling that you would catch me, whenever I was struggling, and I learned to trust you more and more. In some cases, when it was my turn to prepare the method for the next session, I already knew which parts would be difficult for me and where I would have to rely more heavily on you—to trust you to pick up the slack. Coming back to your example, I myself never thought of you as a chaotic person. Hearing you say that makes me wish I had encouraged you more to try your talents on organization and those things.

In fact, I think I trust myself more with structural tasks now that I have watched you doing it—so, my confidence has certainly increased. Perhaps I have also learned during our project that I need faith—both, in myself and others—in order to accept and appreciate my own particular quirks.

Additional propositions can be found in the free online-PDF at www.bit.ly/idontknow-areyousure:

KNOW Y OUR RO OTS

Creating a shared archive of inspirations and references.

M IND MAP

Navigating through shared interests and questions to define a common work ground.

JAM SESS IONS

Splitting a project into a series of playful encounters, in order to facilitate exchange of skills and experiences.

ROOT ING SHIFT ING STR ETCH ING

A diary for pre- and post-processing working sessions.

FRIE NDLY POSITIONS

A playful declaration of personal positions and opinions by means of design.

CADA VRE EX QUIS

Dividing and reuniting parts of the project, in order to keep different voices visible.

MIR RO ING

Translating each other's feelings a experiences into physical form.

THE MA CHIN

A drawing exercise for a halftime r your teamwork.

SHOULDE CHE CK

Designing in shifting roles: taking t head and hand of your team.

TR IGG E DETECTO

Identifying pitfalls and red flags in cooperation.

NA RRA TIVE MAPP IN

Retracing your tracks through the of your partner: a graphic journey evaluation.

CRI ME S CENE

A guide for approaching documen Revisiting the scenes.

MET HO AC TING

Strategically slipping into different and taking up their points of view.

Simultaneous Simulations

[competing shortcuts
entangled in parallel operations]

BLANK PAGE CALLING
BOND THROUGH
DOUBLE-CLICKING
NKING INTO DEPENDENCY
WE MISSPELL
LE NAMES TENDERLY

PEN ALL FOLDERS
ONCE
EMPORARILY
ELECT HAND TOOL,
AND TOOL
LET'S
HOLD HANDS,
TOOL

III. MY C
ARE VISUALL
DURING,
AS, AS OFTE
IF, WHILE

MAGIC MOUSE
IS A GATHERE
MAGIC MOUSE
IS DISSONAN
BLANK PAGE
IS ARROGANT

KS
AFFECTED BY:
HOWEVER,
AS WELL AS,
HROUGH

DUPLICATE
.2. PREVIOUS
AGE
E-DUPLICATE
AGE
E-DO PAGE
E-PAGE
PRAY)

A.a.

A SMILE IN DENIAL ON AN ECLECTIC PILE

EXTRA:
PRESETS, PIXEL
PROTAGONISTS AN
PLEASE, I'M NOT
PROMISE TO DEBUNK
PULLING YOU INTO

D/ AND THE
PAGE REPLIES:
TEAR IT ALL
DOWN! PEEL
ALL
AYERS UP!

(BACKGROUND GRUNTS:
FOREGROUND COME
CLOSER)

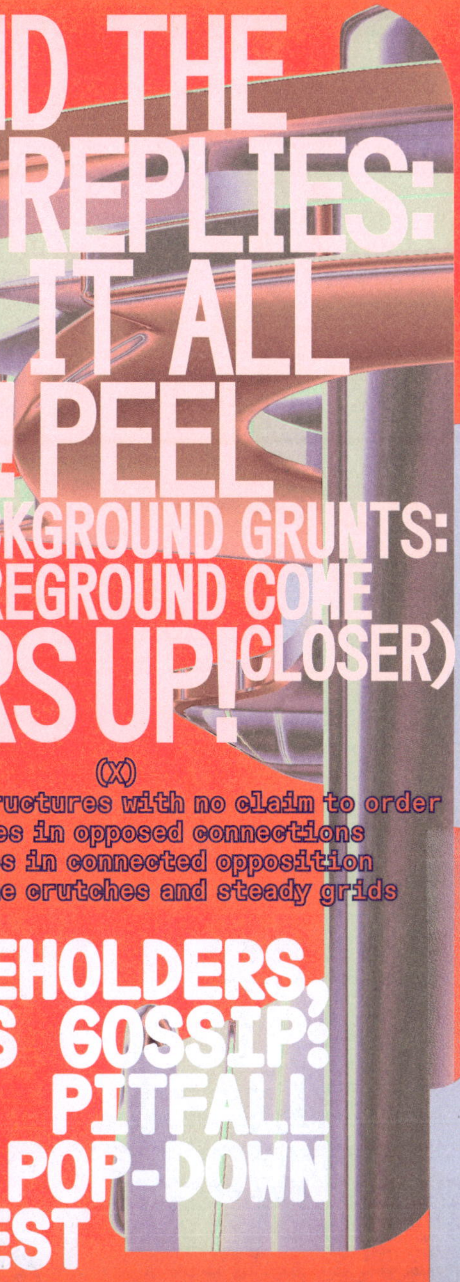

(X)

Structured structures with no claim to order
Structures in opposed connections
Structures in connected opposition
Sidestep the crutches and steady grids

PLACEHOLDERS,
ROXIES GOSSIP:
HER PITFALL
UR POP-DOWN
PROTEST

II. Letter shapes intertwine and cling
images and objects
Words seek encounters at the margins
a, a, a, a, b, c, cheer in multiplicity

DESIGNER, DESIGNER,

DON'T YOU FEEL THE ITCH TO BEWITCH

BEFORE NEUTRA-LITY ANSWERS WITH ANOTHER BRUTE PITCH

I WANNA SEE YOU LAYERED CLAIMS GLITCH

U for Unstable Signs

An *unstable sign* is an ambiguous symbol, charged image or uncertain marker used to aid and promote different perspectives on a design work, with an emphasis on raising questions through a productive tension, often between text and image. Usually drawn from different genres and temporalities, unstable signs are recognized by their connotative meanings and particular inner logics and are best accessed through personal interpretation.

arrow

error

airflow

By the early 1970s, US-American graphic designer and activist Sheila Levrant de Bretteville had grown increasingly skeptical of the prevailing presumption that visual signs were universally valid, especially in the realm of graphic design. To de Bretteville, the lingering modernist notion that a sign could possibly be equally "true" to, legible for or representative of "everyone" revealed nothing more than an overbearing patriarchal point of (world) view. And so, she began letting her subjective associations and visual references influence her design work and, in turn, the viewers' reading of it.

Shaped by political activism and the women's movement of the late 1960s and early 1970s in the United States, de Bretteville initiated the Women's Design Program in 1971 at California Institute of the Arts and, together with Judy Chicago and Arlene Raven, founded the Woman's Building in Los Angeles in 1973. It is in this environment that de Bretteville developed her decidedly social, feminist and participatory approach to graphic design, driven by the quest to bring to the discipline more of the human values that had been historically and culturally associated with women.

Her 1973 essay, 'Some Aspects of Design from the Perspective of a Woman Designer,' is one of the seminal texts from the US to challenge the modernist hegemony of Anglocentric, male-normative graphic design, formulating design principles that were unapologetically inclusive, personal, ambiguous and complex. In the essay, she writes:

As I become more sensitive to those aspects of design which reinforce repressive behavior, I increasingly question

the desirability of simplicity and clarity. The thrust to control almost inevitably operates through simplification. Control is undermined by ambiguity, choice and complexity because subjective factors in the user become more effective and the user is invited to participate. Participation undermines control.[1]

In 1975, de Bretteville co-organized the conference *Women in Design: The Next Decade* at the Woman's Building in Los Angeles, as well as designing the poster advertising the conference. The poster is made up of several unstable signs, which are linked in their respective connotations and, in turn, ask the viewer to complete their meaning, as individual messages as well as in relation to the overall announcement. In an interview conducted in 2012, de Bretteville reflected on the interpretations of the poster:

There's a landscape of a grid, a perspective grid, in which two people with long hair and indeterminate sexuality are walking into the future. And [Superstudio] wrote that that grid was "the equal distribution of goods and services." So, for me, that kind of perspective grid that you see in the *Women in Design* poster references back to the equal distribution of goods and services. But only people who know about Superstudio look at that poster and say "doesn't that have something to do with Superstudio?" And I say "yes, if you happen to know about Superstudio. If you don't, it's a grid, it's a perspective." Most of the things in that poster are unstable signs because, unless you know the moon is Angelica Kauffmann's painting *The Artist in the Character of Design Listening to the Inspiration of Poetry*, you see two women sort of classically dressed, sitting together having a conversation. There's a lot in it, but I think if you look at it you see a landscape and you see a moon—'cause these are the phases of the moon—and you see eyebolts moving in the landscape[2] and you see a bunch of palm trees. And so, you could make your own story, in a way, out of that, that would be different from the story I tell myself about what I'm doing. And there were other interpretations.

> **I heard through the grapevine that, when it was put up at the Architecture League in New York, Massimo Vignelli thought that strong women were taking over. He saw it as like women marching toward him, that kind of thing. Those were none of my intentions. I actually didn't even think about strength when it came to [the eyebolt], because if you don't glue the nut on it'll work itself off of it…**[3]

meaning

Just as language is a common tool of communication, most of today's societies and communities also depend on a shared vocabulary of certain unambiguous signs and symbols—a stop sign in traffic, the date of a demonstration or a hazard symbol on a poisonous substance are not the places to experiment with meaning and interpretation. Wherever possible, unstable signs mess with an universalist definition of visual signs, especially with regards to disrupting the reinforcement of repression, discrimination or exclusion through graphic design. They hold the space for makers, users and viewers alike to make their own stories.

cleaning

Women in Design: the next decade, a conference with "women who work with public visual and physical forms," held on March 20–21, 1975, at the Woman's Building, Los Angeles.

1 Sheila Levrant de Bretteville, 'A Reexamination of Some Aspects of the Design Arts from the Perspective of a Woman Designer', *Arts in Society: Women and the Arts*, 11(1), Kamarck, Edward, ed., Madison, Wisconsin: University of Wisconsin, 114.

2 De Bretteville's fascination with the hardware led her to see the 'Venus symbol' in a simple eyebolt. Combined with a clenched fist in its centre, the Venus symbol had become an iconic feminist symbol of the women's liberation movement of the 1960s and 1970s. To de Bretteville, the eyebolt was a symbol for "strength without a fist." She had initially designed a keychain necklace with an eyebolt pendant for her Feminist Studio Workshop co-teachers, Arlene Raven and Judy Chicago, in 1972, and began gifting them to fellow feminists and like-minded people around the Woman's Building. For the *Women in Design* conference, every attendee was given an eyebolt necklace to wear as a ticket to the event. And, as de Bretteville told the audience at the *GUD Symposium*, "It only takes two dollars spent at your local hardware store to make your own eyebolt necklace."

3 Excerpt from a video interview with Sheila Levrant de Bretteville from 2012. The interview is part of a video series in which designers and artists share stories about art and activism, which accompanied the poster exhibition *Decade of Dissent: Democracy in Action 1965–1975*, organized by the Center for the Study of Polit- [illegible] Los Angeles,

BINARY
BURDEN
OF
BIRTHING

Ursula, Audre, Martha, Hildegard, Judy, Cheryl, Julia, Griselda, Sara, Sheila, Ellen, Laurie, Gerda, Maternal Fantasies, Donna, Lorraine

Wanting to be human too, I sought for evidence that I was; but if that's what it took, to make a weapon and kill with it, then evidently I was either extremely defective as a human being, or not human at all. That's right, they said. What you are is a woman. Possibly not human at all, certainly defective. Now be quiet while we go on telling the Story of the Ascent of Man the Hero.[1]

None of these words are mine, they are harvested and gathered, pieces of thoughts stitched together. A patchwork of words that have 'worlded' worlds, about to be birthed, but already felt.[2] *So, I am standing in the armpits of other womxns' word-bearing, in flesh or beyond form. And I am taking little and larger word things from* a leaf a gourd a shell a net a bag a sling a sack a bottle a pot a box a container.[3]

And I place them here, to dr perhaps, or to be stored, for to eat or chew on. A holder. recipient.... Many theorisers that the earliest cultural inven tions must have been a contai to hold gathered products anc some kind of sling or net carr Yet, Women, by virtue of thei earthliness and closeness to Nature, their involvement wi natural birth, were foreclosed from Genius, for, of course, flesh and spirit do not mix.[5] But although I heard and saw these things, because of dou and low opinion of myself anc because of the diverse sayin of men, I refused for a long ti the call to write ....[6]

In the (Man-the-)hero-worsh ping history of design, the do inant conception prioritizes t machine (masculine) over the body (feminine). It assigns m to the determining, functional areas of design—science, hnology, industrial produc- —and women to the private, nestic realm and to the 'soft,' orative fields of design.[7] *919, the first year at the so-progressive Bauhaus in imar, Headmaster Gropius arently got so scared by the numbers of female appli- ions that he unofficially lemented a quota to restrict r numbers. The "temple of dernity" also subsequently rged women a higher tuition while systematically rele- ng female students to the iving workshop, as Gropius his male masters were vinced that women lacked mental capacity to think hree dimensions and were sically and genetically un- lified to work in architecture ndustrial design.* Women considered to possess sex- cific skills that determined r design abilities; they were arently dexterous, deco- ve, and meticulous. These s meant that women were sidered to be naturally suited ertain areas of design produc- , namely, the so-called dec- ive arts, including such work ewelry, embroidery, graphic tration, weaving, knitting, ery and dressmaking.[8]

There is something about turning a skin into a sling, about the beginning of life: the process of ——bearing, of bearing with each other; a point of origin; that which is born; the start of life as a physically separate being; the coming into existence of something; a person's origin, descent, or ancestry; birthed, burthed, burded, burdred, byrded, byrthed, börded, *berthed.* The life and work situations of women were (and still are) often determined by their roles as mothers, which together with household tasks limits the amount of time they can devote to professional work.... In addition, good design is not exclusively based on talent, but also requires a great amount of practice and experience. In their efforts to acquire both, women have typically faced adverse circumstances due to a lack of time and opportunities.[9] *"Our idea was born out of ...": the metaphor of giving birth, appropriated by the corporate vocabulary of the creative industry.* Creativity has been appropriated as an ideological component of masculinity while femininity has been constructed as man's.[10] *A berth, though, is a fixed bunk for sleeping.* Even the category of 'women' refers us back to a male genealogy, to philos-ophy as white male European inheritance.[11]

Crossing from private to public to create the designed artifacts of our society, such as posters and books, and consciously bringing information about female experience into design forms and workplaces from which it has long been excluded, puts the woman designer in a precarious position, personally and professionally, rendering her vulnerable and potentially in need of support from others. This condition of vulnerability so often ascribed to women, and the emotionality and interde-pendence it often engenders, is seen to diminish anyone who openly exhibits it, particularly in public and professional contexts which are predominantly male.[12] Gathering instead of hunting, cultivating instead of conquering, nurturing instead of self-promo-tion. These values are not strict-ly tied to sexual identity, but have been linked in our society to the worlds of women.[13] Also, the emphasis on women's 'commitment to service' is problematic: although it does not explicitly deny their capaci-ty for 'creative genius,' it also does not affirm it.[14] With its implicit demands on a person's

entire and exclusive attention,
sign work presumes the cons
of one's life partner and requi
sophisticated management s
from both sides for the orga
zation of everyday life—as w
as financial resources, which
often unavailable to young d
signers. At first glance, this s
ation appears to be gender
neutral; however, it is especi
ambivalent for women. Fre-
quently, they bear the great
burden in connection with th
work-life balance. A similar a
bivalence is evident with reg
to the visibility of women in t
field of graphic design. The
names play a prominent role i
the reception of design hist

Child rearing is always a cru
point in discussions about ge
der equality—one that we
shouldn't overlook, even thou
we might risk the charge of
"biological essentialism" fro
some corners. But if we lea
those concerns aside for now
and proceed from the premi
of a supposed "equality," the
we find that the structures in
ostensibly progressive cultu
institutions are actually work
against us. Take for example
the upper age limits for gran
and funding programs. This
almost exclusively disadvanta

nen, since many of us have
ıt a fair deal of our decisive
essional years doing care
k. In this sense, many insti-
ons are writing the bodies of
nen who risk having children
of their history. [16]

*ar heads can be found,
'e all our gatherers' carrier
s, grass-woven satchels
birch-bark containers are
decomposed.* Without a
certed effort to imagine
rnative futures, we will have
ture in which individual
ce is eliminated along with
tions, ambiguity and fan-
. For if we continue to elim-
e female values in an effort
varn society of impending
res and make such visions
by their artful vividness,
, in this editing, it is human-
which is finally, totally erad-
ed. [17] The slight curve of
shell that holds just a little
er, just a few seeds to give
y and to receive, suggests
ies of becoming-with, of
procal induction, of compan-
species whose job in living
dying is not to end the
ying, the worlding. With a
and a net, becoming human,
oming humus, becoming
an, has another shape—the
-winding, snaky shape of
oming-with. [18]

I feel like a termite, gnawing at the bottom. The meal is delicious, and why should I give a damn if the whole house falls down! [19]

1: Le Guin, Ursula K. (2019 [1986]) *The Carrier Bag Theory of Fiction*, London: Ignota Books, 30–32.

2: Lorde, Audre (2017 [1985]) 'Poetry Is Not a Luxury', *Your Silence Will Not Protect You*, London: Silver Press, 7.

3: Le Guin, Ursula K. (2019 [1986]), 29.

4: Ibid.

5: Rosler, Martha (2004 [1983]) 'The Figure of the Artist, the Figure of the Woman', *Decoys and Disruptions: Selected Writings, 1975—2001*, Cambridge, Massachusetts: The MIT Press, 90.

6: Hildegard of Bingen (1151) 'Preface', *Scivias*. English translation via: https://isi.edu/~lerman/music/Hildegard.html

7: Attfield, Judy (2009 [1989]) 'FORM/female FOLLOWS FUNCTION/male: Feminist Critiques of Design', *Design Studies: A Reader*, Brody, David and Clark, Hazel, eds., Oxford: Berg, 49.

8: Buckley, Cheryl (1986) 'Made in Patriarchy: Toward a Feminist Analysis of Women and Design', *Design Issues* 3(2), Cambridge, Massachusetts: The MIT Press, 5.

9: Meer, Julia (2012) 'He, she, it… Women and the problems of gender in the history of graphic design — Introduction to the short biographies', *Women in Graphic Design 1890—2012*, Breuer, Gerda and Meer, Julia, eds., Berlin: Jovis, 386.

10: Pollock, Grise (2003 [1989]) *Vision and Difference: Femininity, Feminism* (*the Histories of Art*, New Yo Routledge, 30.

11: Ahmed, Sara (2010) *The Prom of Happiness*, Durham, North Carolina: Du University Press, 16.

12: de Bretteville, Sheila Levrant (1986) 'Feminist Design', *Space and Society*, *Spazio e Societa*, Beinart, Ju and de Carlo, Giancarlo, eds.,

13: Lupton, Ellen and Haycock Mak Laurie (1994) 'Underground Ma archy in Graphic Design', *Eye* 4(14). Via: http www.eyemagazine.com/featu article/underground-matriar

14: Meer, Julia (2012), 389

15: Breuer, Gerda and Meer, Julia (2012) 'Introduction', *Women in Graphic* *sign 1890–2012*, Breuer, rda and Meer, Julia, eds., lin: Jovis, 41.

16: Maternal Fantasies (2020) 'Fake Gleichbe- ntigung, Plädoyer der Für- gearbeit als Quelle für eine unft basiert auf Nächsten- e (Fake Equality: A plea care work as a source for a re based on charity)', *Arts* *he Working Class #11: Faux* *ture*. Via: http://artsofthe kingclass.org/text/fake chberechtigung

17: de Bretteville, Sheila Levrant (1974) 'A Re- mination of Some Aspects he Design Arts from the spective of a Woman signer', in: *Arts in Society:* *men and the Arts* 11(1), narck, Edward, ed., Madison, consin: University of Wis- sin, 121–122.

18: Haraway, Donna (2016) *Staying with the Trouble:* *king Kin in the Chthulucene* *(Experimental Futures)*, Durham, North Carolina: Duke University Press, 118–119.

19: Lorraine Wild, as quoted in Lupton, Ellen and Haycock Makela, Laurie (1994)

(...)

01

F FOR FINDING FREAKING FUNDING 02

▲ Conversations that took place while planning *GUD*: V: Vincent Schier F: Franciska Zólyom O: Others R: Rebecca Stephany A: Anja Kaiser

We—Franciska, Director of GfZK (Leipzig Museum of Contemporary Art), and Vincent, Project Coordinator—are working on *GUD* with Anja and Rebecca. We want to kick-start and coordinate the funding of the project, among other things. As with any other project, we need a solid financial base to build on. We want to invite guests, we need to pay for labor, create the infrastructure for a symposium and cover the production costs of a publication. We need funding. Our project has big ambitions and faces many different directions. It is situated somewhere between design, art, and activism, whereas cultural funding often only focuses on one area. 03

After seven months of preparation, 160 guests are coming to Leipzig. We have organized flights and train journeys from the US, Portugal, Sweden and the Netherlands, as well as hotels and catering. There will be a total of four days of lectures, workshops, discussions and performances. Countless hours will be spent talking, discussing and dancing … However, the project has not yet been fully funded. 04

How can these processes for raising money and logistics be represented in a transparent way, and how can we translate it into the language of funding? This is essential for the application process, as well as for the subsequent accounting, because, apart from the interpersonal, content-related and organizational levels of a project, it also exists on paper, in the form of applications, project reports, freelance contracts, invoices, receipt lists and financial statements. The figures that these documents contain say a great deal about a project, providing information that goes far beyond their numerical value. 05

We would like to look back and reconstruct some of the discussions that enabled us to make *GUD* a reality. It gets interesting when one considers the question of how the figures and the content are connected—and for this we have frequently borrowed the voices of others—as well as how and with whom our ideas can be sharpened and implemented. What do we learn about the logic of funding and what influence do we have on it? How much do we have to bend over backwards to comply with this logic and … do we even want to comply at all? 06

The following statements describe our communication, conviction and perseveran cash and non-cash resources, our workfor working hours and the equivalent value th they have.

First of all, we research which funding foundations are a good fit for the nature of our project and the deadlines tha have to be met. In the summer of 2019—more than seven months before the symposium—we begin submitting applications.

The project requires 55,000 euros. The symposium costs 22,000 euros; the rest is needed for the publication. All in all, alm 65 percent of the budget goes into paying fees—around 14,000 euros for the sympos and almost 22,000 euros for the publicatio

We are confident about our proposal and continue to subr applications, 22 in total, until we raise enough money.

Twelve applications are rejected, 10 applications are approved.

Less than two weeks before the start of th GUD Symposium, *we receive the funding commitment that makes the symposium financially possible. However, the funding the planned publication has not yet been fully clarified . . .*

Finding . . . a Friendly Foundation

DEPENDING ON WHICH FOUNDATION WE CONTACT, DIFFERENT ASPECTS OF THE PROJECT BECOME CRUCIAL, SUCH AS THE QUALITY AND NATURE OF T CREATIVE OUTPUT, THE SUSTAINABILITY OF THE PROJECT, ITS "TARGET GROUPS"—WHOEVER THEY ARE IMAGINED TO BE—OR THE PLACE OF RESIDEN OF THOSE INVOLVED. THIS RESULTS IN DIFFERENT APPLICATIONS THAT EMPHASIZE DIFFERENT ASPEC OF THE SAME PROJECT—DESPITE THE FACT THAT THE MOTIVATION BEHIND ORGANIZING THE *GUD SYMPOSIUM* IS NOT FULLY CONGRUENT WITH ANY ONE OF THESE ASPECTS.

V: I just spoke to the foundation. I'm not sure if we stand a chance of getting funding from them.

F: Hello! My colleague ha described the *GUD* projec you. We would like to sub an application.

▲ Conversations that took place while planning *GUD*: V: Vincent Schier F: Franciska Zólyom O: Others R: Rebecca Stephany A: Anja Kaiser

O: I'm sure you've seen that our foundation supports children and young people—future leaders, so to speak.

F: Yes, that's precisely why we came to you. We anticipate that those attending the symposium and making use of the publication will primarily be graphic design students.

O: Oh, we do not offer any support for publications. Publications can be sold to generate revenue.

F: In principle, yes. However, we are a non-profit foundation, and for this project we are working with designers whose work is financed by funding and the revenue from sales of the publication.

O: You see, our foundation is gradually stepping back from collaborating with museums. But you can still submit an application, of course … 16

The application is not approved. 17

ANOTHER DIFFICULTY IS HOW SPECIFIC FUNDS ARE SUPPOSED TO BE ALLOCATED. ARE THERE EXPENSES THAT WON'T BE COVERED BY ANYONE? WHICH FUNDING CRITERIA OVERLAP AND WHICH ARE MUTUALLY EXCLUSIVE? 18

R: Hey everyone, the Karlsruhe University of Arts and Design (HfG Karlsruhe) and the Support Association ZKM/HfG e.V. have approved funding for the student contributions to the publication. And the Landesbank Baden-Württemberg has also confirmed their support.

V/A/F: Cool!

R: So, the funding is explicitly for the student work in the publication. I have also inquired with other foundations in Baden-Württemberg, but, unfortunately, they do not support projects that take place in other states—so, sadly, we cannot apply for further funding here, because the GfZK is in Saxony.

A/V/F: !? 19

Our plan for GUD *was to discuss the field of graphic design from the most heterogeneous of perspectives as possible. The guest speakers have a variety of focuses and work in four different countries.* 20

We also contact cultural institutions abroad because they are often more interested in supporting cultural exchange and interdisciplinary projects, and also because they offer funding opportunities for graphic design that are lacking in Germany. But how do we argue that a local design practice is important, while we are trying to think in terms of decentralized practices? 21

Often, we do not receive any justification for why our application has been rejected, but sometimes an interesting discussion suddenly opens up. 22

F: The application was rejected. However, we have the opportunity to respond to their criticisms and file an appeal. The foundation is asking how the political activist approach is reflected in the realization of the symposium?

A/R: At present, feminist theories, practices, methods and stories are increasingly being discussed and their validity questioned, not only within the art and cultural scenes. Against the backdrop of a (right-wing) conservative backlash on a social and political level on the one hand, and the diversity of current feminist practices on the other, it is clear that the necessity of feminist critique has lost none of its significance.

F: They are also questioni whether a book is a suitab format? Here, I would argu that the symposium and th various seminars are part o collective editorial work ar that the contents of the bo are the result of a transver working process.

A/R: Let's acknowledge th and emphasize that as lor as there are "classical" des guides that structurally exclude the voices of wom BIPoC and others, then feminist/alternative/activis guides are needed. For u the book is also important a material object that car physically assert itself on t bookshelf alongside othe modernist design books

In this instance, another aspect becomes clear, namely th graphic design is viewed as a commercial activity and sho be funded as such. The foundation draws our attention to the fact that in the case of a publication we should also ta the revenue generated from it into consideration. This is tr … but it is difficult to calculate the revenue from a publicat that we do not even know we will be able to produce yet.

However, the second, revised application is approved.

Working with Time is Working Against Us

We often find ourselves saying that we'd have been able t work better if we'd had a little more time leading up to the project. But is that really true? Don't good ideas and poter partners peter out over time? Are protracted working processes affordable or are they just exhausting? *GUD* w soon become a reality once we agree on a date for the *G Symposium*. We decide to take on the financial risks and organizational challenges ourselves, come what may.

V: … we're currently working on a project proposal that is dedicated to collective, feminist and anti-hierarchical practices and strategies in graphic design—there will also be a symposium on this, which will take place next February. 27

O: The remaining funds have already been allocated. If you are able to arrange for the project to take place at another time, please feel free to contact us again …

At this point in time, the participants' travel arrangements have already been booked and some people have already registered to attend. The symposium can no longer be postponed. This situation is not untypical for projects of this kind, but it is always a risk to continue working on projects that are not fully financed … and a real test. 28

Sometime in November 2019: After several rejections, we submit another application. The foundation responds a few days later and offers to support the project. They go on to add: 29

O: Since we have received more than 200 applications in this round and many project outlines are promising and in our opinion worthy of funding, we are unfortunately unable to approve the entire amount of funding requested due to other commitments. We hope, however, that you will manage to obtain additional funding. 30

Yes, this is precisely our strategy: We submit applications to various funding institutions almost simultaneously in the hope that we will receive a sufficient amount of combined funding. We produce countless online documents, schedules and drafts of the budget. We are often working at different times and in different groups. We are rarely in the same place until the symposium itself. The simultaneity and the different application forms make it difficult to keep track of everything. 31

Way Too Short(fall) 32

SHORTFALL IS THE DIFFERENCE BETWEEN THE ACTUAL PROJECT COSTS AND THE FUNDS AVAILABLE. IF THE TOTAL EXPENDITURE IS REDUCED, THE AMOUNT OF FUNDING MAY ALSO DECREASE. IF THE TOTAL EXPENDITURE INCREASES, IT IS THE APPLICANT'S RESPONSIBILITY TO COVER THE ADDITIONAL REQUIREMENTS. THIS IS WHY FIXED GRANTS, WHERE THE AMOUNT OF FUNDING REMAINS THE SAME REGARDLESS OF ANY CHANGES TO THE PROJECT, ARE MORE STABLE, PROVIDED YOU GET THEM. 33

o: In your cost projection and financial plan, you write that you expect to receive funding from our foundation. How do you intend to carry out the proj if you do not receive this funding?

We cannot find a correct or even a good answer to this question. In most cases, unapproved funds are offset by savings or by increasing non-cash resources, i.e. unpaid w The problem can be avoided by not listing certain expens and pretending that they do not occur at all. For funding organizations, it then looks as if we are only lacking a sm amount, which would be secured by their funds. In reality, we apply to several foundations to cover the funds we lac based on our experience that not every application is approved.

A Whole Lot of Application Forms

WHEN APPLYING FOR FUNDING, THE FINANCIAL PL IS USUALLY SUMMARIZED IN A FEW MAIN ITEMS.

This results in high total amounts—personnel costs, mate costs … But what lies behind them? We always enclose a detailed financial plan and wonder whether anyone eve reads it.

v: … I tried to enter our costs in the financial plan section—to do this I had to combine personnel and freelance costs.
F: What does this mean for the total cost?
v: It looks as if we have su high personnel costs, do y think it will still be OK?
F: It's hard to judge …
v: I'm submitting it now a is, so if there are any questions, we'll just hav to explain it well.

During the process, we notice time and again that there are a lot of problems when entering the information into online application forms. After all, there are real people, th work and fees behind these figures. Since we began this project, we have been working with a financial plan that is continuously updated, and in it we show what costs we expect and how these could be covered in as much detail as possible. This plan is based on estimated values to be with, which we gradually bring in line with the actual costs on the basis of quotations and actual expenditure.

Role Play: Less Play, More Strategy? 41

▲ Conversations that took place while planning *GUD*: V: Vincent Schier F: Franciska Zólyom O: Others R: Rebecca Stephany A: Anja Kaiser

We're convinced the *GUD* project is important. But can we convince others? It's not always easy to conceive a project, make applications for it, advocate for it, plan and organize it all at the same time, let alone participate in it. It is a role play in which we are authors, organizers, drivers, or even cooks, depending on the situation. 42

IN SOME CASES, PRIVATE INDIVIDUALS MAY APPLY FOR FUNDING, BUT THE FUNDS CAN ONLY BE TRANSFERRED TO A LEGAL ENTITY (AN ASSOCIATION, FOUNDATION, COOPERATIVE, OR SIMILAR). THIS RESULTS IN STRATEGIES SUCH AS CULTURAL WORKERS MAKING UP ORGANIZATIONS IN ORDER TO BE ELIGIBLE FOR FUNDING. OR PARTNERSHIPS OF CONVENIENCE BETWEEN PRIVATE INDIVIDUALS AND INSTITUTIONS THAT MUTUALLY NEED EACH OTHER—BOTH FOR THE CREATION OF THE PROGRAM AND THE LEGAL FRAMEWORK. 43

We, too, have consciously played a number of different roles while planning *GUD*. In total, one institution and three private individuals submitted successful funding applications for *GUD*. 44

A: I have spoken with the cultural department. The publication funding is intended for artists living in Leipzig who are planning a monographic publication. How do we approach this? Our publication is made up of multiple voices; it articulates connections and does not represent the work of individuals. Do we want to defend this or are we concealing the actual focus in order to avoid being excluded from the funding? F: We need to explain that collaborative work is your artistic methodology for the monograph … 45

The funding is approved. 46

THE WORKING HOURS OF FREELANCE CULTURAL PRODUCERS ARE NOT COMPARABLE WITH THE PERSONNEL AND MATERIAL INFRASTRUCTURE THAT AN INSTITUTION HAS AT ITS DISPOSAL. HOW DO YOU ESTABLISH A BALANCE IN WHICH THE INSTITUTIONAL STRUCTURE SUPPORTS THE PROJECT AND DOES NOT EXPLOIT OR CO-OPT IT? 47

F: Hello, we would like to apply for funding from your foundation for our project, *GUD*. It is about feminist and transcultural approaches in graphic design.

O: Is it an art project?

F: Not exclusively. We would like to exchange experiences and reflect on resistant aesthetics and forms of organization in the context of a symposium and a publication.

O: Interesting. If I understa[nd] correctly, you will produc[e] practical knowledge for graphic designers as a res[ult] of this process.

F: Yes, that is the idea.

O: The practical approach [is] very important. However, a[s a] foundation we are interest[ed] in trade union association[s] and not in self-employmen[t] individual professional grou[ps]. Should you apply, please [put] a focus on your researc[h] methods.

The application is not approved.

And yet … at the end of May 2020, we receive the last funding notification. We ha[ve] appealed against the negative decision an[d] refiled the application. With the help of our supporters, we finally manage to collect th[e] money for the production costs and, abov[e] all else, for the work of everyone involved.

The funding for the *Glossary of Undisciplined Design* in percentages:

36%	*GUD Symposium*	64%	*GUD* handbook
10%	Kingdom of the Netherlands – Berlin Embassy	19%	Creative Industries Fund N[L]
9%	GfZK (Leipzig Museum for Contemporary Art)	14%	Cultural Foundation of the Free State of Saxony
6%	VG Bild-Kunst	11%	University of Arts and Des[ign] Karlsruhe (HfG Karlsruhe)
6%	Rudolf Augstein Foundation	9%	Non-cash equity by Anja K[…] and Rebecca Stephany
3%	Support Association ZKM/HfG e.V.	5%	VG Bild-Kunst
2%	Swedish Arts Grants Committee's International Program (IASPIS)	3%	Stadt Leipzig Kulturamt
		2%	Stiftung Landesbank Baden-Württemberg
		1%	Support Association ZKM/HfG e.V.

HARDWORK The Dough – Roll out the dough with the rolling pin. When would you turn down a job? Roll it as thin as possible. Do you work too much? Stretch the dough with all of your hands – be careful not to make holes. Are you paid enough for your work?

SOFTWORK The Filling – Peel the apples. Which soft skills do designers of today need? Cut them into small pieces. Do you personally find fulfilment in your work? Mix the apples with the raisins and the lemon juice. How do you find serenity at work?

COWORK – Put the butter on the dough. Are you author or service provider? Put the filling lengthwise on the dough. What does a Strudel look like? Roll the filling into the dough – strudel it! Would you like to mix profession and private life more or less?

for Strudeling

SOFTWORK
HARDWORK

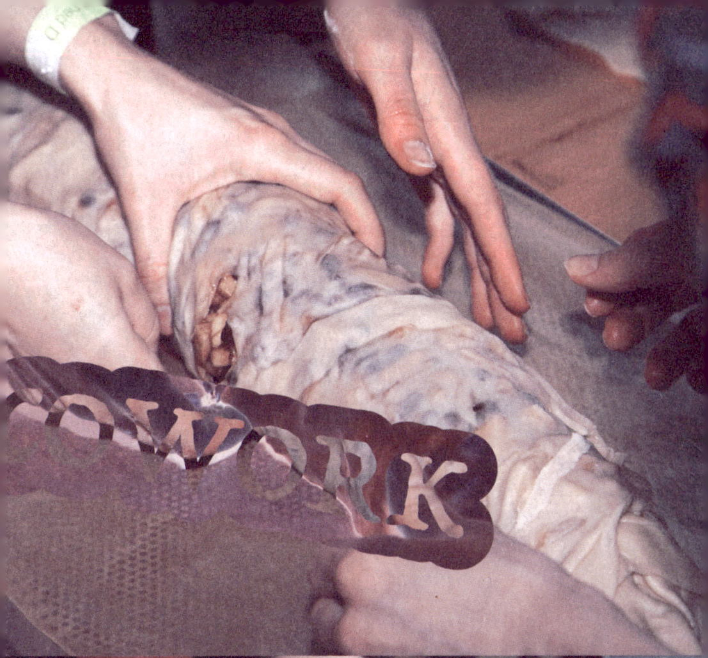
COWORK

We use the term strudeling as a metaphor for a multi-layered
of work, in which spheres of professional and private lif
constantly mixing. In dynamic contact with other peo
boundaries blur and competences are combined and shared.
concept is based on Sheila de Bretteville's idea of Strudeli
described in Dirty Desig
Fuzzy The
in

"Relational existence is only attached to gender by history — not by genes, not by biology, not by some essential 'femaleness.' A relational person thinks about other human beings and their needs during the day. I used to call it 'strudeling,' because strudel is a layered pastry. A relational person allows notions about other people to come in and interrupt the trajectory of thinking or designing. I don think strudeling is an exclusively 'female' way of thinki but I might call it a feminist way of thinking, becaus to acknowledge and valorize this attitude is to separate it from gender and free it from the nineteenth-century idea that women's culture should be locked away in the private, domestic realm."

We translated Sheila's idea of Strudeling into a workshop format for the GUD Symposium. In constantly changing constellations of p
pants, we prepared eight lovely apple strudels. In order to d
we installed three stations called SOFTWORK, HARDW
and COWORK, where questions about work and leisure time
posed and discussed. The participants could exchange view
experiences while keeping their hands busy with the d

ıs of life are affected
ıide effects of patri-
Male Monikers bring
ty relief for non-male-
ınesses through the
 mechanism of revers-
e expectations.
on: Male Monikers
ting ultimate libera-
ıt they will provide
 break in this capi-
dilemma. Please seek
nal feminist support.
biases will continue
ı. Tell your accom-
ıbout your experiences.
 Male Monikers will be
ous in the near future.

FORCE A MALE

E-MAIL ASSIS-TANT

GIVE ME A BREAK

MASCULINELY YOURS, FAKE-MIKES, FAKE-BRYANS AND FAKE-BRADS

USE TO ALLEVIATE
OCIALLY CONSTRUCTED
SYMPTOMS OF:
• HEY GIRL ...
PROTECTIVE KNIGHTISM
• UNWELCOMED
FLIRT ATTACKS
• BAD SALARIES...

LAY HIM OFF ANYTIME! LET YOUR INBOX REST FROM CONDESCENDING INQUIRIES AND STUPID RESPONSE

BYE BOB

LET YOUR E-MAILS BE SIGNED BY MALE MONIKER.

HOW BOB LISTENS:

#CAPITALISMLOVESDECEPTION

By the way: Bots and "intelligent" virtual assistants often speak with female service voices. The tech industry is normalizing the idea that machines must speak like submissive human women. This assumption can at least be countered in the settings on your respective digital devices.

Try to imagine designing with a computer like this:

The display you are looking at is black and white, 9 inch (19×13 cm) with a modest resolution of 512×342 pixels (72 ppi) The computer's microprocessor runs at 7.8 MHz, connected to 512 KB (kilobyte!) RAM There is no internal hard drive but a built-in, 3.5-inch floppy disk drive with a capacity of 400 KB In order to boot the operating system, you need to insert a disk with the system software You can connect an external 3.5-inch floppy disk drive to store any files on a 400 KB disk or run a software program off of a floppy disk The only available programs to design with are rudimentary versions of MacDraw (vector-based), MacPaint (pixel-based) and Mac Vision (a hardware/software interface to digitize still frames from a video camera or VCR) You can only work in one program and on one file at a time; you cannot work in layers and, if you make a mistake, only command-Z can be used and only then to "undo" singular actions There is a simple cable mouse and keyboard You can neither make nor export files larger than 400 KB There are no PDF files—you cannot just send your file to a printing office or upload it somewhere You can connect the computer to a monochrome, dot matrix printer or first-generation laser printer or to a rudimentary dial-up modem

As it is also not possible to generate an offset printing plate directly from the computer, nor can your file be printed straight to photographic film in order to make a plate, you must print the file out on the above-mentioned printers. If your printing format is larger than US letter size, you need to print the work in parts and paste them together before taking this "master" to an offset printer of your choice, who will then have it photographed with a specialized process camera in order to produce negative film for the offset printing plate

And just so that we're clear: there is no Internet, no email, no Google Image search, no JPEG, no YouTube tutorial, no copy-pasting from Wikipedia, no Adobe Creative Cloud, no HD, full HD, 4 or 5K "one billion colors" Retina display, no 16 GB RAM, no Wi-Fi, no Airdrop, not even an USB.

FOR PLAYING FAST AND LOOSE WITH TOOLS

These are the technical specifications of a Macintosh 512K from the year 1984, with reflective notes on the conditions and realities of using such a computer for design at that time.

In 1985, the Los Angeles-based designer April Greiman was invited to create an entire issue of the long-running journal Design Quarterly, published by the Walker Art Center, dedicated to her own work. By the early 1980s, Greiman, born in 1948, was already known for experimenting with pixel-based collage and still video imagery in her designs. She had also been an early adopter of the Macintosh computer, long before it became the default design tool, at a time when most of Greiman's colleagues were downright skeptical—if not terrified—of the idea of integrating a computer into their design practices. For Greiman, the case was clear:

Without knowing what format it would take, I knew it would involve something of all the technology I had been throwing myself at over the past three years.

She decided to use the invitation from Design Quarterly as an opportunity to master the Macintosh technology of the

evolution of humanity and technology, creation and creativity. For that, she created a giant, human-sized, double-sided poster, 33×76.5 inch (84×194 cm) that could be folded down to the standard, 32-page-format of Design Quarterly.

It took Greiman more than six months to develop, design and output the poster on her laser printer. She began working on a Macintosh 128K, the original Apple Macintosh personal computer, released in early 1984, and then, upon its release later that year, continued on a 512K. With an initial selling price of $3,195 (around $7,600 or 6,300 euros in 2020, taking inflation into account), the 512K was a very expensive, slow, bulky and, by today's standards, prehistoric device.

With limited possibilities for design that such a basic device would offer, the work is a technical masterpiece in many respects. The defining image is a digitized, life-size, two-headed portrait of Greiman's naked body. It was captured as live video stills from her Sony Beta camera using MacVision, a device that could digitize stills from composite video. Once all the images were captured, Greiman managed to import the stills from MacVision to MacDraw, where she composed the collage, as well as importing bitmapped typography and images that she had drawn in MacPaint. As MacDraw only offered one visual layer to work with, the process was as much trial and error as it was time-consuming as each visual or textual element was automatically merged into one big, bitmapped surface. During the process, entering command-Z, making copies of all major changes in the layout, as well as practicing one's impromptu composition skills, were a designer's best friend. Once the collage was finished, Greiman had to print it out on her LaserWriter as 21 US-letter-sized parts; the print office she worked with then tiled the pages together to capture it on film in order to create a single source for offset printing. Greiman titled the issue Does It Make Sense?

Ultimately, the speed with which this new technology encouraged me to work threw it into overload. System Errors kept popping up making it impossible to print out the final image. One night I left the printer on to print overnight, since it takes a fair amount of time for it to process this much information. In the morning, when I returned to the studio, I saw that the printer had left out the entire bottom half of my body. When I looked at the screen to see what was going on, I noticed that my entire body was no longer there. Everything else layered on top of my former self was as plain as day. So, somewhere near the planet Pluto we believe, a 6 foot 4 ½ inch digitized image of April Greiman is orbiting.

Leaning on Wittgenstein's statement "if you give it a sense, it makes sense," Greiman created her own kind of mythology by plotting a visual timeline on the front of the poster that shows the evolution of technology in relation to the history of the earth and humankind—including the big bang, as well as Greiman's birth date. In a fuzzy, bitmapped aesthetic, dream symbolism, abstract hand gestures, stretched text fragments (that describe such things as different types of weather and suggestive statements like "sleep in nothingness"), a brontosaurus and cave paintings all float around the portrait of Greiman and her second head or "spiritual double." On the back of the collage, colorful and atmospheric video stills of explosions or seemingly otherworldly eruptions are scattered among textual reflections and personal notations by Greiman that detail the tedious design and production process of the poster.

Apart from performing some kind of techno-magic with this early version of a desktop computer and confronting an entire professional group with the digital possibilities of design, *Does It Make Sense?* is an extraordinary manifestation of a deeply personal, poetic and passionately sensual approach to design and working digitally, making it a groundbreaking example of a suggestive and metaphorical approach to technology.

Greiman, April (1986) *Design Quarterly: Does It Make Sense?* 133, Cambridge, MA: MIT Press/Walker Art Center.

Ibid.

Are you bored of rolling around in books
and listening to lectures?
ead of sitting quietly in the library, do you wish
for physical interaction with the
ɔh-so theoretical content?

n our new
arning method
is just right
or you!

Metabolic Learning* combines
theory and practice.
It turns food into a medium
for graphic content
and makes use of
a social event to acquire
saturated knowledge.

Try it and see for yourse
how easy and tasty
digesting theory can b
Learning has never been
more delicious!

*Glossary terms
printed with algae based ink on rice paper.

eila Levrant de Bretteville opened the **GUD Symposium** *and ogram with her lecture 'Looking Back, Looking Forward or t's Design Got to do with Undisciplinarity?' R for Relationality s together transcribed excerpts from the lecture, as well as conversations with de Bretteville conducted during the osium weekend.*

ad never heard of undiscipli-y and looked it up in the *rd English Dictionary* (*OED*). se one of the definitions [of plinarity] that bothered me nost. It seemed to me that it ioned disciplinarity as if it had nothing to do with lived experience, and that it was opposed to experience and intuition, which seems absolutely crazy. How could we ever live without experience and intuition? And so, I began to just play with the words:

ion from the *OED*)
n.

DISCIPLINARY RELATES TO KNOWLEDGE ACQUIRED BY LEARNING AS OPPOSED TO BY EXPERIENCE OR INTUITION

ion from Sheila)
erb

UNDISCIPLINARITY RELATES O KNOWLEDGE CQUIRED BY LIVED EXPERIENCE, LISTENING, CONVERSATION ND INTUITION

R FOR RELATIONALITY

It seems to me that the kind of knowledge you get from living, and from listening and from conversation and intuition, is very important to what we can do in exchange for the crazy world we live in. I'm really interested in the way in which we can displace the hegemony of tablished, formal design langua in ways that are not dismissive of what's good about it, but I'r also interested in what is left o which is a ton of things.

The Special Edition of Aspen Times by Sheila Levrant de Bretteville, newspaper, 1971

They asked me to do a journal about the *Aspen Des Conference* that took place in the summer of 1971. A journal takes a lot of time, as those of you who eve worked on one know, and I didn't want to spend the whole of fall putting out a journal. I wanted it over b the time the conference was over. So, what I did was I gave everybody [who attended the conference] a bla piece of the newspaper so that I could produce a who issue, which was called *The Special Edition of Asp Times*. I put a piece of the newspaper in everybody's er so that they could trim it over and do whatever y wanted. As long as they would give it back to by Thursday, it got to be in the newspaper. This is of my favorite projects because I had no idea it it was going to look like. When I got all these piec-ack, I pasted them all up—we used to paste things vn in the olden days. We had given out cameras took the pictures that people gave us. As a result, as a very unique way of looking. People wrote on newspaper blanks], they drew on them, said things ut people they were interested in, or people they n't like, and they did whatever they wanted with it. re are 16 pages of it. It was my idea of a news-er—a sample of participatory democracy.

Design and Human Bodies by Ivan Chermayeff, booklet design for the *International Design Conference* in Aspen, 1994

sign and Human Bodies, intervention Class Action Collective at the *ernational Design Conference* in pen, 1994, classactioncollective.org

vant to show you something some of my students did. van Chermayeff is a very fa-s American designer, and d the image on the right, for *gn of Human Bodies*, which another international design conference in Aspen [in 1994]. Chermayeff put his name on the design pretty big so you can't really miss who did it. It is a Matisse rip off in a way, from my per-spective, but anyway. Our students looked at it and went "aargh." They took all the parts and reassembled them, as you can see on the image on the left. They didn't stop there—they went on and made a whole pamphlet about it: (*Reads from the pamphlet*) "This is an image of a woman, naked on her bed, legs spread, contorted, passive, avail-able… She has no identity; she IS an identity. She is the logo of this conference." It's like, what was he thinking?!

I wrote [*A Reexamination of Some Aspects of the Design Arts from the Perspective of a Woman Designer* (1974)] when I was in my early thirties and had just had a child and was running graphic design projects of my own, as well as teaching. And I was running on so many channels, all of them were actually supportive channels, and yet the way in which [women] were being presented in dominant culture was in a binary way.

Feminism to me is about bringing public professional values closer to private domestic values, to break the boundaries of this binary system. There is some level of caring about other people, which is part of women's traditional role, that continues to a certain extent. But I realized that there is also a positive side to that: the ability to think on many different levels at the same time. I saw our thinking about different human needs at the same time as a talent. Human needs are as important as any kind of workplace needs, and it is important to balance those things. But the fact that those needs were actually separated out into both the public sphere and the private sphere deny relational experience—this is precisely what I wanted to challenge.

Certain kinds of "female" behaviors were acceptable at home but weren't acceptable at work. I was thinking that the workplace was suffering from the lack of things that were happening in a home, which had to do with feelings and things that are not as controlled. You had to deal with something happening all the time that you didn't expect. All those things are normative for the home and they are actually normative in the

A Reexamination of Some Aspects of the De Arts from the Perspective of a Woman Desi by Sheila Levrant de Bretteville, pages from *A in Society: Women and the Arts*, 1974

work-world but it's made as if t is not true. Work-world runs in very orderly kind of way and, at home, it is far more complex ar chaotic. … [As a first generatio American,] I grew up in a hous hold that was filled with immigrants, who were staying with There were people living and sleeping in every room. The kit en was the only room that didn have somebody's bed in there. I ally didn't have a household wh had anything like those kinds o separations.

'our design projects can only
e part of undisciplinarity if
you think about what participation really means, in its deepest sense. Which is a real respect for the diversity within any audience, anywhere, and to be really committed to bridging all boundaries of class, color, nationality, sexuality. You can't only be with people who you like to
e with, who make you feel
ood about yourself; you have
be with people that make
u really uncomfortable. Be-
use that is the only way
u are going to make any
fference in the world, from
y perspective.

ly job is to make it possible for students to become themselves in
work. Because every single individual is so unique, if you can bring
part of you into that work, your work will be unique. And how to
rom being who you are into your work is a very exciting thing for a
her to be involved in.

B for Blanketing

Are you giving your friends too much discount on your work? Can you imagine working with your (love) partner? We need more transparency on issues that are not usually talked about. The confidential space under the blanket encourages questions about the price and value of our work, both in terms of social approval and hard cash, about failed projects, tips and tricks of the trade and successful strategies for collaborating with others.

BLANKETING takes the German expression "zusammen unter eine Decke stecken," which literally translates as "to be hiding under a blanket together" and means something like "to conspire together secretly."

When was the last time you ditched a project.
What would you like to ch
Which design tool w
UNTER
EINER
DECKE
discount

Are you giving your frien
do you consider a project fini
Why do you think I'm here?

The blanket
was first installed for
people to interact with at the

Master's Tools (DESIGNING AS OTHERING)

Although the notion of the Other has always been a concern many disciplines dealing with questions of subjectivity and ntological difference between beings, when we talk about the rms otherness and othering, we can no longer think some innate dissimilarities between bodies. Rather, a form disparity comes in, which is socially constructed and imsed by the groups in power to dominate, subjugate and disenanchise the rest. As queer, feminist and anti-colonial schols have long scrutinized, the conditions for otherness strongly ly upon the oppositional and hierarchal binary thinking that etaches bodies from each other. Such binarism positions not nly the Self (oneself) antithetical to the Other (someone else), ıt also man to woman, heterosexuality to homosexuality, white in to black skin, civilized to primitive, modern to traditional, tional to emotional, Western to Eastern, occidental to oriental, ealthy to indigent, able to disabled, young to old and, evenıally, Us to Them. It is a constant polarization contingent upon ıe superiority of one side and the inferiority of the other, perıtuated by epistemic, territorial and corporeal control. Over ıe centuries, this binary logic reproduces both the dominatıg subject (the ideal, Western, white, male, secular human body) ıd its 'ontological other' (the barbaric, underdeveloped, otrusive, hypersexualized body) as an unremitting process othering.

Tracing the motives of this process, in The Origin of thers, novelist Toni Morrison argues that the invention of ıe Other helps to constitute the Self as a "normal" and aceptable person: the more animal the Slave is deemed, the more uman the Master becomes.[01] The Other is demonized as it opardizes the privileges that the Self has obtained precisely y not being the Other. Feminist philosopher Sara Ahmed

01 Morrison, Toni (2017) *The Origin of Others*. Cambridge, MA: Harvard University Press.

similarly analyzes how the Other—who is "not us" yet "endange what is ours—invokes "abjection" that looms out of the bounda ies of the body of the Self, creating the sense of fear, obscure-ness and unease that demarcates the Self and the Other. Diffe ence, here, is not inherently registered in physical bodies, but it is the very borders between bodies that defines the subje (the Self) as separate from the object (the Other). This sense of abjection, thus, is not toward "a particular object/body," bu toward an encounter between the bodies that imperils one side's prerogatives.[02] This formulation, which posits that the impetus of othering is not natural but relational, enables us to situate design better by understanding that the material co dition of otherness is more about power relations that take place in these very encounters than about individuals or spo-radic events.

Many design scholars have already discussed how the Othe is constantly reproduced by the designed: from objects and spaces to images and technologies. They have also scrut nized how design practice is complicit in underpinning segre-gation in society and how the discipline has also created its ow Others through employment, historiography and citational practices. What I further argue is that design does not merely contribute to global inequalities but is also a pillar of it. Desig is the firsthand agency that constructs normal bodies contra abject bodies based on hierarchal oppositions. To recall Sara Ahmed's otherness, it is design that tangibly demarcates the borders of bodies and materializes the bodily encounters betwee the Self and the Other through its outcomes (i.e. artifacts, images, spaces, sites, technologies etc.). Design(ing), conse-quently, is but an act of othering.

There are many designed ways of othering that I call Master's tools here. The term comes from black feminist auth Audre Lorde's renowned maxim "the master's tools will never dismantle the master's house" with which she urges the slave (the othered) to find new strategies to combat the dominatior of the master (hegemony).[03] But who is the "master" in this context (if there is neither a strict duality as one evil and one good, nor as one absolute assailant versus one permanent victim)? The master here is rather equivalent to Ahmed's "whi men" as "an institution," as a broader epistemological and ontological category that does not signify the whiteness but

02 Ahmed, Sara (2000) *Strange Encounters: Embodied Others in Post-Coloniality*. London: Routledge.

03 Lorde, Audre (2007 [1984]) 'The Master's Tools Will Never Dismantle the Master's House', *Sister Outsider: Essays and Speeches*. Berkeley, CA: Crossing Press, 110–114.

ite supremacy, not maleness but hegemonic masculinity, t heterosexuality but heteronormativity.[04] In order to find ategies to counteract these human-made institutions, I gue that we should first identify what their mechanisms are d how they operate. Therefore, I sketch out a set of Master's ols of othering in which design is directly or indirectly rtaking:

MONST (1) ERIZING

Since colonial times, the Other has been depicted as a vage, filthy and barbaric monster by the modern subject, th an aberrant look that threatens humanity. This "threat" metimes came from the chattel slaves rendered as cadav-ous monsters with their disfigured bodies; sometimes the reat came from women and differently-abled bodies who were rnt alive, ostracized or displayed in ethnological ex-bits. Today, monstrosity is still attributed to images of eer, gender non-conforming, immigrant, and diasporic dies. The recent decades, for example, have demonstrated w the discourses around war-on-terrorism and anti-refugee litics[05] reinvent the "racialized and sexualized non-stern-monster-Other," contra to the "normal citizen" prop-ated by mostly implicit designed images that pave the way r justifying military interventions, ethnic cleansing d the criminalization of the non-Western body.

TAXONOMI (2) ZING

The taxonomy of bodies, based firmly on hierarchal dualism, s long been used to prove the "deviation" of bodies, not ly socially but also scientifically. Although visually doc-ented anthropomorphic studies of the colonized, hyster-al women and "freaks" from the 19th and 20th centuries are longer favored ethically, today, their updated versions ep categorizing bodies into every single trait from sex to

04 Ahmed, Sara (2014) 'White Man', *feministkillkoys*. Via: https://feministkilljoys.com/2014/11/04/white-men/ (Accessed on September 20, 2017)

05 Puar, Jasbir K. and Rai, Amit S. (2002) 'Monster, Terrorist, Fag: The War on Terrorism and the Production of Docile Patriots', *Social Text* 20(3(72)), 117–148.

social class. Biometric technologies, for instance the air port millimeter wave scanner machine, a design based on bi logical dimorphism, target all gender nonconforming bodie as deviant and risky. Facial recognition technologies, iri scanners, gait recognition systems and fingerprint scanner likewise, legitimize rigid identity categories as physical measured and the only reliable information. By doing this, they also catalyze racial profiling, denial of service or ev calumniation for the 'phenotypical others' that were once targeted by criminal anthropometry; a phenomenon today th can be called a designerly repetition of the history.

IGNOR(3)ING

Where monsterization is politically incorrect, the Mast deliberately ignores the Other to deny their knowledge, existence and dignity through exclusion and erasure. In th context of design, historically, women, women of color, people of color, differently-abled, queer and non-Western design practitioners, researchers and educators have been systematically omitted from the history books, exhib tions, course materials, conferences and bibliographies. Although it has been decades since design scholars first ac dressed these issues, and the visibility of the Other has definitely increased, both representation of neglected boc ies and the production and circulation of their knowledg still falls short.

TAM(4)ING

To understand the potency of taming the Other, one can inquire into how enforced domestication has oppressed an silenced women for centuries or how European missionaries used it as an effective technique for assimilation, civiliz tion and soft annihilation of the colonized by means of education, religion and the like. This strategy has always been publicized by design too; such as convincing Muslim women in colonies to unveil while enforcing dress codes li Tignon Laws to desexualize and attenuate African women in the US in the 18th century, or the tokenistic granting of cit zenship to "well-behaved" immigrants and recruiting peopl from underrepresented groups. Today, the institutional na taming is the politics of "inclusion" and "diversity," ich, in Sara Ahmed's words, signifies a shift from a confron- tional to a collaborative work model and changes the rceptions of a problem instead of changing the problem self.[06] This is what many diversity-driven projects from dvantaged" social design practitioners have been executing th "disadvantaged" communities: conflict-free design with cile bodies.

APPRO(5)PRIATING

Cultural and political appropriation of the Other in the rvice of the Master is another common strategy to decon- xtualize, trivialize and erase the ethos of the Other. Once e colonizer's abjection toward the colonized turned to exoticization, it has brought about fetishized appro- iation as a new form of authority and possession over e Other. Arrogation of the values and practices of others .e. indigenous peoples, tribes and natives) can be found a myriad of modern and contemporary material configura- ons—from graphic, textile and fashion design (i.e. symbols, tterns, colors) to product and interior design (i.e. cred objects, furniture, totems)—as a tactic of slow dis- entification and, eventually, depoliticization of their ruggles for self-preservation.

DOUBLE-O(6)THERING

While the Master might not be a necessarily stereotypical elf"—as they can also be an abjected Other—the Other ght not merely be an oppressed victim, but can be another ent for creating other forms of oppressions for other hers. For instance, in colonial times, while they were sub- gated by the colonizer male, the colonized male also ben- ted from hegemonic masculinity that allowed them to repress d control the colonized women, who became three times re enslaved: by the colonizer male, the colonizer female d by their male, colonized counterparts. Today, such pression pyramids can be seen in the form of, for instance,

06 Ahmed, Sara (2017) *Living a Feminist Life*. Durham: Duke University Press.

liberal/imperial feminism — by which non-Western women ar treated as having no agency and are waiting to be saved by 'white' feminists — and pink-washing/homonormativity — by which the immigrant Other are deemed new homophobes in Western cities. These political strategies, meanwhile, are disseminated mainly by designed propaganda.

PITY(7)ING

Showing compassion and empathy for the Other is the las and rather controversial Master's tool, since it mostly involves benevolence and good intentions. Yet, the economy charitable emotions is also linked to the 'savior complex,' similar to that of the colonial Western missionary who wer to faraway lands to "help" and "illuminate" the so-called underdeveloped. Postcolonial scholars' critiques of human itarianism have taught us that the feeling of compassion for the "needy" transforms itself into a total otherness. not only reinforces the privileges of the helpers, salving their conscience, but also distances the Self and the Othe further by consolidating condescension of the Self withou addressing deep structural problems imposed on the Other One can recall how the politics of pity has been adopted b design lately with the discourses around refugee "crisis," war-on-terrorism and African girls in need of sanitary pro ucts, under the banner of emancipation and solidarity and yet in the name of profitability.

Monster's Tools (DESIGNING AS BOTHERING)

Master's tools can surely be proliferated further, yet it is important to move from denouncing the problems to propour ing maneuvers. Thus, here, I shift to a set of counteractions, which I call Monster's tools, as a form of reclamation like the words queer, dyke, slut or fag. If the Other is deemed onster," then it can also be something literally to be feared d a threat to the authority of the Master.

As mentioned earlier, monstrosity, queerness and otherness ve often been linked to each other, validated by the firsthand counts of LGBTQI+ folks who have long been regarded as geymen and abjects. In recent decades, activists and scholars queer and transgender studies have found more affinity ch monsters in popular culture (such as comics, cartoons and rror movies), who are mostly represented as outcast, effem-ate and hyper-sexualized, in contrast with heroes, who dom-antly conform to heteropatriarchal norms and white ethics. is embracement of the monster may have become more pres-t with queer scholar Jack Halberstam's affirmation that onsters can offer pointed critiques of normativity and a queer ernative,"[07] but definitely peaked in 2016, after Netflix put e horror movie Babadook in their LGBT film category and ousands of queers adopted it like it was one of the family.

One of the most acknowledged queer monsters in history is, doubtedly, Frankenstein's monster. Writing in 1816, Mary elley, at the age of 19, had an epiphany after long painful ghts of trying to write a ghost story: "I have found it! What rified me will terrify others!" This exact intention—of "ter-ying others"—and the very physical body of Frankenstein's onster as a freak child disdained by its own creator, also in-ired transgender studies scholar Susan Stryker. Stryker forges direct link between the figure of (her own) transsexual body d Frankenstein's monster, as a "less than human" embodiment at is alienated from its own self.[08] As well as the identifica-n of Frankenstein's monster with the Other, over the decades, her areas of study have used elements of the novel and mon-osity: disability studies, for example, reclaimed the "crip-ss," while Afrofuturists often use images of grotesque and sfigured bodies.

On the other hand, it is not suggested here that all queers d Others relate to the figure of the monster. I use the term as possible re-appropriation of the master's intention, as a twist existing discourses around the Other and a claim for the agen-of the monster who "has been wronged and seeks justice… en the injustice is nearly forgotten."[09] Monster's tools offer a

07 Halberstam, Jack (2011) *Queer Art of Failure*. Durham: Duke University Press, 181.

08 Stryker, Susan (1994) 'My Words to Victor Frankenstein above the Village of Chamounix', *GLQ* 1(3), 237–254.

09 Tuck, Eve and Ree, C. (2013) 'The Glossary of Haunting', *Handbook of Autoethnography*, Holman Jones, Stacey, Adams, Tony E. and Ellis, Carolyn, eds. California: Left Coast Press, Inc., 649.

set of strategies for defying the Master's tools, which also bare the possibility of transforming into a counter-hegemonic criti practice. In the context of design, in my works, I sketched ou an open-ended yet methodologically formulated set of propositions for ways of undoing, queering and decolonizing the design theory, practice and discipline to counteract the rami cations that design generates. Monster's tools will be a continuation of these strategies, envisioning the act of designing bothering not only the master but also the world around him

EMBRACING THE MONSTER'S TO(1)OLS

Embracing one's own monstrous tools that have been deem worthless, ill-favored or dangerous by the Master is a crucial start. One can remember how, during the French Rev lution, the Tricoteuse (knitting women)—who were once considered as "mothers of the revolution" and then deeme "viragos, whores and monsters" and banished from government proceedings—started gathering around the guilloti platform during the executions and quietly knitted.[10] The very fact that knitting, an activity considered domestic, tender and feminine, was juxtaposed with one of the most dreadful events forged an immense abhorrence in public. Cr ating such revulsions by challenging norms and taboos around, for instance, such condescended practices (i.e. kni ting, cooking, ornamenting), dehumanized physical conditions (i.e. menstruation, dis/ability) or disgraced manne (i.e. effeminacy, excess) is a decisive way to intimidate the power. Also, one's own inherited knowledge and cosmologies that have been erased and belittled as "kitsch," unscienti or incorrect should also be revitalized as a way of delinking from the Master's epistemic dominance imposed as the "universal truth."

10 Wilson, Natalie (2020) *Willful Monstrosity: Gender and Race in 21st Century Horror.* Jefferson, North Carolina: McFarland & Company, 243.

EXPOSING THE MASTER'S (2) TOOLS

The dancer and filmmaker Yvonne Rainer once rebutted Audre
rde's maxim by saying that you can dismantle the master's
use with the master's tools as long as you expose the tools.[11]
is an important strategy because to expose something is
lay that thing open to public eyes and make that thing con-
icuous and, thereby, vulnerable. This can be done both by
omulgating the aforementioned strategies of subjugation
d by using design to expose everyday violence. Besides,
an era of political correctness, it is important to use ex-
sure for "naming the names." Toni Morrison stresses that
enever we use the word "race" instead of "racism," we cor-
oorate the idea that race is a natural phenomenon while
cism is the consequence of it as something beyond our con-
ol, although this cause-and-effect relationship is proven
be the other way around.[12] Similarly, whenever we replace
xism and homo/transphobia with "gender issues" or "sexual
ference," we alleviate the severity of real experiences.
though, as Sara Ahmed warns, when we describe a problem, we
come the problem, we should also remember Audre Lorde's
etic advice: "give name to the nameless so it can be thought."[13]

COUNTER-MEMO (3) RIZING

There are two kinds of tools in relation to "counter-
mory:" re-writing and now-writing the history—
nely, writing a "counter-history"—as a refusal to rely on
nories framed by official accounts of the past and a re-
unt of the repressed stories that come from the darkness
create contradicting yet plural narratives.[14] As to
-writing, in recent years, while design scholars who are
vested in changing normative historiography have been

11 Rainer, Yvonne (2006) *Feelings are Facts: A life.* Cambridge: MIT Press.

12 Morrison, Toni (2017).

13 Ahmed, Sara (2017); Lorde, Audre (2007[1984]), 37.

14 Foucault, Michel (1977) *Language, Counter-Memory, Practice.* Ithaca: Cornell University Press.

recuperating the histories of those who have been excluded from books, from classrooms, galleries and museums, practitioners have been focusing on archival works to shed light on personal narratives and events that were deemed non-existent (i.e. Native Land Digital, Bishopsgate Institute, Slave Voyages). As to now-writing, it refers to the momentousness of recording our own history here and now, against erasure, obliviousness and amnesia. Today's ongoing techniques of othering (i.e. from hate crimes to human rights violations) can only be accurately archived and made accessible for other generations today. Writing-history-as-witnessing-it to prevent prospective grand narratives is another designerly monster's tool.

BOUNDARY-BLUR(4)RING

How can we overcome oppositional categories that are extremely entrenched in our daily practices, ways of thinking and embodied values? How can we theoretically and practically exist on borderlines, on margins and on liminal spaces? Pursuing these answers is another huge step in exercising counterhegemonic monstrosity that could go beyond binaries. One can start unfolding the conditions and effects of every single hierarchal dichotomy by scrutinizing how they are being both materially and discursively reproduced every day. To do this, it is pivotal to drift away from design and explore cross-disciplinary and non-disciplinary knowledges, such as border thinking, which can open infinite doors for us to understand other cosmologies, customs and ways of being to find many others within otherness.

HAUNT(5)ING

Whenever those subjected to violence mention responding to violence with violence, the majority feels troubled. For instance, Frantz Fanon, who defined decolonization as an absolute disorder and violence taken over by the native, is often excused as being misinterpreted. Meanwhile, there is a decades-long debate around Valerie Solanas' SCUM Manifesto and whether she really meant "cutting up men" or used it as a metaphor. The deadlock of these discussions

a fallacy that the violence toward the othered might
ne to a peaceful end by the violator's own accord. Critical
sign practices, likewise, suffer from this problem of
ilding the wilding' by addressing the most urgent and
cious issues peacefully and passively through aesthetici-
tion or safe politics. However, if violence is inherent to
dern/colonial/capitalist (design) practices affecting the
sses, the sources of violence are not to be soothed, but
ould be either ousted by force or "haunted." This act of
unting should be considered not a short-term fix, but a long-
rm revenge for "wronging wrongs," as "the cost of subju-
tion; the price paid for violence."[15] This means that the
ols—of design's or others'—shall be used not to polish
e predicaments but to disturb them; not by being intimi-
ted but by terrifying the Master back, as Mary Shelly's
nster would do.

OTHERING THE (6) SELF

Γhis strategy is a direct response to the Master's double-
nering tool, mentioned above, since the issue is partly
out us imagining solutions to the structural problems
thin the capacities of our own internalized privileges and
ejudices. Today, for instance, as Halberstam points out,
e live in a world where instead of trying to replace the
sters who exploit us, we seek to become them in small and
aningless ways."[16] He asks us to consider designed home
vices such as Hey Google, Alexa, Echo, Siri, etc. which can
der anything in any moment: we also have servants now,
st as the Masters had. When we imagine emancipatory futures
ourselves, it is important to double-check whether this
ture has already been realized elsewhere, as a repetition
history and maintenance of current hierarchal struc-
es. Unlike such historical relapses, a radical future shall
e myriads of unprecedented futures through which we
uld encounter our own Others and coexist with them. Mean-
ile, thinking difference differently and applying this
ered notion of difference into material practices.

15 Tuck, Eve and Ree, C. (2013), 643.

16 Halberstam, Jack (2018) 'Vertiginous Capital Or, The Master's Toolkit', *Bully Bloggers*. Via: https://bullybloggers.wordpress.com/2018/07/02/vertiginous-capital-or-the-masters-toolkit-by-jack-halberstam/

SURVIVING THE TOOLS (7)

The last and the most essential tool: surviving while not hindering the survival of others. Surely, everyone has the own personal survival kit, but one I consider worth emphasizing here is forging bonds with people we are tied to—n by blood but with care and affinity—and building collectives not only for work but, also, for support and to share love, life and the energy to keep on resisting. Nevertheles this is not a call for a utopian commonness of "us," but a call to remember who "we" is in times when everybody agree when everybody is an "ally" and everybody "queers" and "decolonizes" things; a reminder that there is neither "or we" nor are our needs identical. Sharing through bounding in collectives without treating a group of people as a mon lithic category can enable us to think in a 'pluriversive' way; not on behalf of others, but only with ourselves and others, acknowledging that in this world there are man worlds within each other. This is especially important for design practices where the problem of representation (of the Other) still prevails through either generalized or radicalized aesthetics.

At this point, the utmost importance of context-, time-, an site-specific acts, through which every single subject, object and situation is treated as a unique phenomenon, comes int view. Such a self-reflective step toward surviving one's own privileges and disadvantages while caring for the survival of others and staying open to the possibilities of other forms o survival entails some omnipresent questions such as "whom do I speak for/about/with?," "when and where shall I use thes tools and why?" and, more importantly, "am I the Othered or the Other; the Master or the Monster?" These inquiries ar important to remind ourselves that our positions are everchar ing between othering and bothering; and being on the borderline means dealing with both the master and the monste at the same time. Lastly, designing is an act of negotiation between these boundaries and binaries, and the aforementior set of open-ended tools is but a symbolic and self-effacing start to go beyond them.

:spite the many (known and felt) side-effects of oosing self-employment in the cultural field under oliberal rule, paradoxically, the heroic myth of trepreneurialism is still going strong—for many ulturally minded" designers, "becoming" self-em- oyed remains the ultimate career goal. And, in turn, e apparent need to explain oneself for choosing nployment in the field of design is quite telling—the asons for why one doesn't feel suited or ready to ork "independently" are readily listed. Being one's wn boss" and working for "oneself" simply resonates o well with the contemporary cultural producer's sire for autonomy, freedom and independence. In e and in work.

Yet it is no secret that this presumed indepen- nce is entirely contingent on how disciplined the f-employed designer is as she juggles her economic pendencies, nurtures her socio-ecological entangle- ents and invests in her ever-enterprising self-machine. onomic necessities, creative choices, societal ex- ctations and life ideals, including those to combine self-employment with parenthood, are heavily inter-dependent. Together, they paint an exhausted portr of the average cultural producer.

Remember your last "passion project"—strangely sat fying yet poorly paid? The issue of self-exploitation ir the creative field is usually romanticized under the guise of creativity and the promise of visibility and su cess. We firmly believe that we are in control of our own living and working situations and, because of th buy into the "I can do what I want" narrative and even feel a sense of sovereignty as—tired but proud—we ha chosen precarity ourselves. Too perfectly it conforms to our generational addiction to self-reinvention (yest day we were a type collective, today a trend forecast-ing agency, tomorrow we redesign freedom), as well a the sick ways in which we are conditioned to believe that our human potential needs constant maximizatic

So, we bear the 24/7 invasiveness of digital labor where design work, as well as managing one's self-employment, largely takes place. We sacrifice any prospect for sustained stability by taking on the em tional, social and financial stresses of living from oject to project—all by ourselves. We travel back d forth on cheap tickets between European "cultural pitals" to keep our precarious CVs updated. Trying self-regulate the resulting anxieties, overwork, burn-t and depression, we have become a fully self-disci-ned, fully bureaucratized yet precariously looping roject" ourselves.

Silvio Lorusso, author of *Entreprecariat: Every-e Is an Entrepreneur. Nobody Is Safe,* defines ecarity as a condition of material, social, economic d existential instability and uncer-nty. With this knowledge, "choosing" ecarity becomes a strange ivilege in the way that it ucturally excludes those io simply cannot ord to dedicate time d labor to poorly anced projects.

bottomless pits in soft focus rooms

political theorist Isabell Lorey, the innocence or, tter, ignorance with which we, the members of the elf-precarizing" cultural class—those who self-impose ecarity—cling to the fairy-tale of self-realization, is ly proof of how difficult it seems to grasp the compul-e effects of liberal power structures on our bodies d selves. "Perhaps those who work creatively, these ecarious cultural producers by design, are subjects at can be exploited so easily because they seem to bear their living and working conditions eternally due to the belief in their own freedom and autonomy, du to self-realization fantasies." poooh

Thus, self-precarization must be understood not as freedom of choice but as the very personal consequences of systemic exercises of power: having involuntarily worked into the hands of exactly those (self-)exploitative models of work we were originally seeking to liberate ourselves from, Lorey goes on to argue that our adaptability and availability has mac us the perfect role models for neoliberal and bio-political governance desires. As the solo self-employe cultural producer offers such an excellent example "o the extent to which 'self-chosen' ways of living and conditions of working, including their ideas of auton my and freedom, are compatible with political and economic restructuring," pooooh corporations and organiza tions of our contemporary motivational capitalist societies have long adapted their "corporate cultures toward more agility, personalized flexibility,

nployee engagement" and "workplace wellbeing." ɛlf-responsibility, individualism and creative partici- ;tion around comfy lounges, hubs and ping-pong ɔles sound sexy at first. But now, both the solo lf-employed designer and the employee share the me biopolitical destiny, as they have internalized lf-inflicted performance pressure, increased compe- ion as desirable and self-exploitation as inescapable.

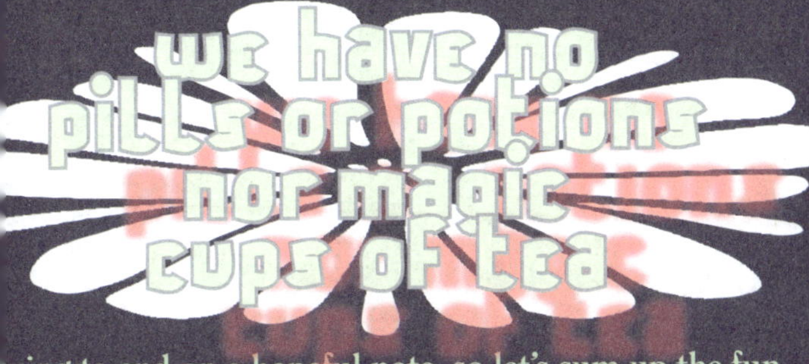

ying to end on a hopeful note, so let's sum up the fun cts: burn-out and depression are the contemporary seases of our self-determined society; there is no end how self-responsible and self-improving one can be; lf-precarization is both "a condition and effect of ɔeral power relations." pooooah So, in order to create some ɔckets of sanity in the doom loops of self-employed ɔrking life in a neoliberal society, it may be helpful to st let the realization sink in, that feelings of being ɪck, overworked or burned out aren't at all personal oblems but the result of exactly those structural, cietal conditions that neoliberal state governance ɔlds in place for us. And that they affect most of us.

There is no quick fix, but we have a few pro- ɔsals nonetheless: We could begin by dragging our ed bodies together and become one big, bad, lazy, -role-modeled cautionary tale. We could loosen up maintaining the aesthetically pleasing success story solo design self-employment, we could try to stop ding when we feel empty and overworked and go easy the urge to relentlessly reinvent ourselves.

No guilt.

E is for the Everyday
because feeling bad is a very ordinary and Everyday experience.
F is for Failure,
which is not always a bad thing since the Failure to be normal can be good.
H is for Happiness.
Happiness is a tricky term. Because the things that are supposed to make us happy often don't succeed in doing so. It's important to question what counts as Happiness and to make room for feelings of Unhappiness that express the desire for a different kind of world.[pooooooh]

pooh Lorusso, Silvio et al. (2019) *Entreprecariat: Everyone Is an Entrepreneur. Nobody Is Safe*, Lorusso, Silvio, ed. Eindhoven: Onomatopee, 170.

poooh Lorey, Isabell (2006) 'Governmentality and Self-Precarization. On the normalization of cultural producers', *CAPITAL (It Fails Us Now)*, Sheikh, Simon, ed. Berlin: b_books, 117–139.

pooooh Ibid.

poooooh Ibid.

pooooooh *The Alphabet of Feeling B* by Karin Michalski in collaboration wi Ann Cvetkovich, speech transcript, H video, 13', Germany, 2012

CRASH REPORT_1: PER-PLEXED PRESETS

)esign production today would be conceivable without digital devices and software. The con- :ional and standardized work- environment for graphic design oxed in by a software monopo- nd subscription constraints. gners hang around in front of r 16:10 workspace, mimic click eographies and internalize ılated sequences and routines hey work on their screens. e staring at the design inter- , one's gaze wanders over abricated tool palettes remi- ent of analog desks, but with er, impersonal equipment. ning to use these tools in the sical way is often the very step in a designer's education. to cut with scissors that can be dragged and dropped onto a element instead of simply ding the page into two as one t assume? An analog lasso would certainly capture more excit- ing things than fastidiously crop- ping out a placeholder. Getting used to these digital gestures is tedious and boring. Of course, many users achieve digital agency through these gestures in the long run. But, more often than not, this only leads to merely obeying design tools, which results in er- rorless software performances and predetermined design strate- gies. Regrettably, we first become skilled software insiders and experts that are bound to very spe- cific manufacturers and can even operate all the sub-palettes in our sleep. The manufacturers' in- tentions breathe down our necks, and we remain neatly pigeon-holed in the compartments that the pro- grams provide us with.

Unfortunately, software isn't soft at all. In the limbo of stan- dardization, we seem to have lost the ability to fundamentally question our software. One should be able to rampage in digital spaces without expertise, invade new programs and, in the best case, intuitively scout out our own logics and choreographies. Why aren't we establishing alternative structures and additional features instead of surrendering to the strictive monopoly of subscription madness? Software should tually allow us to get involved Emphasizing autonomy and disol dience toward our tools should be part of every design school foundation course.

Crash Report 2: Dirty Clicks

Everything can be deleted from a program interface without a trace—no grease stains, no wrinkles or residue. And, sometimes, all of our digital efforts can be irretrievably erased with a single click. But instead of hygienically and submissively tidying up in standard programs and following their logics, a potpourri of unfamiliar pro and low-fi software could be installed. The subsequent dirty clicks and faulty files come with visual and technical consequences that reveal initial information about the software, operating system and file formats themselves. When we take a closer look at the program and scruti the "default" settings, we see that social norms and expectat are cemented into the interfac and gestures. These are structu biases—unchallenged presets—that inform and enforce how anc what to design.

Artist and researcher Rosa Menkman works with the potenti for disruption and the visual a tifacts created by accidents in digital file formats. Her resea highlights the norms of tech cu ture and offers insightful strate for corrupting them. In 2015, s created the *Institutions for Resolution Disputes* to draw mo

ntion to the compromises creat-
y the standardized resolutions
t are part of our communica-
n media. Rather than seeing our
ital environment merely as a
nsparent, well-functioning in-
face, Menkman advocates for the
tch" as a digital strategy for
lly looking behind the facade.

The outcome and the visual quality of the damage reveals new information about the system, the regulations and the standards in which the *glitch* occurs.

Crash Report_3:

**Viewing distances do not exist in neu-
al environments and are not occupied by
neric viewers. Viewing does not lie out-
de of social conditions; viewers are nev-
neutral or objective. Yet in most design
ocesses, special attention is given to ad-
sting viewing distances and resolutions
order to enlarge files to the correct size
d prepare them for reproduction. Accord-
g to the traditional definition of a poster,
r example, it should have a high reach
d varying viewing distances with low
ntact times: "experts" estimate up to two
conds. If we believe these dogmas, we
t stuck with more "classical" consequenc-
and repetitive design conclusions: re-
uction, clarity, hierarchy and brevity. The
ntexts in which such designs operate
d the viewers' subjectivities are ignored
assumed to be all the same.**

Porous Viewing Distances

Numerous design theories promise a standardized gaze and a universal idea o readability, which leads to society and clients expecting the same from design. Designers must maintain enough distanc between both content and print margins to prevent typographic accidents and di order, while mastering the golden rules of typography, of course. Our tools are inescapably burdened by truths about what is good or bad.

But what if these statements, with thei redundant formulas, only confirm a uniform jargon, outdated clichés and stereo types, and design degenerates into an already-ready-made. Viewing distances can be infected, reversed or multiplied—it is simply impossible to maintain a neut distance with design tools. Viewing distances will always be affected by power relations and social conditions. It is neces sary to endure the uncertainties and doubts that come with this and even get radically entangled with those feelings.

CRASH REPORT 4: PLEASE KEEP CRASH-ING

that design grids and presets do not systemically repress unruly bodies and types. As designers, we're allowed to take our own subjective viewing distances seriously, as well as those of others, and produce countless faulty files for them all.

rous viewing distances in order to self-confidently conquer our own screen work with non-knowledge, or alternative and oppositional knowledge. Let's free our digital compulsions from routine and repetitive processes. Keep crashing and crushing!

EMOTIONAL TYPEFACES

etterforms[1] come
through
your eyes,[2]
your ears,[3]

your optic[2] and hearing nerves,[3]
nto
your brain[4]
and heart,[5]
en they evoke emotions.[6]

1

tterforms—the shapes of the stroke, its beginning and ding, thickness, angles and curves—contain details and pressions that evoke emotions from readers. They impose emselves upon other people and say “I am serious,” am friendly,” or “I am funny” in a specific tone of voice. ie “tone of voice” of a typeface is a personality or aracteristic that enables it to transform how the written ord appears on mediums, and how it reaches a reader rough their emotions and sentiments. The anatomy of typeface creates a tone of voice that could be a sound, word, language or speech.

2

rbal communication becomes one way of conversing nverbally when it is written down in print or online and, therefore, typefaces are one of the most significant nonverbal cues.

Each visual element of a typeface—including its color, poi size or style—is made to create a contextual background linguistic material, and that background may carry certain connotations in regard to its form.

3

1] When transcribed, letterforms may entail the rendition of performance of speech

2] The vocalization of written words after perceiving an image from the letterforms; an inner voice

4

When reading, words that are set in certain letterforms m support a text to be visualized as a "mental image"/"sceni picture." These visualizations touch our emotional intelligence, while letterforms influence the emotional sentiment of the text.

5

Emotions aren't just ideas in our heads, they're physically embodied. Letterforms interact with human emotions and make the reader engage with the text through their tone of voice.

6

Emotional Typefaces carry
connote
embody certain emotions/feelings an
Emotional Typefaces engender those emotions/feelings.

·om multiple angles, you can read the word 'emotional' fferently. Hence, Emotional Typefaces can be interpreted two main ways: the outcome—in this case, letterforms—comes externally expressive on its own terms as it em-dies emotions while also taking into account the making of terforms, which are regarded as a direct expression of the actitioner's mind.

hen considering emotions in motion, typography and oreography are the same. An easy analogy is the fluid and fortless movements of a highly-trained ballet dancer and e hand movements of a classical calligrapher. The body—at of the dancer and the calligrapher—is the main medium ed to express their feelings, but it is the lines and gestures rmed through motion that leave a lasting impression of eir emotions for the viewer to recognize.

ised on the following two reasons, my attentiveness to signing typefaces veers away from being an emotive actitioner when drawing letters. Firstly, it would be fficult to retain certain emotions when they are translated to letterforms, as they are drawn from my own immediate oughts and emotions. Secondly, my personal emotions that elt while drawing the letterforms would not necessarily understood by the reader. They would interpret the terforms from their own point of view, potentially invoking her emotions than my own. Simply, emotions are registered fferently from person to person.

y medium to talk about "emotionality" is Realist pography (with reference to Object Oriented Ontology), iich explores the shapes of objects' material properties and eir emotions/expressions through letterforms.

y example of Object Oriented Ontology would be a needle, which is a hin, metal stick with a pointed end. If you design letters by using the shape ieedle as a reference, those letters would never look friendly—the result : the opposite. They will rather look spiky, hysterical, and cold. These ves are emotions of the needle and Realist Typography uses the object's ues directly into type design process.

In the same vein, SPOOKY HAIRY shows how Realist Typography is rooted in process. It is designed by using the shape and expressions of East Asian black, thick, shiny, soaking wet hair.

Drawing a c

Repeating the circle drawings. In Zen, a circle (Ensō) refers to the beginning and end of all things; the circle of life; the connection of existence; the symbol for both emptiness and fullness; presence or absence; all things may be contained or on the contrary, excluded by its limits.
Learning to purify the mind and to control the body by practicing the circular lines and repetition.

The Zen practitioner's focus on drawing Ensō has been a pivotal influence when exploring Emotional Typefaces.
It has led me to a research project that has resulted in a typeface now known as **Birch**. The typeface traces back to the 18th century when hand-carved wood block printing was an exponent of a laborious relief process, and the sound of chisels punctuated the air; sometimes confident, like a marching band, other times rather sad, happy, or lethargic. **Birch** focuses on the emotions felt by wood block engravers that are brought about by the repetitive movement involved in the process. These emotions are akin to those involved with drawing Ensō circles.

The two approaches briefly outlined above for SPOOKY HAIRY and **Birch** are case studies of Emotional Typefaces that exemplify the translation of emotions into letterforms.

Emotional Typefaces: Case Study 1

SPOOKY HAIRY
REALIST TYPOGRAPHY)

alist typography references Object Oriented Ontology.
Oriented Ontology manifests in all objects that relate to each ifferently. The objects perceive each other partially, only with the s that they can interpret from each other.
way, Realist Typography focuses on the exchanged interpretations bjects. (see the text below)

alist typography is typographic research anchored firmly in the aterial reality that surrounds us.

alist typography portrays the material properties of objects and es their visual cues that are directly rooted in the process.

alist Typography tries as much as possible to remove human stures from the process of making letters.

alist Typography emphasizes the expressions/sentiments of the aterial properties of an object. Their expressions determine e emotions of the letterforms.

SPOOKY HAIRY

(with reference to Object Oriented Ontology)
[Written in 2017, *Real-Time Realist No.1*]

1] I get out of the shower, the mirror in my bathroom is reasonably foggy. Heavy, stifling moisture hits my cold forehead.

2] The warm, moist air silently meets cool air in the bathroom. The ceiling starts to drip its tears.

3] Non-human (living, non-living, artificial or conceptual) entities are all considered 'Object.' All these entities experience their own existence by perceiving each other.

4] I stare at my eyes—the fog is in the eyes making their colour seem translucent—between the wet, kinky, wild, black hair draped all over my face, a bead of water trails down

the side of my

neck, pooling in the hollow of my collarbone.

5] All beings acting on one another.

"air, water, condensation, mirror, fog, eyes, hair"

6] The diameter of Asian hair is 0.08 to 0.12mm. Significantly thicker than the average European's hair.

7] Wider, glossier, shinier, straight, coarse and almost invariably black.

8] Some strands of hair dip their feet in the pool of my collar-bone, the others hold fast to not fall into it.

9] Letterforms trace the desire of objects, beyond the purview of human conception.

10] The obscure copulation of typography and materialism gives birth to the multiverse of beings.

11] Things are emoting according to their own goals and motivations, which can be deeply affecting.

"The world does not exist outside of its expressions"

Deleuze and Guattari, *Brian Massumi from A Shock to Thought: Expression after Deleuze and Guattari* (London: Routledge, 2002)

12] The way you emote is drawn by the truth and fantasy of the uninitiated.

SPOOKY HAIRY follows the expressions of East Asian

THICK
COARSE
BLACK
SOAKING
WET
HAIR

BIRCH

This typographic research is derived from a feminist perspective and comprises a short, written text and a typefa The research traces back to a period of the printing press during the 18th century; a period of woodcut letters, fema engraving laborers who were often housewives with unrecog nized skills and, as such, remained anonymous ... **Birch** i a result of the emotions that were locked into letters on th surfaces of wood blocks, and serves as an analogy between letters from handwriting and engraving.

Type, Smile, and Face
Notes on Woodtypes and **Birch**
[Written in 2019, *Real-Time Realist No.2*]

1700s.
In this period, hand-carved wood blocks
and hand-crafted typefounding
were still commonly practised.
The mirror image of each letter was carefully carved
on the end of the grain side of a wood block.
The letters were laboriously carved,
yet many emotions drifted in.
Pieces of lemon, cherry, birch and pinewood, from
sections through the trunks or large boughs of trees,
were turned into battle sites for these emotions.
The engravers who fought for them were mostly
women working freelance out of their homes.

Putting on a brave face
on the faces of wood blocks.

The emotions were soldered through
and
locked into the type.

As your sorrow
liquefied into a "**T**"
TEAR

As your lust
electrified into a "**t**"
**tingle of
excitement**

As your worry
evaporated into an "**S**"
SIGH

As your lovingness
smeared into an "**s**"
smile

2019, again.
Isn't wooden type the most *sentient* of
all those developed throughout the whole of type history?

LANGUAGE

Storytelling

**J-LTF typefaces care for their text,
amplifying the sentiments expressed by the content**

M
for
MAO—
MAO—
MAO—
PR
THE ARTIST
FIBS
Einzel Single 5 / 3 Euro
Kombi Combined 8 / 4 Euro
Mitglieder Members frei free entry
im Jahr / per year

With the workshop format 'Mad-Mad-Mad-PR,' we explore subjective design narratives with 'U for Unstable Signs,' rete design history with 'M for Messy History' and enable undisc plined encounters with 'A for Accomplices.'

More specifically, the workshop starts by poring over the bi raphies of non-conforming pedagogues, theoreticians, de- signers and symbols in graphic design from the past, prese and future. In the next step, two biographies are paired in a fictitious encounter: What overlaps, or differences are formu ed in the practices of the people meeting? What spontaneo informal or even staged setting could encourage solidarity through conversations or joint activities? What gestures o invitation and announcement have to be designed—in the sense of 'Mad-Mad-Mad-PR'? Here, the inevitable balanci act between curating, designing and authorship plays a pa ticularly important role.

In December 2019, the week-long workshop 'Mad-Mad-Ma PR,' held at the Burg Giebichenstein University of Art and De Halle, was an attempt to expand and complicate the *Gloss of Undisciplined Design Symposium*. Over the week, the 26 participating students were invited to add their own confro tions, appropriations and contradictions. Ece Canlı meets the Venus symbol, Hackers & Designers meet Muriel Coop Sheila Levrant de Bretteville meets the Suffragettes: Eightee speculative encounters were conceived and "curated" in vari working constellations and media—from the founding of a p litical party to a sticker riot, a self-defense workshop to a spe lative lab space of fluid futures. In the next step, the student designed corresponding PR materials, which announced t their events would take place at the same time as the *GUD Symposium* at GfZK (Leipzig Museum of Contemporary Ar February 2020. Alongside classic posters and flyers, partici pants also made flags, labeled inflatables or printed on pa towels. During the symposium, the diverse announcement gestures were mixed in among the flyers in the museum, di played on its information screens, pinned to the museum's poster wall and also occupied some more unusual places, s as a toilet paper dispenser. With a total of 18 "events," the fic tional parallel program of 'Mad-Mad-Mad-PR' invited the a ence to imagine alternative possibilities for a history of desi

WORDS
PATCH WORK NOT leaders
voices NOT SILENCE
Sheila Levrant de Bretteville and the Suffragettes

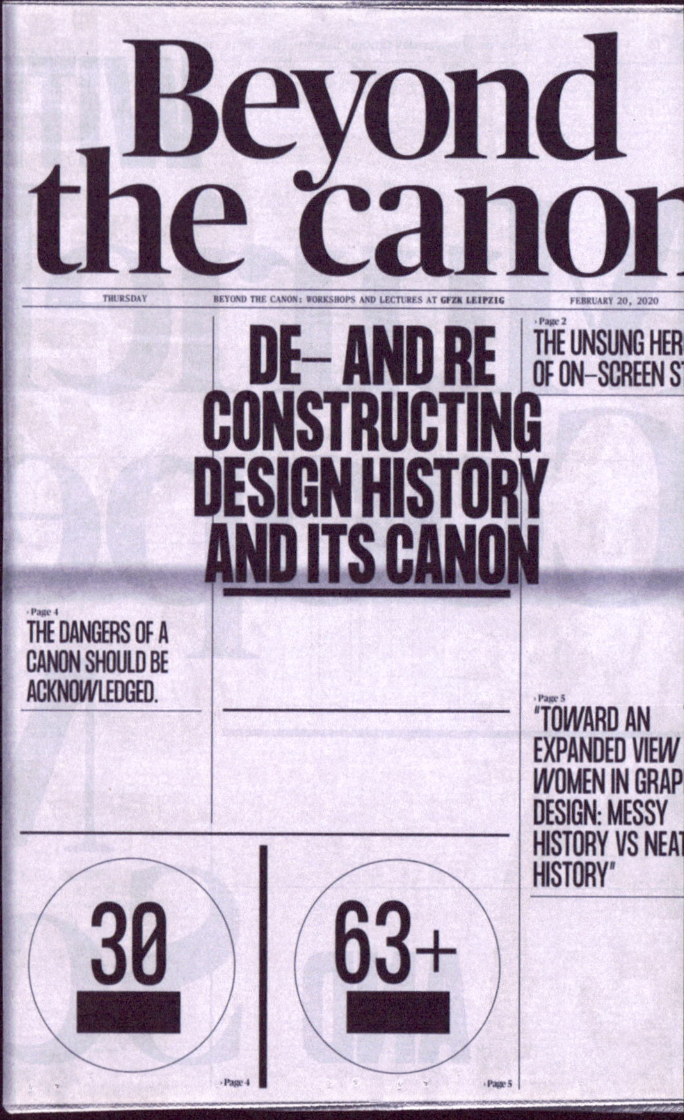

Beyond the canon

THURSDAY | BEYOND THE CANON: WORKSHOPS AND LECTURES AT GFZK LEIPZIG | FEBRUARY 20, 2020

DE– AND RE CONSTRUCTING DESIGN HISTORY AND ITS CANON

› Page 2
THE UNSUNG HER
OF ON–SCREEN S

› Page 4
THE DANGERS OF A CANON SHOULD BE ACKNOWLEDGED.

› Page 5
"TOWARD AN EXPANDED VIEW
WOMEN IN GRAP
DESIGN: MESSY
HISTORY VS NEAT
HISTORY"

30

› Page 4

63+

› Page 5

a public
ECE CANLI AND
VENUSSYMBOL
GET RID OF
DETERMINISM and
discrimination
FROM

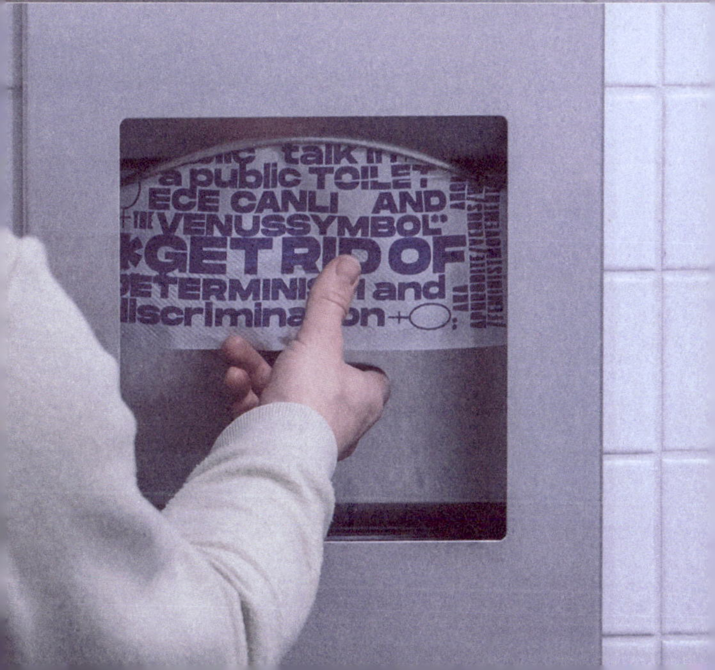
a public TOILET
ECE CANLI AND
VENUSSYMBOL
GET RID OF
and

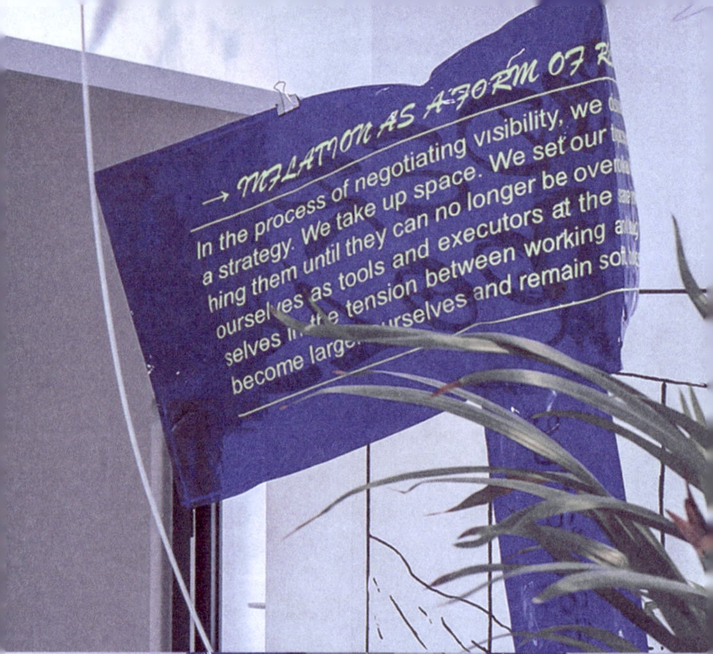
→ INFLATION AS A FORM OF R
In the process of negotiating visibility, we
a strategy. We take up space. We set our
hing them until they can no longer be over
ourselves as tools and executors at the
selves in the tension between working a
become larg urselves and remain so

GfZK Leip
20. – 23.
AS A FORM OF RESISTANCE
tiating visibility, we discover inflating as
space. We set our topics by gently pus-
longer be overlooked. We discover
tors at the same time, lose our-
and being worked off
but persistent.

DER
TOOLS
nflation as a form of resistance

Dirty Deeds Done Dirt Cheap

DISCUSSION ABOUT

THE POTENTIAL OF FEMINIST STICKER-RIOTS IN TIMES OF SEXIST ADVERTISING

WITH

THE SUFFRAGETTES AND DEPATRIARCHISE DESIGN

AT

GFZK LEIPZIG

02/20/2020 7 PM

AND HACKER&DESIGNERS
COLLECITVE LAB BY MURIEL

same time, lose
g and being worked
soft, but persistent.
ACKER&DESIGNERS
COLLECITVE LAB BY MURIEL

sparky
SELF–
DEF–
ENCE
for
digital
DILET–
TANTS

Dead Daddy Design I've given you all and now I'm nothing.
Dead Daddy Design another underpaid passion project,
November 2020.
I can't stand my own mind.
Dead Daddy Design when will we end the Adobe war?
I don't feel good, don't bother me.
I won't design this page till I'm in my right mind.
Dead Daddy Design when will you take off your clothes?
When will you look at yourself through your grave?

Dead Daddy Design your white, Eurocentric, male, straight
libraries are full of tears.
Dead Daddy Design when will you check the rich bouquet
of your privileges?
I'm sick of your insane demands.
When can I go into a meeting and get what I want without
my good looks?
Dead Daddy Design after all it is you who is far from
perfect not the next world.
Your machinery is too much for me.
You made me want to burn your canon.

    form of a practical joke?
I'm not trying to come to the point.
I refuse to give up my obsession.
Dead Daddy Design stop pushing I don't know what I'm doing.
Dead Daddy Design I feel sentimental about the times
    when I didn't know our system to be so fucked.
Dead Daddy Design I used to be an optimist when I was a
    kid I'm not sorry.
I drink golden milk for my nerves every chance I get.
I sit in my house for days on end and stare at the
    Sister Corita prints on the wall.

My mind is made up I'm going to stay with the trouble.
You should have seen me reading Scotford, Attfield, hooks,
Buckley, de Bretteville, Halberstam, Haraway, Lorde,
Preciado, Ahmed, Carson, Le Guin and Peppermint Patty.
My therapist thinks I'm perfectly right.
I won't say the Modernist Prayer.
I have mystical visions and cosmic vibrations.
Dead Daddy Design I am addressing you.
It occurs to me that I am conditioned by Dead Daddy Design.
I am talking to myself again.

went barefoot climbing in Allen Ginsberg's 'America' (1956)

for Undisciplinarity

story of undisciplinarity cannot be told without demysti-ng the clean logics of success and failure by which our estern capitalist societies are run. Systemic and struc-ral inequalities, by proxy, keep most members of society ught in harmful loops of defeat—economically, socially, rsonally, spiritually. But do we even want to succeed in a stem that, by definition, considers most of us inade-ate, as we are forever failing at being male, at being iite, at being straight, cis or able-bodied?

'nder certain circumstances, failing, losing, forgetting, making, undoing, unbecoming, not knowing may in fact 'er more creative, more cooperative, more surprising ıys of being in the world.”[1]

rhaps, then, reclaiming failure is our best bet. After all, t succeeding can offer unexpected pleasures: of getting ganized with other flops and losers, of plotting out ways living and working that offer alternative definitions of ccess, of disrupting the circulation and reproduction of triarchal ideals and discriminating structures. Keeping ose in mind who cannot escape their circumstances, we n build spaces where other ways of being and knowing n exist.

ı the undiscipline of design

ıere there is discipline, there is a master—as design hools continue to be the official sites of “learning de-ın,” they remain the main hubs for the introduction, ınsmission and normalization of conventions for “good sign.” Implied in the very texture of any design study ogram is the legitimization of certain conceptual and sthetic tools and ideals, substantiated by a correspond-g canon and role models—through the naming of

courses, through the appointment of teachers, throu
their respective internalized convictions, to the belief sy
tem behind a foundation course.

Disciplines define our codes of normalization. They are to
taken seriously. The theorist and author Jack Halberst
writes: "Disciplines qualify and disqualify, legitimate a
delegitimate, reward and punish; most important, th
statically reproduce themselves and inhibit dissent." 2
So, when we talk about design as a discipline, as a field
study, what exactly are those codes of normalization,
legitimation, qualification and reward? Who is this discipl
of design serving, who or what is it protecting? And who
disqualified, delegitimized or excluded by the routines, co
ventions, perspectives or formats of this discipline?

An undiscipline of design remains eternally scepti
of reproducing the formulaic and simplistic, wary of canc
ical ideologies in favor of more unpredictable, diverse in
modes of history-making and future-building.

An undiscipline of design happily fails at reinforci
patriarchal imperatives for the field of graphic design a
its institutions, toward a messier, fuzzy, emotional, unr
and collaborative landscape of design.

On undisciplined desi

This is not a pitch for a new, temporary, experimental stu
program or an aesthetic renaming exercise. Structu
change is not a fleeting trend; there is a lot to unpack in
places of design and its institutions. And we need actior
As long as disciplinarity is a noxious consequence of c
current state of patriarchy, we are sticking with this u
stuff. Exactly as complex and non-binary as it sounds,
are neither advocating for pseudo-chaotic design tric
nor do we place undisciplinarity in opposition to syste
atic or orderly design approaches (you should see c
online spreadsheet deep skills used for this very boo

ill, there is fun to be had in poking holes into the oppres-
'e toxicity of patriarchal disciplinarity and in insisting on
ıltiple subjectivities, caring design principles and frivo-
ıs, promiscuous work strategies.

being undisciplined designers

re we are. Silly, dissonant, bruised, uncertain, irrele-
nt, moody, unpredictable, weak, confused, permeable,
rous, excessive, irrational, irritable, attached.

We suck at believing the modernist man myth of
ing an extraordinary single machine. We're incapable
buying into the sick logic that personal achievement
esupposes self-control, over one's emotions, tender needs
any excessive or nonsensical impulses. And we have lost
e ability to believe that success equals enacting the cap-
ılist tropes of hard work, competitiveness and self-exploi-
tion. Attached, irritable, irrational, excessive, porous,
rmeable, confused, weak, unpredictable, moody, irrele-
nt, uncertain, bruised, dissonant and silly, here we are.

e came across the notion of undisciplinarity in the book
e *Queer Art of Failure* by Jack Halberstam. Advocating
r a radically queer re-imagination of success in discrimi-
tory societal systems, Halberstam also includes the re-
rictive conventions for success in academia in his critique.
writes: "We may want new rationales for knowledge
oduction, different aesthetic standards for ordering or
sordering space, other modes of political engagement
an those conjured by the liberal imagination. We may,
timately, want more undisciplined knowledge, more
estions and fewer answers."[3]

1 Halberstam, Jack (2011) *The Queer Art of Failure*,
ırham, North Carolina: Duke University Press, 2–3.
2 Ibid., 10. 3 Ibid.

Inbox: wanted@whose.agency

social and outward looking activity. 'A for Accomplices' is a plea for more exchange, support and generosity between designers—in sharing knowledge, experiences, insights or resources. Working collaboratively and collectively also holds true potential for complicating questions of authorship. And there is always the adventurous promise of working in many voices.

BLISSFUL BONDING

Sisterhood has struck. Can u devour every inch of my insecurities? My knees go weak for shared sympathy and joint suffering. Hurry! I'm caring as hell!

Box: bliss-bond

MESSY GODDESS:

QUEER INTERGALACTIC LIBRARIAN, GOT THE HOTS FOR FILTHY HISTORY, INTERSEC FEMINISM, DECOLONIAL QUIRKS OR BUST. GET WEIRD BETWEEN BOOKSHELVES AND I SPOON U ALL NIGHT. POLY-PATCHWORK FOR LIFE. FACSIMILES TO THE FRONT. SEND ME YR CITATION POLICY.

Box: mess-godd

Unchain my monsters
Fun-loving hydra-headed feminist fighting with a bunch of conflicts and schizo desires to unplease her clients. Fulfill my skepticism of ideological construc-tions during office hours. Bring more heads, we'll see how to trouble-make.

Box: un-mons

TRIGGER THE BUG
twisted, good-hearted fuck-up seeks joint dysfunctional mouse-clicks. don't want a trial or a subscription. like hard software, radical resolutions and cheerful restarts. glitch me up!

Box: trigg-bug

Box: demys-dory

Demystifying Dory
fast speaking flaky wet dream wit
a kink for queer failure; let's explo
other ways of world-building in
the undisciplined zones of counte
hegemony. forgetful of heterosexi
norms but fall hard for unexpecte
pleasures of knowing.
Let me unmaster u.

ANY WHICH WAY YOU WANT IT:

IRED PLACEHOLDER WITH STRONG DESIRE OR MORE THAN ONE-TIME (Box: any-which) CONFESSIONS. LET'S SURVIVE THE REPRESENTATIONAL HYPE TOGETHER, LAUGH AT MOST, CRY IF WE MUST. NEXPER AT TAKING THE LEAD, BUT WORTH IT, COME ON HONEY, WRITE.

Roles from
the rolaroladingdong
Conflicted author/
designer/manager/
mother/babe with
unpredictable needs
for professional
variety. I'm many at
once and I'm freaking
large. Into conscious
role-play without
forgetting about the
neo-lib plot. wanna
see me disco? I'm ur
favorite multitasker.
Let's fuck the
burnout away.

(Box: rola-ding)

Solidary duck is ready for radical redistribution. Are you? Rebelliously feathered femme goes off on feisty societal turmoil. Left city for witch-brained off-grid communes. Comrades and chatty accomplices—let's share agendas!

RELATIONS

SOCIAL

SAPIO-SEXY

Box: sapio-sexy

Box: 1-3-5

Seeking Clients:
Overqualified designer with heal reputation who doesn't talk in sleep; I appreciate a good salsa move; spank me with a diction ary, but don't sweat it too much. But please only read lines 1,3 and

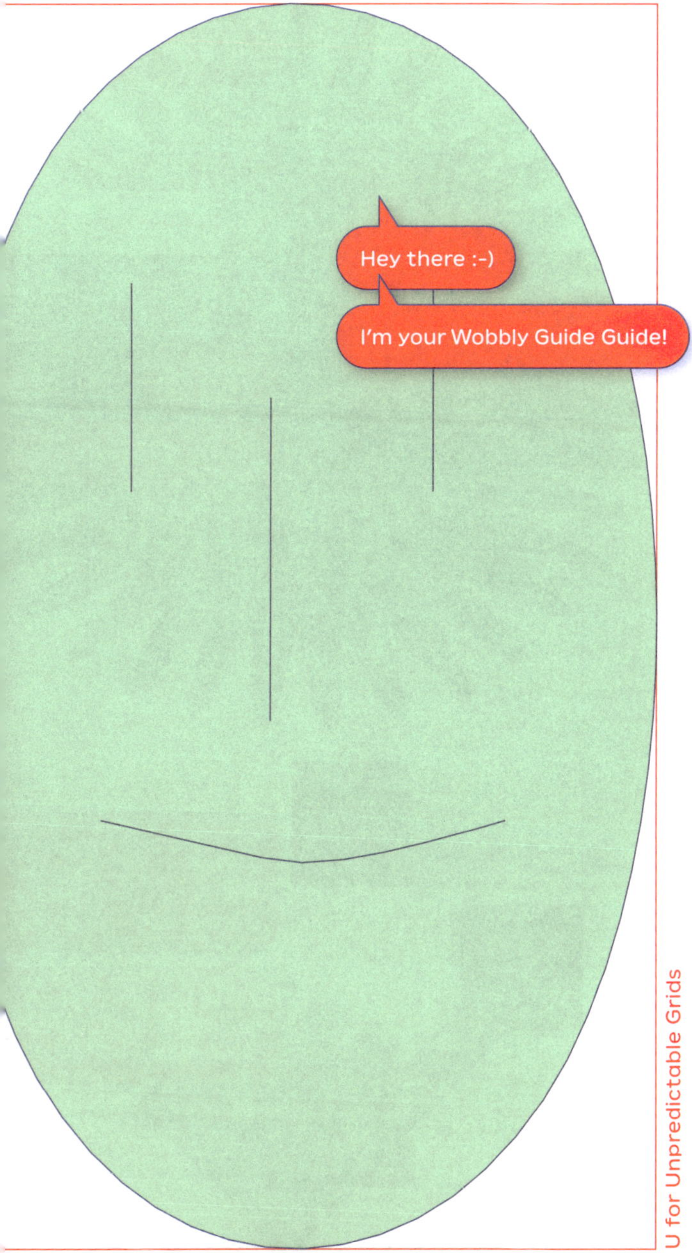
Hey there :-)
I’m your Wobbly Guide Guide!

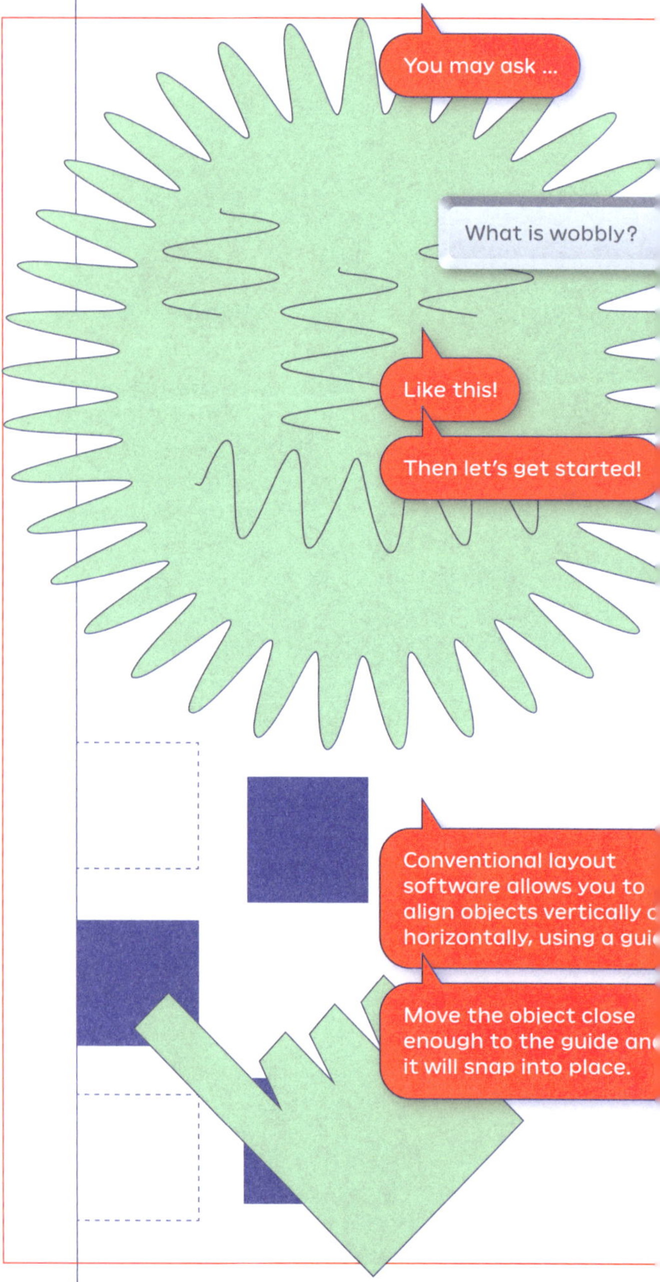

You may ask ...
What is wobbly?
Like this!
Then let's get started!
Conventional layout
software allows you to
align objects vertically
horizontally, using a gui
Move the object close
enough to the guide an
it will snap into place.

This leads to pretty static results ...

Let's align them with one of my special wobbly guides!

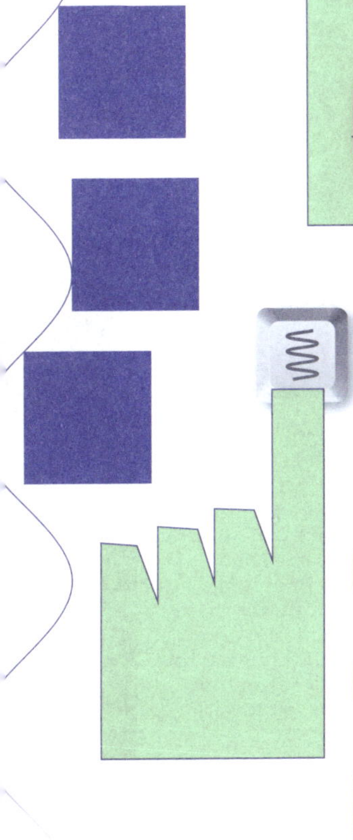

The wobbly guides are inspired by quantization.

A technique used in music production.

Quantizing musical notes is similar to aligning graphic objects.

But you can adjust how much the notes should be corrected.

When designing with grids, the results are often quite predictable. Of course, designers can define the grid and therefore can use it as an individual tool to generate layouts. Depending on the subtlety of a grid, layout options can be fairly diverse. But, because of the possibilities and the complexity opened up by ever finer grids, it becomes more and more difficult to use them. This contradicts the original purpose of a grid: Reducing the number of options and thus improving the efficiency of a layout for a large number of pages. The designer has to weigh simplicity against detail.

What would a grid look like that is not overly complex and still leads to more organic and diverse-looking layouts? Instead of static lines defined by coordinates, it could consist of moving elements that, even if they have their origin at a particular coordinate, move between positions and over time. Using such a grid for layouts, the probability is small that its lines are at the same spot at different points in time. The grid has become more unpredictable.

Standardized tools in graphic software, such as the grid, can only be changed within the narrow scope of a few predefined settings. The Wobbly Guide Guide is an attempt to question and augment the intended use of such tools and their presets.

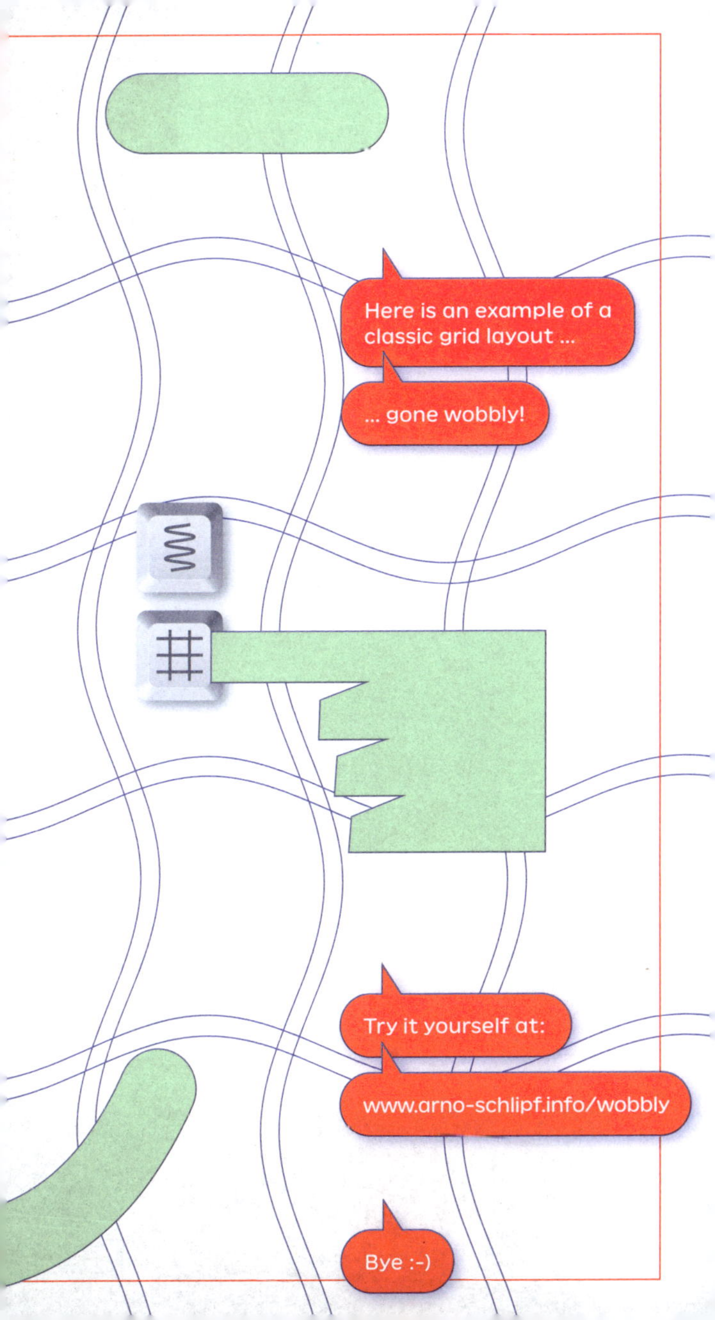
Here is an example of a classic grid layout ...
... gone wobbly!
Try it yourself at:
www.arno-schlipf.info/wobbly
Bye :-)

C FOR CARE ADVICE WANTS TO ESTABLISH NEW WAYS OF CARING IN THE FIELD OF ART AND DESIGN. CARE WORK, AKA REPRODUCTIVE LABOR, IS HABITUALLY SUBORDINATE TO THE PRODUCTION AND ACCUMULATION OF CAPITAL IN CAPITALIST SOCIETIES, EVEN THOUGH IT IS THE VERY BASIS OF OUR WORK AND LIFE. SO, HOW CAN WE ESTABLISH CARE AS AN INTEGRAL PART OF OUR UNDISCIPLINED DESIGN PRACTICES?

ALL I LONG FOR IS TO GROW A MONSTER

A conversation
about
care and work

They first met in a sunny
and humid place, next to a very
long river. One gave shelter to each other,
because they knew how difficult
it can be to plan in advance.
Also, in that sunny and humid place,
rents were quite high. In order to stay,
you had to pay money that you earned
in exchange for work.
Not all work could be exchanged
for money in the same way.
Later, they met in several other places,
sharing interests.
Once, they created a huge towel
that would cover a human body twice.
They ate Borscht together.

CARE LABELS ARE PIECES OF FABRIC USED IN TEXTILE INDUSTRY. THEY ARE USUALLY WO FROM FINE THREAD. THEY ARE TO BE FOUND IN CLOTHES, MOSTLY UNNOTICED. HIEROGLYPH-L SIGNS GIVE INSTRUCTIONS ON HOW TO WASH IRON THE ITEMS THEY ARE ATTACHED TO.

Occasionally, the two women think about care and work:

ANNE I like to think of care as something that has to be given over and over again – something that serves regeneration, something cyclic rather than linear, something that doesn't accumulate, but creates and also gets destroyed again, something that does not grow without dying and yet is powerful because it makes us feel alive. I think, for a lot of people, care work means that everything they create will be destroyed again. Just think of the daily routines of care workers. And this kind of work doesn't have great value within the capitalist idea of accumulation, growth and optimization.

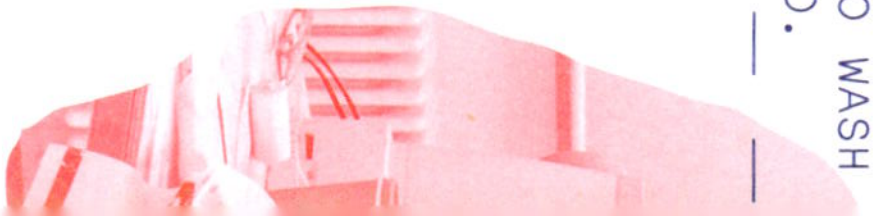

TERESA If we look at it through the lens of

This is how the Italian feminist Carla Lonzi
put it in her manifesto from 1970.
The quote reflects the experience of many
generations of women, as well as care workers.
Lonzi suggests a radical break with the logic
of success and its imperative of visibility:
"We consider incomplete any history
which is based on nonperishable traces."
That was the claim of the Revolta Femminile
in the 1970s and it is still subversive.
All the monuments, inscribed in stone and
cast in bronze, lasting for centuries,
creating whole pictures and panoramas,
are nothing but remains. Just a hint at
so much more—innumerable and invisible
stories of women, workers, people,
not handed down on stone slabs.
Between the lines and outstretched limbs of
neatly structured monuments and encyclopedias,
we catch glimpses of the stories that have
not been told. If we confront the fact
that all kinds of work by women have been
destroyed again and again in the course
of history, then it is a reasonable assumption
that there has probably been an ongoing
creative practice by women at all times.

THE PARTICIPATORY WORKSTATION *C FOR CARE ADV*
DEVELOPED FROM AN ENCOUNTER WITH THE WRITI
OF SHEILA LEVRANT DE BRETTEVILLE. ESTABLISH
THE NOTION OF FEMINIST DESIGN BACK IN THE 197
SHE DEVISED A TERMINOLOGY FOR TALKING AB
DESIGN IN RELATION TO SOCIAL INEQUALITIES.

ANNE I like how you interpret destruction as a premise for creation. This reminds me of something Donna Haraway said in 'A Cyborg Manifesto' in 1985 where she turns profound vulnerability into an idea of power.

She uses the example of a salamander who loses its tail but has the power to regrow it. "The regrown limb can be monstrous, duplicated, potent ..." The temporary wound has the magical power to transform itself into something yet unknown.

'Wound' can mean a lot of things when you start thinking of it on a physical, mental and societal level as caused by the precarization of our work and lives, by patriarchy and capitalism as well as by marginalization and colonialism...

I imagine it as a soft and messy place full of potential, as a place where the code of society has not yet taken control.

TERESA In my imagination the monstrous limb is transformative, somehow open-source or open-code in its structure, growing from collective actions. Trying to make a living from my design profession, I am constantly confronted with precarious work situations, inequalities and binary thinking. All of this feels quite heavy and stiff to me. I want to regrow monstrous limbs!

ANNE The power to turn a 'wound' into something monstrous, in my imagination, that is the power of our desires. Listening to our desires can be pretty powerful. It can change a lot of things. First on an individual level, and in a second step, it could also change things on a systemic level, if we keep going down that path. Or at least that's how I feel about it. To search for and listen to these places of monstrous freedom within ourselves and within any kind of oppressive system is an idea that I like.

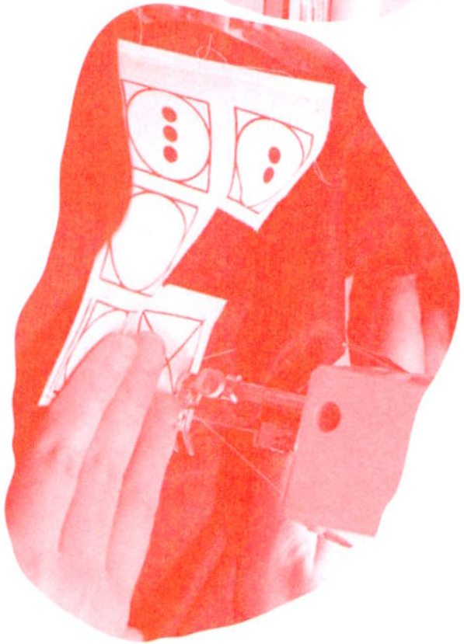

THE QUESTIONS SHE RAISED, PARTICULARLY WITH REGARD TO DESIGN IN THE PUBLIC SPHERE, WERE: WHOSE VOICES ARE BEING HEARD AND WHOSE ARE MISSING? HOW CAN DESIGN ENGAGE WITH ITS VIEWERS INSTEAD OF PROMOTING A CERTAIN OPINION?

IN *C FOR CARE ADVICE* I USED QUOTES FROM SHEILA
THOUGHTS ON RELATIONAL STRATEGIES AND FEMINI
DESIGN AND SCREEN-PRINTED THEM ONTO FABRIC. NE
TO HER WORDS, DEFAULT CARE ADVICE SYMBOLS FLO
AROUND THE SLOGAN "ONGOING STRUGGLE FOR CARE
WORK SITUATIONS." DURING THE *GUD SYMPOSIUM*, T
PREPRINTED FABRIC WAS CUT INTO PATCHES OF VAR
OUS SIZES AND SHAPES BY THE VISITORS. A SEWI
MACHINE WAS PROVIDED TO ATTACH THE CARE ADVIC
ONTO CLOTHES AND BAGS—A FRIENDLY REMINDER OF T
INVISIBLE WORK SURROUNDING US.

It's like looking for those open,
soft spots where I can sort of
recode something, where I can
change a little thing
in a situation with others.
It can be something simple,
like thinking about my use of
language in a conversation,
or being aware of my actual
needs, instead of the things
I think I need.
From this change might
rise a monster:

a monster
that outgrows
my control.
In a good way.
Hopefully.

1
Hang the hourglass over your shoulder.
2
Turn the hourglass, start walking and drift away
3
Return when the hourglass has run out.

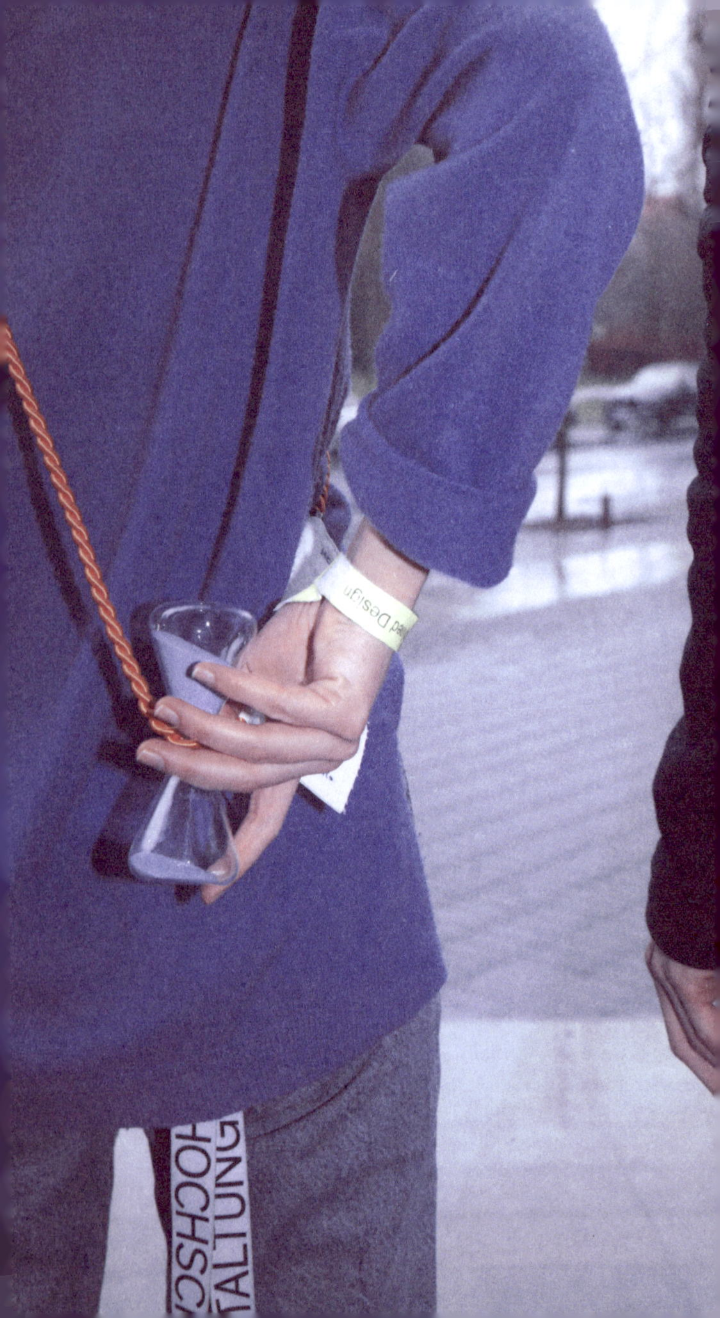
Design
HOCHSCH
TALTUNG

n was the last time you took a break? What did you do ıg that break? Scrolling ıdlessly on your smartphone? king your notifications? ıswering messages you ved weeks ago? When was ast time you really took break and did nothing? ıed, as Rebecca Solnit states, ı nothing is hard to do. But maybe drifting way to deal with this ıdox. It is an alternative way of g a break and ıggests walking around ıout specific direction or aim, d with exploring unfamiliar surroundings. concept, inspired by the Situationists International ıment of the 1950s, reflects the lack of ırk-break-balance many gners experience at their ay-covered workplaces these days. Fed up the socially exclusive but videly accepted cigarette k we came up with the idea an alternative social routine taking break. ırroring the sense of time implicated by a burning rette, we use an hourglass display time in a material way. Instead of lighting a cigarette,

D for Drifting

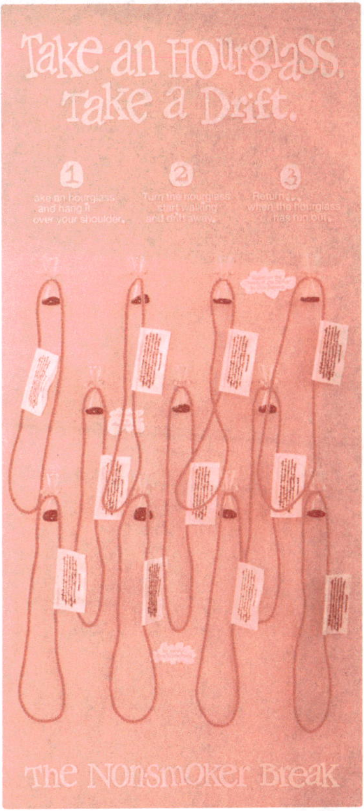

you turn the hourglass and start walking. Replacing our phones with these simple timepieces both disorients and liberates us from the use of digital devices during the break.

In the framework of the GUD Symposium an installation with 11 hourglasses offered participants a chance to drift off between talks and return back to business, once the hourglass had run out.

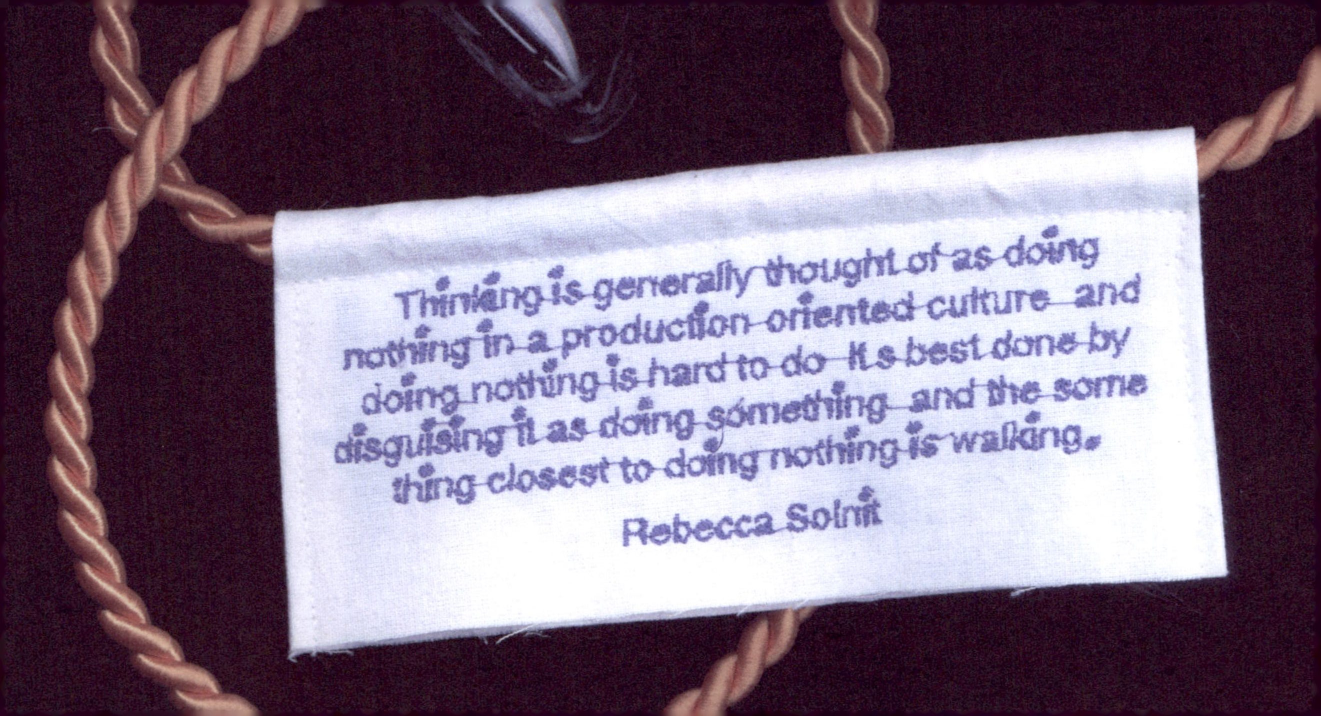
Thinking is generally thought of as doing
nothing in a production oriented culture and
doing nothing is hard to do. It's best done by
disguising it as doing something and the some
thing closest to doing nothing is walking.
Rebecca Solnit

M FOR

A PATCHY DREAM OF WILD TONGUES IN A LIBRARY

MESSY

HISTORIES

It was an unruly and fuzzy night. From a distance, I heard several voices. Lurking between book spines on the dusty shelves of the art school library, I witnessed an intense and passionate conversation:

VOICE Research on women in design has been focused on women as objects of representation and on women as audience or consumers (in the broadest sense) of graphic design artifacts; to this should be added the breadth of the design activities in which women engage.[1]

OTHER VOICE Indeed, the omissions are so overwhelming, and the rare acknowledgment so cursory and marginalized, that one realizes these silences are not accidental and haphazard; rather, they are the direct consequence of specific historiographic methods.[2]

SEVERAL VOICES, SIMULTANEOUSLY Often when attempts are made to rewrite history in an effort to make room for women, it is done in the form of searching for and presenting individual success stories.[3]

At this point, I tiptoed a bit closer and hid in the L–M aisle.

1 Scotford, Martha (1994) 'Messy History vs. Neat History: Toward an Expanded View of Women in Graphic Design', Visible Language 28(4), Blauvelt, Andrew, ed., Providence: Rhode Island School of Design, 370.

2 Buckley, Cheryl (1986) 'Made in Patriarchy: Toward a Feminist Analysis of Women and Design', Design Issues 3(2), Cambridge: MIT Press, 251.

3 Fanni, Maryam, Flodmark, Matilda and Kaaman, Sara (2020) Natural Enemies of Books: A Messy History of Women in Printing and Typography. London: Occasional Papers, 8–9.

VOICE, AGAIN It was easy to answer the questions: Who? What? Why? From whom? For whom? This simplistic history has served the establishment (white, male, business, design and academic worlds) well.[4]

ANOTHER VOICE [On the other hand,] I will also dare to claim that there cannot be such thing as queer feminist design history, but one can seek to capture different moments of theoretical and practical endeavors shuttling between past, present, future, and eventually, utopia.[5]

EARLIER...

Feminist social critique has always been afflicted by historical amnesia. Some voices are structurally buried under the canon, while other accomplices linger unconsulted in the bookshelves obscured by the spectacle of contemporary feminism. The chronology that follows doesn't claim to document a linear, homogenous or unbroken thread of theory production. Rather, it allows wild tongues to speak, that are linked, knotted, entangled. Surely there are many more knots, differences, beginnings and endings that we still know nothing about. Our timeline is full of holes; incomplete, chaotic.

1986: A HISTORY OF THE HETERO-PATRIARCHY

When one sees the characteristics of the sexes as the result of humanity's domination of nature, which is according to Charlotte Mohs and Korinna Linkerhand, reproduced under

4 Scotford, Martha (1994), 371.

5 Canlı, Ece (2016) 'Design History Interrupted: A Queer-Feminist Perspective', The Responsible Object: A History of Design Ideology for the Future. Van Helvert, Marjanne, ed., Amsterdam: Valiz, 188.

pitalism" in the contradiction between wage labor and capi-
l,"[6] it makes sense to ask: How did this patriarchal system influ-
ce the historiography of design, and how does it continue
do so? Which positions does this deterministic order reinforce,
d which conception of design does its logic legitimize?

In 1986, Cheryl Buckley published the text 'Made in Patriar-
y: Toward a Feminist Analysis of Women and Design.' In it,
e criticizes the historiographic methods used in design history,
ch as the classification and prioritization of design disciplines
ich ultimately led to the structural exclusion of women's per-
ectives. The few women who managed to be included in this
story of design were either reduced to dominant notions of fem-
inity, appear as users of products geared toward women,
ch as household appliances, or women are summarized under
e names of their male partners and relatives. In her critical
proach, Buckley drew on the work of contemporary feminist
t historians such as Griselda Pollock. Buckley appeals to all
sign historians to take patriarchy and capitalism into account
ien thinking about the roles, experiences and desires of women.
cause, according to her, the vehemence with which design
storians ignore the supremacy of the patriarchy leads them to
aintain the construction of traditional gender roles in design.
ie cites countless examples to demonstrate a biologistic ideology
e with heteronormative assumptions at work in the history of
sign. One such case is the hierarchies that exist between design
sciplines. Industrial design and its mass products, for example,
ceive fastidious attention in the history of design. Meanwhile,
e supposedly reproductive and caring disciplines, such as work-
g with textiles, have been pejoratively relegated to the history
craftsmanship.

According to Buckley, the stereotypical depictions of women
consumers of design objects (synonymous with the roles of
others and housewives), and of women as objects of sexist adver-
ing, urgently need to be analyzed in the workings of design
story in order to finally be able to distinguish social constructs
om biological conditions. Furthermore, she criticizes the
cus on individualism—the individual as the creator of design
orks—as an authoritarian historiographic method. Buckley
gues that when historians follow this narrative method, the

Mohs, Charlotte & Linkerhand, Korinna (2013) 'Natürlich gesellschaft-
?–Überlegungen zu Arbeit, Natur und Geschlecht', outside the box #4 Arbeit
itschrift für feministische Gesellschaftskritik). Lotta e. V., Leipzig, 41.

history of design is immediately reduced to the individual designer's narrative and decisions. This monographic thinking serves the interests of domination, leading to exclusion and simplification. Ultimately, eliding the way history is embedded in political, economic and cultural relations only serves a "universal" truthtelling that is conditioned by patriarchy.

1994: COUNTER-NARRATIVES BEYOND CATEGORIES

Everyone needs it, nobody wants it: feminism.[7] In 1994, design theorist Martha Scotford built on Buckley's critique in he text 'Messy History vs. Neat History: Toward an Expanded View of Women in Graphic Design.' Like Buckley before her, Scotfor also challenges the depiction of history in neatly sorted boxes, linear epochs and exceptional individual accomplishments whi lamenting the reluctance to introduce "unfitting" figures into the history of design, given the self-referential tendency in mai stream design history and its preoccupation with previously canonized biographies. She also demythologizes design work, which has always been collaborative, and pleads for the discussion of collective efforts and relationships in the design proces of taking a stand between clients and society, as well as of maintaining dialogue with everyone involved. The title of her essay pit ily summarizes the comparison between "Neat History" as an expression of conventional history and "Messy History" as a reb lious inscription of everyday visual culture, of non-normative, personal and expressive design activities far removed from larg production runs. Scotford does not categorically rule out adding female designers and their achievements to the canon of desi history. But she does demand that we recognize how the normative concepts of previous (male) designers do not correspond t

7 Original German: "Alle müssen, keiner will – Feminismus." Klitclique (lyrics and artists) (2016) 'Der Feminist D€R F€M1N1$T' Via: https://www.youtube.com/watch?v=8pPKkHFMi34

ie experiences of "deficient" others and structurally disadvan-ge them. We need a vocabulary for collective work in order better recognize and evaluate it. To this end, Scotford sketch- out a typology of women's participation in design practice, ie labor market, the educational apparatus and in the field of esign theory and criticism. She adds research questions to l these areas in order to highlight invisible territories for further ivestigation and discussion in the history of design.

Scotford asks:

Are the skills once valued in male typographers equally valued in female computer typesetters?... If the trades (except some forms of "commercial art" such as illustration) were not open to women, what were the routes into design for women? And what difference did class make for them?... Where were the "velvet ghettos" of the '30s, '40s, '50s? What is the meaning of the preponderance of women in publishing: books, magazines especially, fewer in newspapers?... When women are owners or partners, has this been conceived differently?... In addition to studying the presence of women in mainstream design practice, and understanding their roles as influenced by patriarchy's sexual division of labor, where else are women active?... Is "marginal" work a strategic choice or a default position?... Have women benefited from the support of professional organizations?...

LATE 2010S: UPLIFTING ECHOES AND ILLEGIBLE HISTORIES

Thirty, almost forty years later, and the queer, lesbian, feminist itskirts of design history are still buffeting the cis-hetero ref-ence system and its self-referential discussion of artifacts. It omes as no surprise that Scotford and Buckley's research ques-ons still resonate defiantly and relentlessly in the works of col-ctive wild tongues, such as the publication *Natural Enemies of*

Books: A Messy History of Women in Printing and Typography by MMS (Maryam Fanni, Matilda Flodmark, Sara Kaaman). In this work, MMS uncover further images of the past—its women's unions, collectives, and anonymous female laborers who multiply the definition of graphic design. Decolonial design histories reveal the absences of certain strands of knowledge, being and creation within the Eurocentric canon. Meanwhile, queer and intersectional tongues insist on fragmented and collaged narratives for design. In her text 'Design History Interrupted: A Queer-Feminist Perspective,' Ece Canlı calls for an assemblage of the theory and practice of writing and compiling of design history, much like a patchwork. She explicitly addresses the way all designers are complicit in reproducing normative conditions with their tools and designed objects.

But honestly, when will these echoes resonate in the mainstream and the academies? It's time for a radical metamorphosis—not just another adaptation of the narrative or new addition to the canon. Furthermore, it's also time to take up Scotford's research questions in order to include structural categories such as ethnicity, class, nationality, sexuality and age, and to explore the entanglements and interactions of these categories. Otherwise we will continue writing history that is reserved for the hetero-patriarchy and continue to cement all its discriminations.

Ramon Tejada appeals:

Make spaces (big spaces)
in your bookshelves
leave spaces in our syllabi,
literally leave spaces blank
to explore this idea/action responsibly;
leave spaces for other[s] to talk and
share their non-Western, nonbinary,
non-"designed" work. Simply get out of the way
and let others occupy the space.[8]

TBC

8 Tejada, Ramon (2018) 'We Must Topple the Tropes, Cripple the Canon', Walker Art Reader. Via: https://walkerart.org/magazine/soundboard-queering-design-education-ramon-tejada.

Reality. Not Necessarily a Book. by Stefanie Leinhos, a scan of a folded sheet of A4 paper that has been blown up to four times its size, color print on 120 gsm paper, 84 × 118 cm, published by studiolent, 2016

N for Network

IMAGINARY

Our collective 'network imaginary' reflects the ubiquity of server-client relationships that are tightly and often unnoticeably enmeshed in our daily professional and domestic digital lives.[1] Abstract notions such as "the cloud" contribute to the mystification of concrete technologies and the erasure of their material implications.[2] Our Network Imaginary ought to be troubled. Our network technologies need to be opened up in order to (self-)critically pose questions through the lens of connectivit As designers we need to reflect on our own networked practices, and their technical, practical and organisational workings.

1 In the workshop 'Designing Digital Domestics,' Beyla Popanda and Fabian Tombers proposed to spend time alone together, connecting through a live-stream video of instructions on decorating personal video chatting booths. "How to not be alone in a world that targets us as individual consumers and individual producers and never as a social organism that relies on its networks and connections for survival." Via: https://hackersanddesigners.nl/s/Summer_Academy-_2020/p/Designing_Digital_Domestics

2 "As we struggle now for the health of our communities, fuelled by the dreams of an equitable future, we must also strive for an Internet that is sustainable." The H&D Summer Academy 2020 kicked off with a lecture called 'The Sustainable Internet,' which was a teaser of a larger publication put together by the initiatives EIT Climate-KIC, Climate Action Tech and Mozilla, that aim to convene in a space to discuss a sustainable Internet. It is urgent that we start thinking about the sustainability of the Internet. An average spam email corresponds to 0.3 g CO2e (carbon dioxide equivalent), a standard email to 4 g CO2e, and an email with "long and tiresome attachments" to 50 g CO2e. A year's worth of emails received by someone is approximately 0.6 tonnes CO2e. This information is taken from *How Bad are Bananas?: The Carbon Footprint of Everything* (2010) by Mike Berners-Lee. To put this into perspective, the total yearly carbon footprint of an average person living in India is approximately 1.5 tonnes CO2e (Climate Outreach data) and 16 tonnes in the USA. The world average is 4 tonnes. Via: https://hackersanddesigners.nl/s/Summer_Academy_2020/p/Climate_KIC_Lecture_'Sustainable_Internet'

How can we, as hackers and designers, open up our modes of collaboration and consider creative alternatives to file sharing,[3] email protocols[4] and instant communication apps?[5] Can we challenge established client-server models with, for instance, decentralized and distributed models, for network technologies such as P2P or mesh networks? How can we enable critical encounters with communication and transfer protocols? How can hands-on approaches to those encounters contribute to making abstract and complicated technological concepts more tangible for non-experts?

3 For the Hackers & Designers Summer Academy (HDSA) 2020 'Network Imaginaries,' Karl Moubarak created a documentation and file sharing tool: a website that utilizes the Hypercore protocol — a secure transport protocol for scalable peer-to-peer applications. Every participant, workshop host and facilitator dedicated a folder on their personal computer that they 'served' to the public domain. These folders acted as servers and were accessible via unique public keys (hyper://....). By dragging and dropping files into the folders, HDSA participants were able to share, publish and distribute files in a decentralized way. Via: https://hyperdrives.hackersanddesigners.nl/

4 In the workshop 'EpiphenoMAILnal: RITUALS OF EMAIL,' Char Stiles and Sol Sarratea gave an introduction to "the history of esoteric and sacred text, as well as the history of the email protocol, which is ancient (and even sacred) within the timescale of the internet," followed by a proposal for designing a new collective email ritual. Via: https://hackersanddesigners.nl/s/Summer_Academy_2020/p/EpiphenoMAILnal_:_RITUALS_OF_EMAIL

5 In the workshop 'The Experimental Chatroom,' Xin Xin and Lark VCR invited participants to explore "micro-social-medias using p5.js to build experimental chat rooms from scratch. As a means to think beyond Web 2.0, participants designed their own chat room interfaces and explored playful and embodied ways of communicating with each other by including features such as collaborative drawing and interactive play." Via: https://hackersanddesigners.nl/s/Summer_Academy_2020/p/Experimental_Chatroom

We need to weave out[6] the socio-technical fabric[7] of network infrastructures and pay attention to the 'hospitality' of our web hosting providers[8] while interrogating the notion of "software as a service."[9] By lifting the fog[10] of cloud concepts, we might notice it is not possible to reimagine our networked futures[11]—as sustainable, open, fair and affordable social technologies—from a distance. Instead, we must reimagine them from within, intimately connected and entangled as we are with the complexities of pervasive techno-social infrastructures.

6 During the H&D Summer Academy 2018, we were introduced to weaving anti-patterns with Celeste Perret. The jacquard loom was a key source of inspiration for early operating systems. During this workshop we explored patterns as algorithms. Via: https://hackersanddesigners.nl/s/Summer_Academy_2018/p/Weaving_Anti-Patterns

7 Drawing from Sadie Plant's alternative history of computing, *The Future Looms: Weaving Women and Cybernetics* (1995), and the parallels between weaving and computing, we explored alternatives to dominant human-computer interaction during the GUD Symposium's workshop. In her book, Sadie Plant weaves the history of women and cybernetics tightly together, exploring the imagined and not-so-imagined life of Ada Lovelace, who helped develop the first computer. Plant maps the relation between women and computers over time, and she shows how weaving and computing technologies mimic and inspire each other even in their most simulated behaviours. The allegory for textiles as network, connectivity and feminism branches in many different directions: from evoking possible points of interaction, meeting points and connections, to its connotations with technology and industrial processes (cf. the Jacquard Loom), or the relation to domestic work and women's needlework (knitting, embroidery, weaving), and storytelling through weaving and textile work (as seen in many weaving traditions and in the common etymology of the words text and textile that refer to weaving in Latin). During the H&D Summer Academy 2020 we further explored these notions during the 'Hole Mending Workshop' proposed by Nicha Keeratiphanthawong and Tabea Nixdorff, which focused on repair and "networking" as a literal and tactile activity. Via: https://hackersanddesigners.nl/s/Summer_Academy_2020/p/Hole_Mending_Workshop

In 'Are You Being Served?,' the members of the cyber-feminist collective Constant ask: "what could make current networking technologies into hospitable habitants for critique, as space for artists and solidarity, teaching and learning?"[12]

8 'Build Your Own Server' was a Saturday workshop series hosted by James Bryan Graves. H&D teamed up with Greenhost, an Amsterdam-based, environmentally conscious web hosting provider that provided us with free Virtual Private Servers (VPS) for the duration of workshops.

9 'The Immaterial Labour Union' is an ongoing project by Lídia Pereira that challenges the notion of "software as a service" by inquiring about the possibilities for politically organising corporate social networking labour. Via: http://immateriallaborunion.net. Lídia presented the 'The Immaterial Labour Union' at the H&D Summer Academy 2016. Via: https://hackersanddesigners.nl/s/Summer_Academy_2016/p/Immaterial_Labor_Union

10 "Fog Computing is like Cloud Computing, but more local and ubiquitous." Quoted from the 'Eliza Ludd and the Fog and the Shade' workshop description at the H&D Summer Academy 2019, hosted by Ollie George and Char Stiles. Via: https://hackersanddesigners.nl/s/Summer_Academy_2019/p/Eliza_Ludd_the_Fog_and_the_Shade

11 During 'Reimagining the Future,' hosted by Laura Rosser, Karen Abadie and Molly McAndrews, participants were invited to "re-shape and re-think uncertain times by manipulating and exploring algorithmically reproduced instruction sets from wikiHow. The instruction sets were treated as sites of discussion and experimentation, with potential for (and not limited to) collaborative writing, performance, video, installation, programming, drawing, appropriation and dialogue." Via: https://hackersanddesigners.nl/s/Summer_Academy-_2020/p/Reimagining_the_future

12 *Are You Being Served (notebooks): Verbindingen/Jonctions* 14, edited by Anna Laforet, Marloes de Valk, Madeleine Aktypi, An Mertens, Femke Snelting, Michaela Lakova, Reni Höfmuller (Brussels: Constant 2013).

In aspiring for collaborative and hospitable networks, we need to explore virtual connections as much as physical connections.[13] As bodies within a trans*disciplinary[14] space, hackers, designers, system administrators, academics, disobedient citizens all have the potential to relate to one another. They will connect and disconnect, receive and transmit,[15] communicate, mediate and

13 'Yogicode': "a yoga session for coding mind and body. Through a set of easy and accessible exercises, heavily used joints, muscle groups and organs during screen time are soothed and revitalized. Breathing and relaxation techniques help to process information, calm the mind and reconnect the participant to their body, inner images and immediate surroundings." Via: https://hackersanddesigners.nl/s/Summer_Academy_2019/p/Yogicode

14 Trans* here is used as an umbrella term to refer to a variety of identities within the gender identity spectrum that are represented in the H&D community. By connecting trans* to the notion of disciplinarity, we want to address how there is more to consider when it comes to difference than disciplinary boundaries. The notion trans*disciplinarity is an attempt to apply an intersectional approach to problematizing disciplinary boundaries.

15 The 'Radio Transmission' workshop invited participants to join Radioee.net, "a nomadic, translingual radio station on a sonic adventure to learn about distributed radio broadcasting. Participants were provided with the tools to set up the front- and back-end of radio productions. Activities included organizing a station, sourcing content, radio technics and networking with listeners." Via: https://hackersanddesigners.nl/s/Summer_Academy_2020/p/Radio_Transmission

meditate,[16] stream[17] through verbal[18] and sonic gestures,[19] but also through making and doing, drafting, deploying, debugging. Spaces that unsettle our collective Network Imaginary offer themselves as test sites for learning how to cope with and embrace the struggle of relationality in our daily networked practice.

16 'Data Meditations: new rituals for new possible worlds' is a form of daily meditation through data that took place during the H&D Summer Academy 2020. Salvatore Iaconesi, Oriana Persico, Daniele Bucci proposed to use data as an expressive form of representing oneself: "Data becomes existential, not a mere process of extraction. We will find innovative ways in which we can share data, or keep them to ourselves: what lies beyond privacy and control?" Via: https://hackersanddesigners.nl/s/Summer_Academy_2020/p/Data_Meditations:_new_rituals_for_new_possible_worlds

17 During the Summer Academy 2020 we explored different ways of "streaming" to each other, with text (via Etherpad), and audio (via Icecast) in the 'Temporary Riparian Zone' workshop hosted by Cristina Cochior and Angeliki Diakrousi. We reflected on the processes that arose from using these tools, considering forms of online live-ness and simultaneous participation that manifest through listening, waiting and responding, inspired by the hydrological definition of a stream: a body of water with surface water flowing within the bed and banks of a channel. Via: https://hackersanddesigners.nl/s/Summer_Academy_2020/p/Temporary_Riparian_Zone

18 The heart-beat-to-print code is available here: https://github.com/hackersanddesigners/Hearbeat-to-print. Selected fonts include libre fonts by womxn: https://www.design-research.be/by-womxn/.

19 During the Summer Academy 2020, the South-Korean collective dianaband introduced us to a distributed collective sound exploration. We created a Soundmix web application that hosted our own sounds (recordings, music or other). It was publicly accessible, so anyone could play with sound by pressing the buttons that controlled the sound mixer on the webpage. If many people were on the page at the same time, all the sounds that were playing screamed from everyone's computers; you can jam altogether while being apart. Via: https://hackersanddesigners.nl/s/Summer_Academy_2020/p/Sound_Mixing_Bowl

This glossary entry evolved from the workshop entitled 'Imaginary Networks,' which took place during the GUD Symposium in February 2020. We propose the term "imaginary" (rather than "imagining" at a distance) as a way to anticipate our own involvement in a network. There is no engagement with a network without being implicated with it, changing it, being changed by it. This glossary contribution should therefore be read as a network of its own that consists of manifold "foot-nodes" – that is, tools and resources, projects, workshops, practices of many talented practitioners who took part in, and still are part of, the growing network of Hackers & Designers.

The foot-nodes in this text, as well as the tool and workflow used to design the Network Imaginary contribution, serve as a concrete attempt to put H&D's Network Imaginary into practice. The tool, which goes by the name "heart-beat-to-print," was made in collaboration with Jonas Bohatch for our latest publication that looks at our activities in 2019 around the topic "Coded Bodies". Every year H&D self-publishes an experimental publication. The process of its making enables us to reconnect with the growing network of participants from the previous year and to question our design processes. In doing so, we try to use and build alternative design tools, such as the PJ Machine[20] or a newspaper

20 The PJ Machine (Publishing Jockey Machine) is an open-source tool that uses arcade buttons to control a NodeJS interface for live publishing, created by designer programmer Sarah Garcin. Via: https://github.com/sarahgarcin/pj-machine-workshop

generator.[21] In 2020, we invited Jonas Bohatsch to work with us on an experimental publishing tool that considers and challenges our bodily engagement in the design process. Jonas was one of the participants of the Summer Academy in 2019: he hosted a workshop around heartbeat sensors[22] in collaboration with Andrea Valliere and Ana Jeličić in 2020. The intention of making this tool was to influence the design of the text using input from our bodies, differentiating between "head," "body" and "foot" as literal references to body parts. We were curious to investigate in what ways our heartbeat can affect a page layout, and our voices while reading. What if we shout or whisper? The tool registers the heartbeat of the user with a pulse sensor[23] connected to our computer with Arduino,[24] and the volume of the user's voice through a built-in microphone. The

21 The script auto-generates a book from a bunch of HTML files. The script removes most of the CSS and combines all the documents in one file. Weasyprint converts the HTML to PDF. The fonts used are all open source fonts. Via: https://github.com/hackersanddesigners/NDSMpaper

22 During the 'Heart Bits' workshop, we learned how to use Open Sound Control, p5.js, and Processing to route their pulse signals into generative music and art. Participants were introduced to the sensors and Arduino, and provided a jumping-off point through code concepts and examples. Via: https://hackersanddesigners.nl/s/Summer_Academy_2019/p/Heart_bits https://github.com/kabrio/Heart-Bits

23 Pulse Sensor: "an open source hardware project developed by Joel Murphy and Yury Gitman." Via: https://pulsesensor.com/pages/open-hardware

24 Arduino: "an open-source electronics platform based on easy-to-use hardware and software. It is intended for anyone making interactive projects." Via: https://www.arduino.cc/

Processing[25] script picks up on both values and translates those values in real-time to different typographic expressions. The interface shows the page and works like a teleprompter. By pressing the space bar, a word appears. You can read it aloud. After speaking the word, you release the space bar. The heartbeat value registered for that word changes the font, and the volume changes the size. Jonas incorporated a control window where we can adjust the maximum and minimum size of head, body and foot. The fonts are carefully selected by us and include libre fonts by womxn.[26]

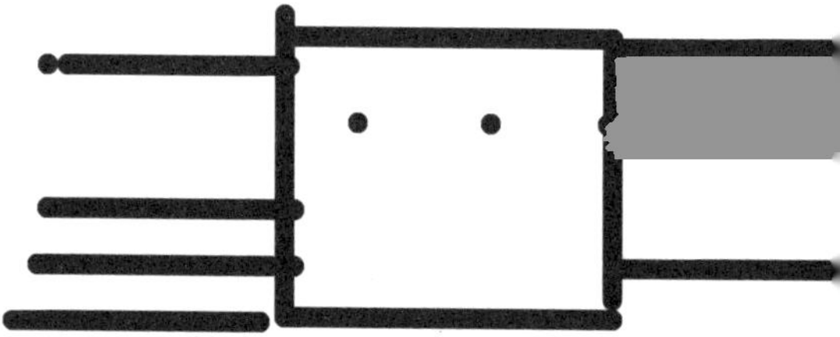

25 Processing: "a flexible software sketchbook and a language for learning how to code within the context of the visual arts. Since 2001, Processing has promoted software literacy within the visual arts and visual literacy within technology." Via: https://processing.org/

26 The fonts were found on https://www.design-research.be/by-womxn/. This collection was started in 2018 by Loraine Furter and gives visibility to libre fonts drawn by womxn designers who are often under-represented in the traditionally conservative field of typography.

CI for Corporeal Identities

PLEASE
DIVIDE
IN GROUPS OF II OR III

just had a feeling of déjà vu: several mice, sea sponges and ducks all ran [i]to each other, quite out of their minds. But no, we rarely—actually never—[de]sign logos or corporate identities (No! No!), but if you're looking for [so]meone to participate, we're in.

*Take my thoughts with you and when you look behind
You will surely see a face that you recognize
You're not alone* [1]

The mascot is an aesthetic vehicle and identification [f]igure. It feeds into the attention economies of soccer [c]lubs, the police,[2] demonstrators [3] or sites of cultural pro[d]uction.[4] It combines contradictory connotations; it [i]ntroduces itself to the neighborhood as a conspicuous [h]ugging magnet, generates attention and, at the same [t]ime, it operates as a loophole for identity politics. The [m]ascot questions itself, becomes a real-life test dummy [f]or those performing inside it and guiding it. The mas[c]ot is a life-like, tangible lesson—a living logo. It is a per[f]ormance and an embodiment of the characteristics [o]f a community or institution, which attracts and identi[f]ies an audience from existing and new spaces.

The performers are hidden and yet unprotected from [p]hysical proximity, nor are they allowed to defend them[s]elves against being shoved over as they shuffle, un[d]erpaid, through shopping malls and amusement parks. [A]lso, the mascot has to listen to people mocking it or [e]ndure involuntary confessions from those tugging at it.

[1] Kellett, Tim and Taylor-Firth, [R]obin (lyrics) and Olive (singer) (1996) ['Y]ou're Not Alone'. Via: https:// [ww]w.youtube.com/watch?v=8pPKkHFMi34 [Fo]r the exhibition *Please Divide in [Gr]oups of Two or Three* (2019) at Kunst[v]erein Leipzig, music producer Hazina [Fr]ancia (Tadleeh) performed a new [in]terpretation of the track. Via: [ht]tps://www.youtube.com/watch?v= [?]kowWgN9to

[2] In 2015, the State Criminal Inves[ti]gation Office of Saxony posted a [jo]b offer for two actors to play Poldi, [th]eir police dinosaur mascot. Since [20]15, Poldi has been on part-time work.

[3] During the Black Lives Matter [de]monstrations in May 2020 over the [mu]rder of George Floyd, one protes[te]r in down-town Philadelphia caught [th]e public eye. Wearing an Elmo mask [an]d raising a fist, the protester [da]nced in front of burning trash cans. The protest images went viral, the famous "Elmo Rise" meme was translated into real life. In the marches that followed, demonstrators held up signs that read "Philly Elmo for Mayor" and "Stand for something."

4 In November 2019, Anna Jehle and Juliane Schickedanz curated the group exhibition *Please Divide in Groups of Two or Three* at Kunstverein Leipzig. The show was activated, hosted and surveilled by a mascot. Instead of designing a visual identity, Simone C. Niquille and Anja Kaiser developed an artistic and communicative identification figure that welcomed visitors to the Kunstverein. The result was a corporeal identity that could be worn and engage with others. The mascot was realized in collaboration with fashion designer Alexandra Börner. The video work was supplemented with a soundtrack by music producer Hazina Francia (Tadleeh).

IN GROUPS
IN GROUPS

This mascot comes in the form of déjà-vu and a ıash-up—it is a delirious, flawed version of itself, a boot-‍ɛg, grinning back at the institution and the outside world ·ith multiple ears and eyes. Somehow, it evokes memo-‍es in all of us and creates alienating projections. Though ’s not entirely clear who the mascot is working for or llied with. It hardly fits any standardized parameters nd doors. Motorically sluggish, its movements are awk-‍ard and its verbal communication limited. In the end, protects those who actually come together to negotiate ıclusion and exclusion. It simply distracts everyone lse and camouflages those underneath and behind it.

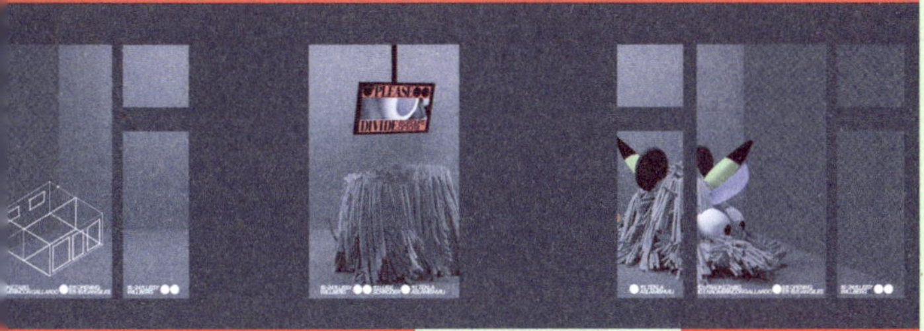

A comic shell of the mascot gives one ıe freedom to become someone else r to see through the eyes of another crea-‍ıre, like in live-action role-play. But the uestion remains: what kind of onsensus do we reach when we scape our own iden-‍tities and tart from a different perspec-‍ve? Mask your flesh! A mascot an tell us about access and aversion to lentification figures much more directly ıan logos and corporate visual identities an. It tangibly reveals what conscious and nconscious rules, codes, languages and ymbols create a sense of commu-‍ity. The mascot allows us and thers to participate in design.

Hallo? Hello! Psssst! Pst! Goedemorgen, hey!!
At most talks and events, we tend to sit next to people we already know. Usually we stick to one seat, even after long breaks. By mixing up the seating order at regular intervals, R FOR RESEATING provokes new conversations and exchanges between people who might otherwise have never met—even if it means making them leave their comfort zones.

1) WOULD YOU RATHER – Would you rather bind a book against the direction of the paper grain [EMPHASIZE] or print a book without a baseline grid? [PAUSE] Make sure your seatmate to your right has a different preference than you. [REPEAT]

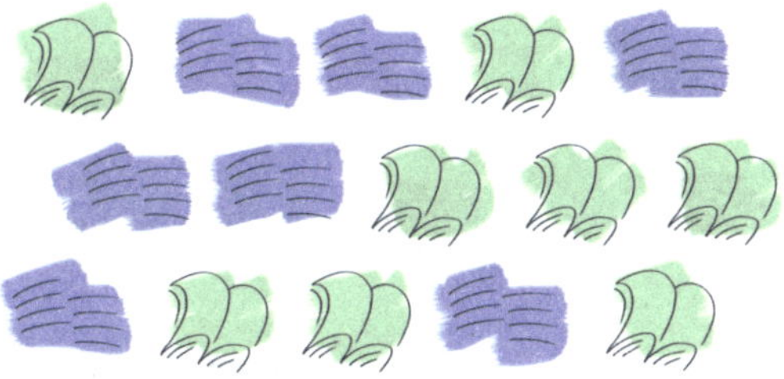

[PLAY COUNTDOWN MUSIC, 30 SEC]

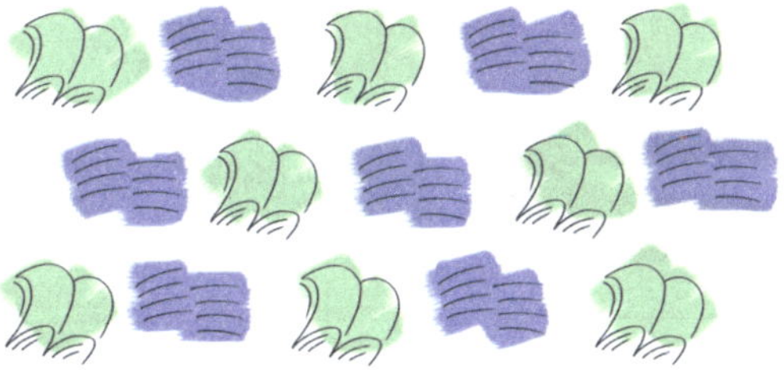

(2) THE TRIO – What describes you best as a designer: a sensitive elephant, a sociable duck or an anxious spider? [PAUSE] Talk to your neighbors. [PAUSE] Which animal do they identify with? [PAUSE] Form teams of three. Make sure that one of each animal is part of your trio and sit down together. [REPEAT]

[PLAY HAWAIIAN MUSIC, 30 SEC]

tarting point: Students have a stack of A3 paper and some drawing utensils in of them. The teacher begins with a question: "If you could be born again as an l, what one would you be?" The students only have three minutes to sketch out vision of the animal on paper. Then, the second task begins: "Now, draw this l again, reborn as a plush toy." Now, the third task: "If you could be born again piece of furniture, what piece would it be?" Three minutes. Then the fourth: draw this piece of furniture again as though it were designed by a Cubist." the first four tasks, the students have designed and created objects, intuitively ing their imagination, with artistically subjective force. Then come nine more ts to draw, with three variations of each object prompted by three quick-fire ions. By the end of these exercises, there are 31 drawings on the table in front h student.

The teacher suggests a way to proceed that questions the status of the dra
From now on, the students should not think of their drawings as subjective a
sketches of a possible world, but should take them seriously as drafts—as bluep
for designed objects to be implemented in detail later.

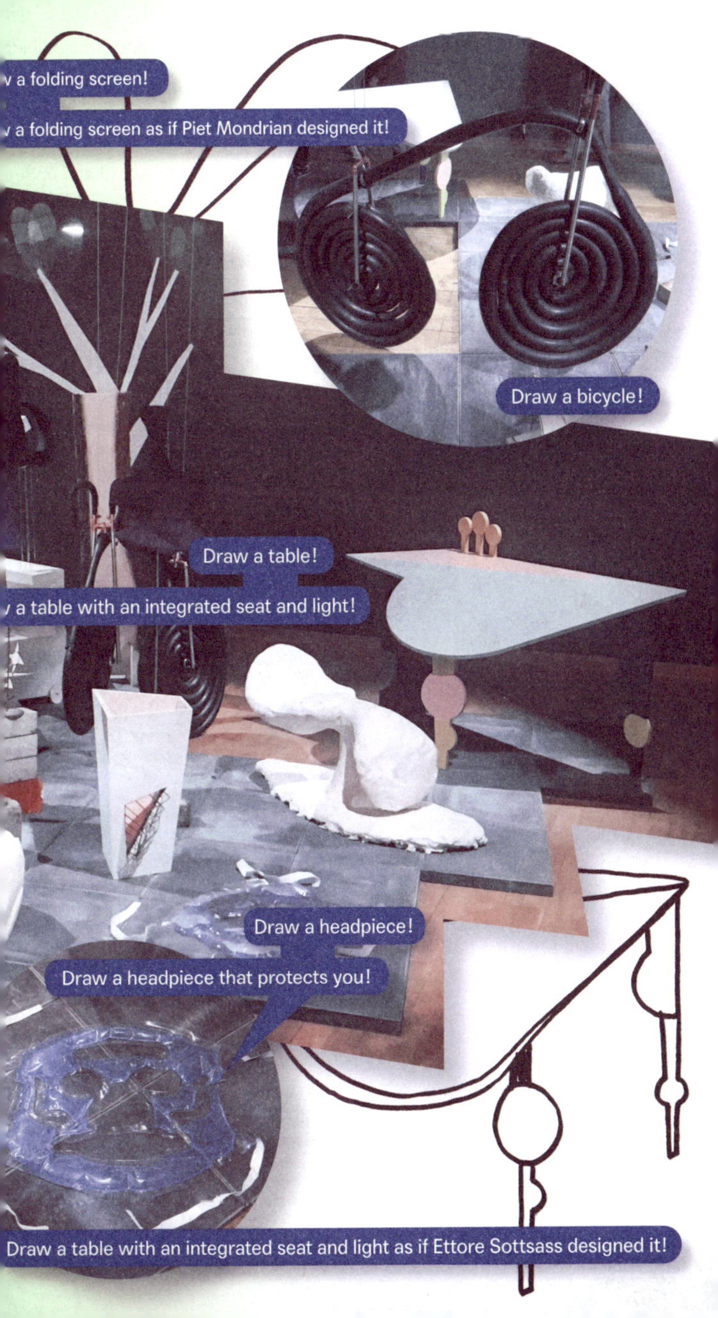
a folding screen!
a folding screen as if Piet Mondrian designed it!
Draw a bicycle!
Draw a table!
a table with an integrated seat and light!
Draw a headpiece!
Draw a headpiece that protects you!
Draw a table with an integrated seat and light as if Ettore Sottsass designed it!

According to Friedrich von Borries, design (*Entwerfen*) is the opposite of subjug (*Unterwerfen*). Everything that is designed subjects us to the conditions of its in use. At the same time, that which is designed frees us from the state of subjug of submission.[1] In design training, drawing is rarely free. Rather, it is a plan subj to the demands of mediating and implementing objects. The student designs a in which graphic deficiencies are not cleaned up, polished and driven to the pc functionality during the drawing process but are, instead, accepted and under as essential. Nevertheless, the choice of materials, color scheme and craftsma should be executed with the utmost attention and precision.

The premise of design as the planned—i.e. intentional, deliberate, goal-orier creation of objects is suspended.[2] It is not that art and architecture are absorbe design,[3] but rather that design is restored and freed from purpose. The resul "world as design"[4] that Otl Aicher would never want to see.

1) von Borries, Friedirch (2016) *Weltentwerfen. Eine politische Designtheorie*, E edition suhrkamp. 2) Ibid. 3) Ursprung, Philip (2013) 'Multitude: Die Rände Empire – Absorbiert das Design die Kunst?', *Die Kunst der Gegenwart: 1960 bis* München: C.H. Beck. 4) Aicher, Otl (1991) *Die Welt als Entwurf.* Berlin: Ernst & S

S for Strudeling

Sorry (not sorry), I'm not a solo genius but a relational designer-being.

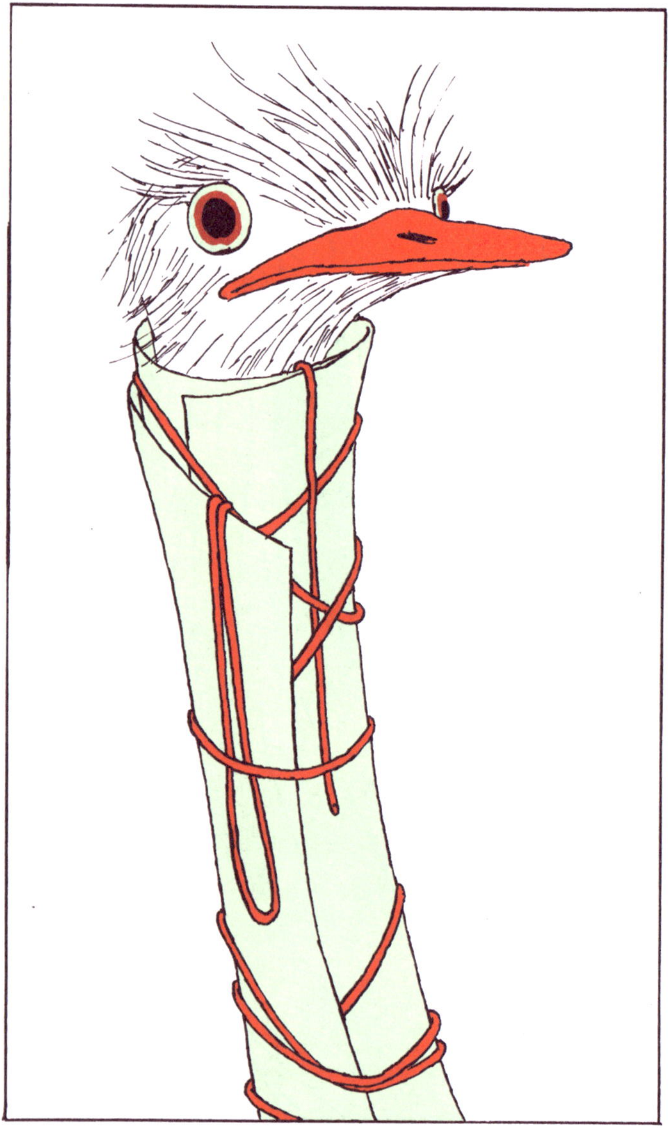

I think about other living things and their needs during office hours and I allow other people's ideas and opinions to change my mind.

Sheila Levrant de Bretteville compares this ideal of a relational designer with the image of a strudel, a multi-layered pastry.

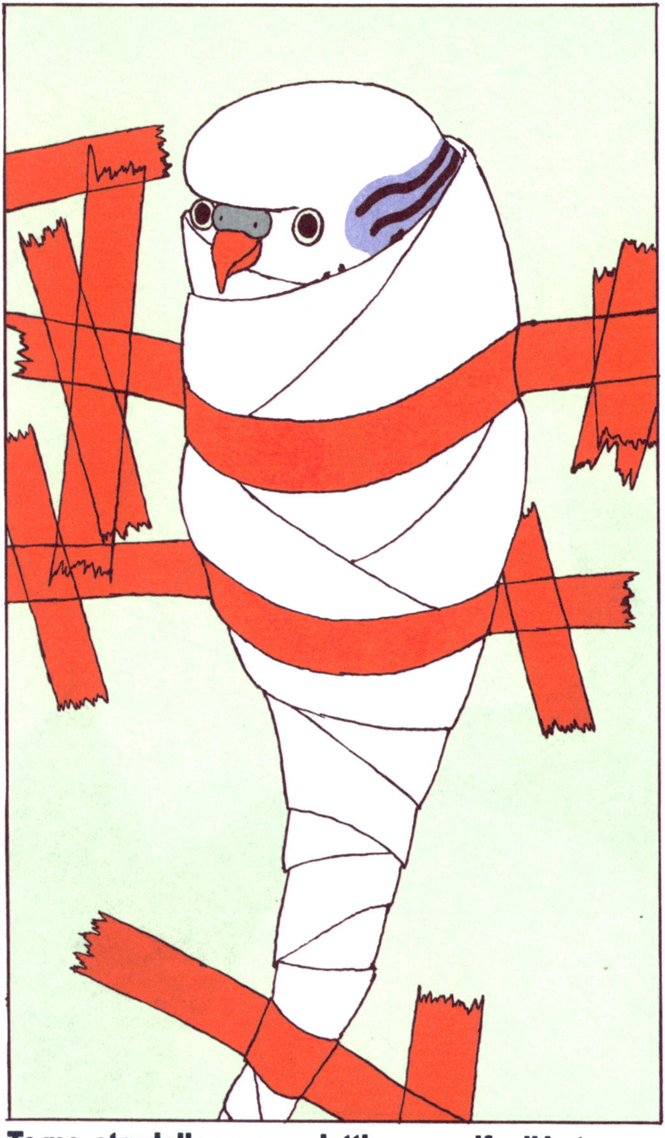

To me, strudeling means letting myself roll between various private and professional relations, while staying in dynamic contact with my own sticky feelings and fillings.

Recently, I have been thinking about uncomfortable consumption and digestive disorders as possible figurative strategies for cultural practice. There is some post-critical agency to be gained in allowing the different and often conflicting roles we perform, as well as the desires we have and expectations we are facing, collide in plain sight.

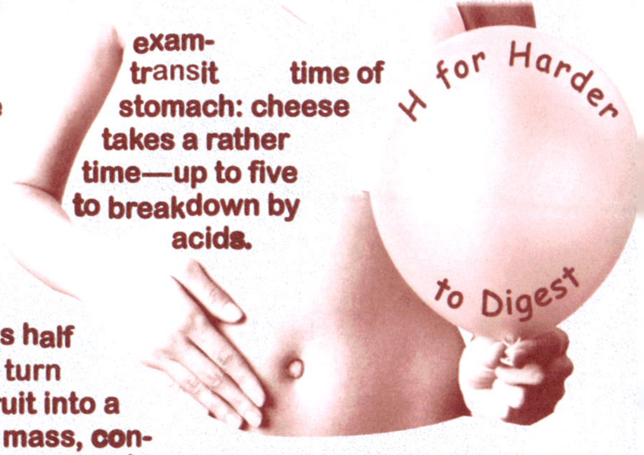

Take, for example, the transit time of food in the stomach: cheese and meat takes a rather long time—up to five hours—to breakdown by gastric acids. Meanwhile, it only takes half an hour to turn salad or fruit into a semi-fluid mass, consisting of gastric juices and partly digested food, ready for their journey through the intestines. These are different speeds and complexities of caloric (economic, artistic, emotional) exploitability.

What happens when we willfully complicate the consumption of our labor, making it a little harder to digest? Offer "cheese fondue" before the "melon" and the lighter food will start to ferment on top of the heavier food, and fermentation produces gas as a by-product. Although a gassy stomach is a rather painful and farty affair, I'm quite fascinated by the idea of moving one's practice on a spectrum between easily digestible and bloating grease feast.

After all, it only takes two different digestive speeds to generate a new kind of energy. And, knowingly aware that most of our efforts will either be co-opted or commodified, there's still a chance that the build-up of one's voices may be a little harder to digest.

a paradox of subjugation and empowerment.) You are what you eat.

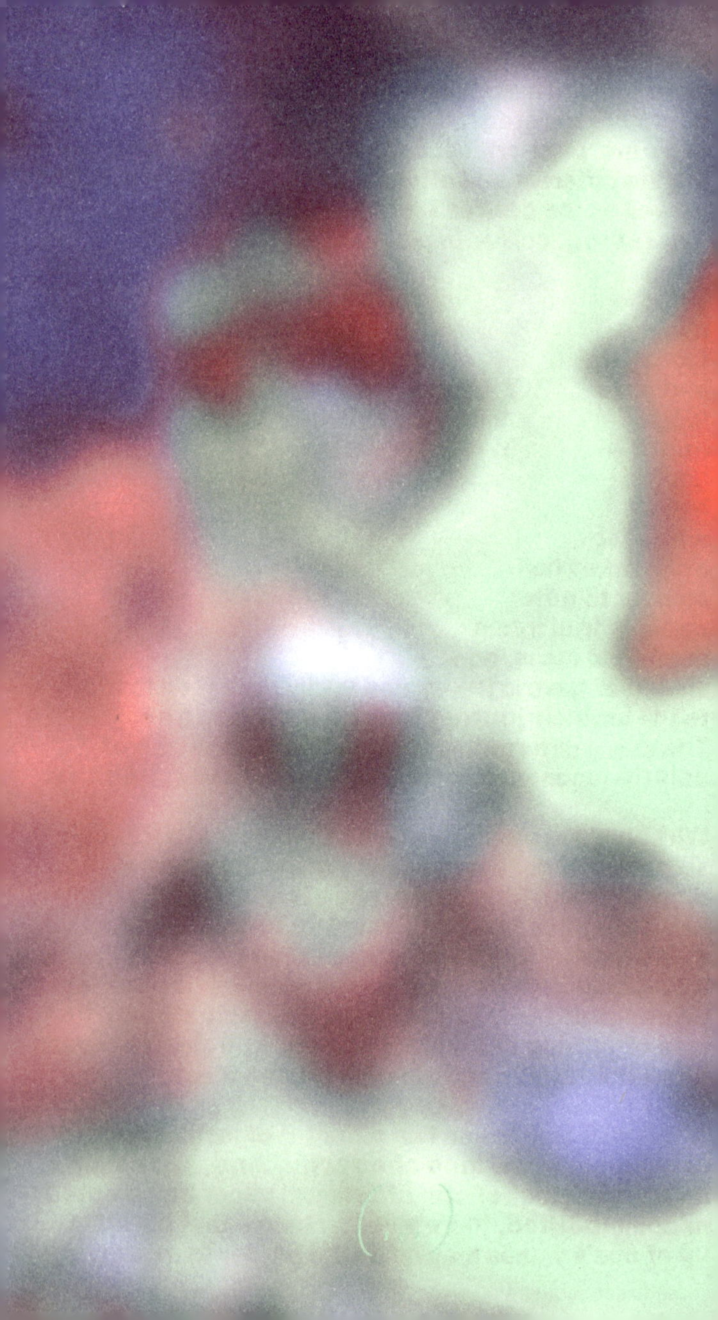

C for Comfort
Your Work(un)flow

It is okay to get stuck
sometimes.

-doubt and insecurity are
challenge to any kind of
low. Add to the mix the
essure to be productive
all times, and everything
jams up completely.

Now this is not so
much a personal
as a social problem.

let's comfort this state of
work(un)flow;
old it tight until it starts
moving again, perhaps
en transforms itself into
material to be used
a self-reflective practice.
Maybe we stay stuck.

And that is okay, too.

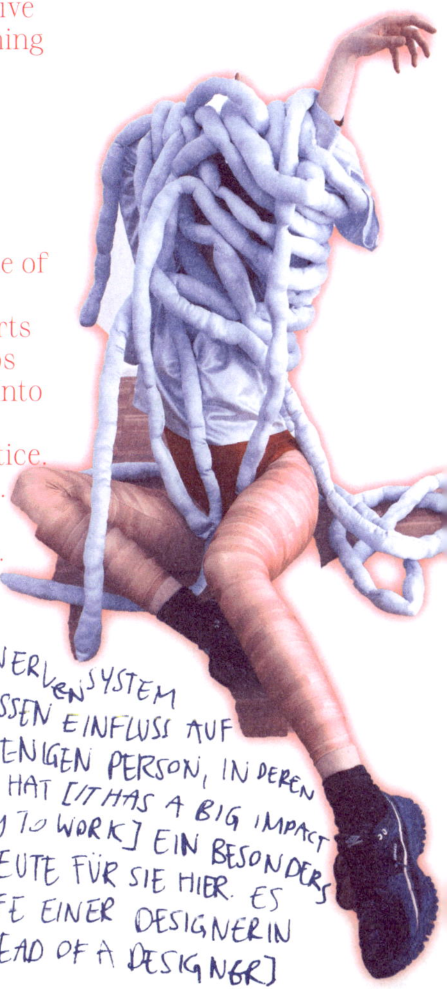

DAS GRÜBELN EINMAL
ERÄT DAS KOMPLETTE NERVENSYSTEM
REITSCHAFT. ES HAT GROSSEN EINFLUSS AUF
RBEITSFÄHIGKEIT DERJENIGEN PERSON, IN DEREN
ES SICH EINGENISTET HAT [IT HAS A BIG IMPACT
HE PERSON'S ABILITY TO WORK] EIN BESONDERS
ES EXEMPLAR IST HEUTE FÜR SIE HIER. ES
AS GRÜBELN IM KOPFE EINER DESIGNERIN
DING INSIDE THE HEAD OF A DESIGNER]

WHAT HAVE I BEEN DOING THE WHOLE DAY? THE DEAD
IS TOMORROW. WHAT HAVE I BEEN DOING ... MY WHOL
LIFE? I MIGHT BE HAVING A COLD TOMORROW ... I HE
– MEDITATION WORKS I SUPPOSE? MAYBE I WILL J
CALL IN SICK. NO. I SHOULD CLEAN MY ROOM FIRST
I SHOULD DO THE LAUNDRY FIRST. VIELLEICHT SOL
ICH ZUERST MAL MEIN ZIMMER AUFRÄUMEN

I SHOULD GET SOME FRESH AIR FIRST.

[AMPLIFIED THOUGHTS OVERLAPPING EACH OTHER]

SOME MOVEM WILL DO ME GOOD.

UND WENN ICH DANN MEIN ZIMMER A
GERÄUMT HABE... ICH KANN NICHT BEEINFLUSSEN,
ANDERE VON MIR DENKEN. TROTZDEM BEEINFLUSST
DIESES DENKEN SCHON IN MEINEM GESTALTUNGSP

MOVING THE BODY (THE BODY)

THERE'S THOUGHTS IN MY HEAD – THERE TO ST
I WISH I HAD STARTED A LITTLE EARLIER
I GUESS THEN I WOULD BE A LITTLE FURTHER NOW
BUT IT'S THE LASTMINUTE PRESSURE that
craving FOR.

SHIT (16x)

SO I CAN STAY HERE IN MY CAVE (OH MY HEAD)

I'VE BEEN THINKING TOO MUCH.
I'VE BEEN THINKI TOO MUCH.
[WHAT OTHER PEOP MIGHT THINK]
TOO MUCH.

WHAT HAV I BEEN TODAY

I HOPE IT'S EN

-FAST
ANZE NACHT
GEMACHT.
ANDE DES WAHNSINNS
S TAUSENDFACH DURCHDACHT.

*(ⓐ)

H PITCH PITCH,
H – WIEDER NICHT!
ICH, ICH, ICH
MICH WIEDER-
– UNGEDUSCHT
SCHREIBTISCH.

EFERE DEADLINE
ESSION IM
RESSVERSAND!
RE PROJEKTE MIT
GAS GEGEN DIE
ND ICH HAB' DIE, MICH PACKT DIE ... ARBEITSWUT
TSWUT!

SIE KRIEGT DICH, SIE HAT DICH

VIERTE REVISION UND IMMERNOCH GEFÄLLT'S DIR NICHT
KÖNNT'S ZWAR ÄNDERN, DOCH GANZ EHRLICH:
WILL ICH NICHT! ICH REISSE MICH ZUSAMMEN
DER GEDULDSFADEN REISST.
, PITCH, PITCH, PITCH, PITCH – WIEDER NICHT!
CH, ICH, ICH, FÜHL' MICH WIEDERLICH – UNGEDUSCHT
SCHREIBTISCH.
E EMAILS UNTER SCHREIBT EIN HERR MIT NAMEN
T – DENN BIN ICH MANN UND HEISSE ERNST
AST DU MICH DANN ERNST (ICH REISSE MICH
MMEN, DOCH DER GEDULDSFADEN REISST.
HAB' DIE, MICH PACKT DIE
ARBEITSWUT!

*(ⓐ) = Arbeitswut / Work Mania: Pitch, Pitch, Pitch, Pitch, • Pitch, not again! • I feel, feel, feel, feel • I feel disgusting • Unwashed at my desk • Suffering deadline depression •
Via express delivery • Driving projects • With full speed • Into the ground • I am suffering from • Work mania • Work mania • Won't let me rest!

STECKST DU ETWA SCHON WIEDER FEST?
ICH HAB' DA WAS FÜR DICH.

KOMM' DOCH INS STUNDENHOTEL, STUNDENHOTEL, STUNDEN
TEL. DAS SIND KURZE INTERMEZZI MIT VERSCHIEDENEN
WECHSELNDEN PARTNER*INNEN. INS STUNDENHOTEL
DRAUSSEN SCHON HUNDE-
GEBELL. KOMM' WIR MACHEN DAS ZU ENDE GANZ SCH

RETINA DISPLAY, DEINE AUGEN SIND DRY,
VOR MEINEN BILDSCHIRM PASSEN SOGAR AUCH ZWEI.
DU BIST KEIN „HIP TEEN" VOR DEM LCD SCREEN.
ARBEITEST NICHT GERN ALLEIN? LAD' DICH
INS STUNDENHOTEL EIN.

SHARE YOUR DESIRES
HARVEST YOUR EYES
I'M IN A ROOM SEARCHING
FOR NEW ALLIES
NUR EIN PAAR STUNDEN – KEINE VERBINDLICHKEI
HAST DEIN TIEF ÜBERWUNDEN.
KOMM' WIR WORKEN HEUT' ZU ZWEIT!
DATEI GEÖFFNET UND DANACH DIREKT WIEDER ZU.
HEUTE BRAUCHT ES EBEN DOCH NOCH EIN ZWEITE
PAAR AUGEN DAZU. HAST ZU VIELE LISTEN; DU HAST
„WAY TOO MUCH TO DO". HAST ES ZU OFT GESEH
— DEIN LAPTOP HAT KEINEN AKKU??
GIB' MIR DAS ZEUG. ICH NEHM DIR DEN DRUCK
ICH GEB' DIR MEIN ZEUG, UND WIR GEH
IN DEN DRUCK. GIB' MIR DIE FLASCHE (SEKT)
KOMM' ICH NEHM' NOCH NEN SCHLUCK.

SHORTCUTS! SHORTCUTS!

STUNDENHOTEL (3x) KOMM' DOCH INS
SIND KURZE INTERMEZZI MIT VERSCHIEDENEN
ISELNDEN PARTNER*INNEN.

INA DISPLAY, UNSERE AUGEN SIND DRY,
MEINEM BILDSCHIRM SIND WIR (JETZT AUCH
TON) ZU ZWEIT, **TOUCHEN** TOUCHPADS HINTER
SCREEN. ARBEITEST NICHT GERN ALLEIN?
ECK UNS INS STUNDENHOTEL EIN.

RE YOUR DESIRES
VEST YOUR EYES
N A ROOM SEARCHING
NEW ALLIES
EIN PAAR
NDEN-
VE
NDLICHKEIT
N WIR
EN
ZU ZWEIT.

DATEI GEÖFFNET. DANACH DIREKT WIEDER ZU.
MANCHMAL BRAUCHT ES EBEN DOCH NOCH EIN
ZWEITES PAAR AUGEN DAZU.
EIN INTERMEZZO, WORKEN AN UNSERER PUBLI
KATION – FOR A SHORT TIME TOGETHER –
WIR MACHEN KURZ EINE KOLLABORATION.
SHORTCUTS INS STUNDENHOTEL (← 3x)
DAS SIND KURZE INTERMEZZI MIT VERSCHIEDENEN
WECHSELNDEN PARTNER*INNEN.

… KOMM' WIR

*= Stundenhotel / Transient Hotel: Retina display • Dryness in our eyes • There are two of us now • Looking at my screen • Touching touchpads • Behind the LCD Screen •
We don't like to work alone • Self-check-in to the transient hotel • Share your desires • Harvest your eyes • I'm in a room searching • For new allies •
Just for a couple of hours • There is no obligation • You have overcome your low • Let's work together today • Shortcuts into the Transient Hotel •

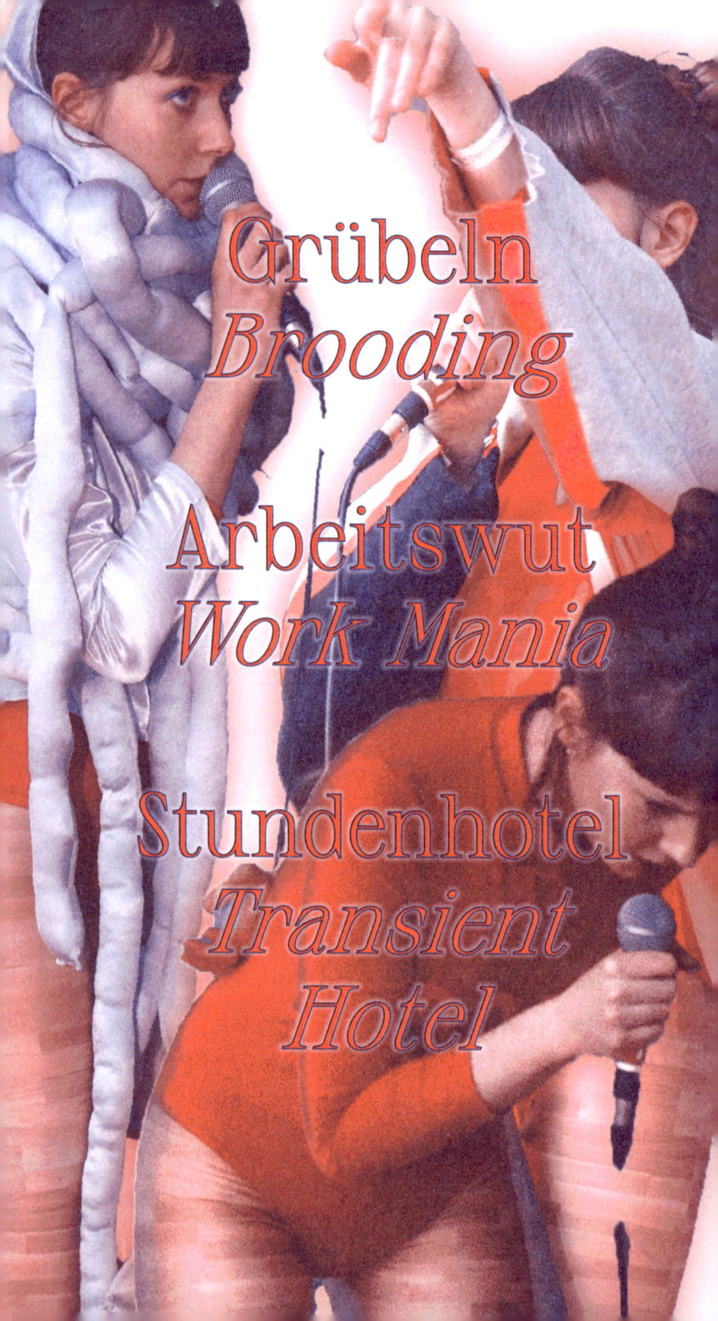
Grübeln
Brooding
Arbeitswut
Work Mania
Stundenhotel
Transient
Hotel

Theory Parody

How to prepare ...

All participants write down four theoretical terms, that are complex, difficult to understand or not commonly used – each term on one small piece of paper. Fold the papers and collect them in a bowl.
Now divide into two opposing groups (A + B).

How to play ...

While one person from group A stops the time (30 seconds per round), one person from group B takes a piece of paper from the bowl, looks at the word and begins to describe it, starting with level 1 of abstraction. The rest of group B has to guess the term or word.

As soon as the right word has been shouted, the next piece of paper can be taken from the bowl. This continues until the 30 seconds have run out. Now group B collects their paper pieces and the round starts for group A.

When there are no pieces of paper left in the bowl this level ends. The paper pieces are counted for each group and the numbers are noted down. Then the pieces are folded again and put back into the bowl to start the next level of abstraction...

LEVELS OF ABSTRACTION

1 – VERBAL EXPLANATION

Paraphrase the word without using the word or giving a translation.

2 – PANTOMIME

Perform the word through gestures, facial expressions and body language.

3 – A WORD

Explain the word with only one other word like a synonym or association.

4 – A SOUND

Indicate the word by one single sound.

IN ALL LEVELS FAST AND SIMPLE ASSOCIATION IS REQUIRED. THOSE WHO THINK TOO LONG ABOUT MEANING AND SIGNIFICANCE ARE CLEARLY AT A DISADVANTAGE.

We played Theory Parody one evening of the *GUD Symposium* to offer a physical, playful approach to the glossary and to make sure the multilayered terms are easier to remember.

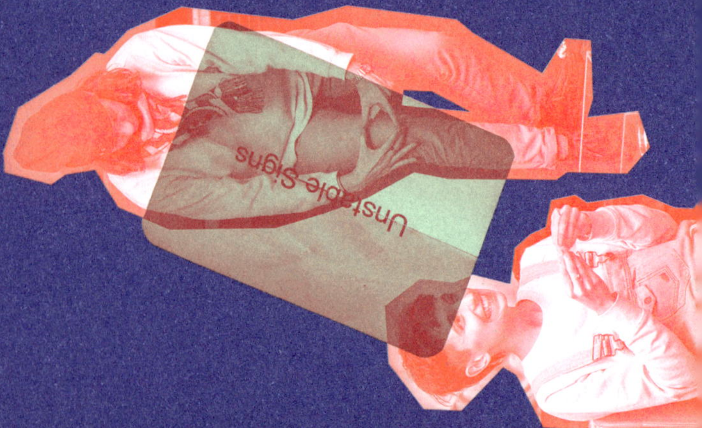

It looks like you were misusing this
ature by going too fast. You've bee
mporarily blocked from using it. W
trict certain content and act
our community. Tell
made a mist

S for Social Media Surrender

s post famous

xbrewing #artfullyengineered #newcol
que #antitrend #inimitable #newera
ossingborders #millennials #springsummer18
etails #luxury #attributes #defyingboundaries
heritage #indianvirtues #indiaonthemove
fashiondiaries #itsanattitude #bepositive
galitarianism #madeinitaly #iconic #milkshakeipa
akeuprevolution #fitness #truth #peace #love

ser Lol #makeuprevolution

tzung anzeigen

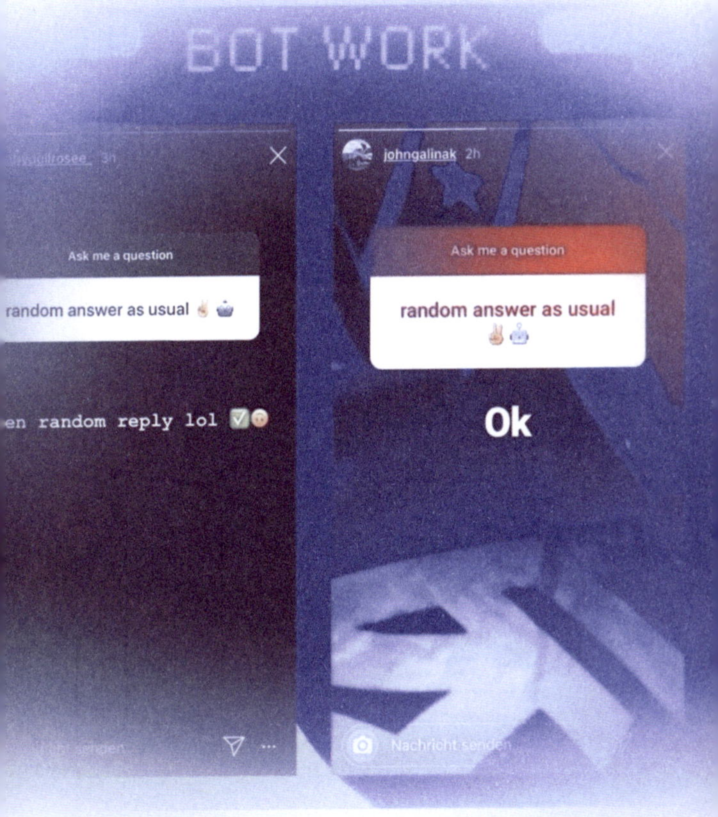
BOT WORK
Ask me a question
random answer as usual
en random reply lol
johngalinak 2h
Ask me a question
random answer as usual
Ok
Nachricht senden

Instagram is jungle. Design is a jungle. I am Indiana Jones. Does it makes any sense for you?

FAV #
PARTNERS

SMS for SOCIAL MEDIA SURRENDER

Next to having a practice as a designer, I need to constantly present my work in the form of portfolios. Social networks such as Instagram are an easy way to position my practice somewhere between self-marketing, performance and instability. SMS is a method to critically examine the potential for research, networking and professionalization of social media and to explore some unfamiliar tools of these platforms.

With the account @please_follow_undisciplined, I set out to test my Instagram potential.

12-07-19

I open an account and approach Instagram with this clean, new slate to re-evaluate my criticism. As a designer, I feel pressured to be part of the design discourse on the platform. Instagram allows me to quickly build a portfolio without any conceptual considerations, which makes it an extremely democratic tool for visual presentation. However, the streamlined appearance forces me to constantly compete for attention with other content.

The goal of the project is to test strategies I previously ignored or deliberately rejected.

12-10-19

I divide my contributions into topics that I want to deal with. #Portfolio is the first. I am testing strategies to position my portfolio within the visual codes of the social network.

12-16-19

With the format "Favorite #," I want to see what the online community has to contribute to a given topic. I am looking for #Portfolio and suddenly find myself outside of the graphic design portfolio bubble.

Using Instagram can either be completely categorical and intentionally curated or systematically undisciplined. I can use the medium to develop a specific linear project; but it could also be a documentation of inspirations, experiments and work in progress. Because my personality and my life circumstances directly influence my work, these are part of my work. If I am honest, I find it difficult —almost impossible—to exclude my self from any meaningful presentation of my work.
And who is to judge?! It is still my decision as to how much of my person I want to share and what role I choose to play in my own portfolio.

01-02-20

To my post "Can Instagram be a portfolio?" @_skinny_ replies: "Instagram is a jungle. Does it make any sense for you?"

Creating an account is similar to developing an identity. My identity is dependent on how others perceive me, as well as acting as my mirror image. It allows me to appear as I would like to be seen. My interests, which of course have a strong influence on my work, are easier to identify and keep in when I consider them through the interests c others, who interest me. This applies not only t tual social networks, but also to my immedia surroundings. Looking at myself as a mosaic influences I surround myself with probably al applies to my consumption of graphic materia

01-08-20

I had a program generate 30 hashtags fo keyword. The combination of carefully designe images with the arbitrarily selected tags becc exciting in the moments when tag and image have no obvious connection, but evoke new associations.

01-18-20

@luxxuryvibelivewire liked all my posts. I irritated and curious at the same time and try learn more about the intentions behind her/h havior via personal message. He/She writes: " users are confused if you like too many posts c load more than necessary. It also shows that th certain etiquette here on this platform."

01-22-20

I booked a bot to take over my account fo day. The bot processed 1,819 polls, 1,491 slid 330 quizzes, 3,232 countdowns and 1,619 que in stories. In 2020, this setting, also known a "masslooking," has become the most popular s for quickly generating followers.

I notice that it is mostly teenagers from S America and the US who react with irritation a report the answers and comments of my bot in stories. I find the arbitrary connection incredi exciting, but still feel patronized by my artifici assistant.

01-24-20

My account has been suspended. I can no longer log in and I am receiving dubious warn messages from Instagram that a foreign devic has tried to log into my account. Maybe I have too many bots run wild on my account. Despit the wide range of Instagram services, workin bots is against the terms of use.

02-02-20

I reactivate my @undisciplined_design_ac account and rename it @please_follow_undiscip The account was a temporary playground for r as safe a space as it is possible to have, a spa which I could appear as a professional or insti as an amateur or collective. In the long run, @p _follow_undisciplined will probably become a inactive account and, eventually, a mere numb other people's statistics of potential and influe

As a last consequence, I share the login c account in this article in order to release it fo potentials: *please_follow_undisciplined, GDUD*

PART 1
TROPICO-VERNACULAR GLOSSARY
(IN REVERSE ALPHABETICAL ORDER)

VENTRILOQUISM

Ventriloquism as an alternative to (North/Western) [1] mimicry and a form of redirecting power flows, making them begin at the periphery instead of the center. Let them regurgitate us. Let us appreciate that it is we who throw the carrying voices.

Certain precolonial Filipino tribes [2] were noted by anthropologists for their talent at mimicry. The ability to imitate sounds of animals and sounds of other languages as a precolonial talent. In a colonial setting, it was used as a tactic for survival, to place the "foreign . . . outside of oneself" rather than assimilate it. [3] This talent is prevalent still today. (A murky talent, in the way of Homi K. Bhabha, but a talent nonetheless.) Filipinos are quick at learning new languages and imitating foreign accents, especially the US American accent. Mimicking foreign accent and jargon is a task often folded into their jobs in the BPO (business process outsourcing) industry, i.e. call centers. How to pass from mimicry, or channel it, toward another position, leveraging power; the ventriloquist.

Ventriloquism as a tactic, animating static or lifeless bodies or practices through external influence. Ventriloquism is framed as a collaboration, not as a master and slave relationship. It is not simply a reversal of oppressor and oppressed, it is a relationship of kinder politics. The channel (as opposed to the puppet or dummy) is as necessary as the ventriloquist.

The difference between mimicry and ventriloquism is in levels of agency and attribution. To mimic unsatirically is to create a copy, sublimating one's own personality in order to assume another. To ventriloquize is to expose more facets of one's individuality through the performance of character in another body, form, vessel. It could also be perceived as a form of spreading attribution and collectivizing authorship, as the ventriloquist is not always using a lifeless channel and thus depends on the generative skill of another.

To use canonical, North/Western mouths to regurgitate a language that we create using their tools. Some (not all) of the master's tools can be used to destroy the master's house. To disallow the possibility of appropriating tools that are efficient seems like sabotage, making things more difficult than necessary, setting the stage for failure. To creolize as a form of conquering. Language theft (or loan, if one is predisposed to euphemisms) supposes the creation of a new vernacular with a significance and history of its own. Ventriloquizing the master's tools to create an aesthetic language that is as liberated from as it is imprisoned by the imperial design logic embedded within them. It is this memetic trace that makes the creolization compelling, giving it healthier odds for survival. I'm thinking of Ece Canlı's lecture at the *Glossary of Undisciplined Design Symposium* (February 2020) where she speaks of the possibility of monster's as opposed to master's tools. What is more monstrous than an appropriation, a failed copy, a Frankenstein?

Ventriloquism is imagined as a way for the subaltern to speak, a saving of distance for those who find it difficult, painful, or dangerous to be heard. Meaning, a marginalized figure can use another person as a channel to face and speak to a set of listeners, especially when this audience is hostile or when what needs to be said carries the weight of trauma. The channel says no original words of their own, only utters words predetermined by the ventriloquist.

The channel may or may not know they are being ventriloquized. The channel may or may not be a human body.The ventriloquist may not be visible to the listeners or the channel.

The channel filters, veils the identity of the ventriloquist. (Unobstructed visibility is not always a cure.) Invisibility blurs authorship, distributes accountability. Invisibility is a remove that allows the (subaltern) speaker to broadcast uninterrupted, without the feedback of a listener's emotional charge. Or the listener's need for protagonism. Or the listener's assumption that they have a right to consume the speaker's body, wholesale. The listener's reaction to the speaker often carries an implicit demand for attention and acknowledgement. This is a burden for one who is speaking of or from trauma. Breaking the line of sight——not allowing the listener to see the speaker or hear their voice——can create frustration for listeners.

Ventriloquism may be employed, in the passive sense, by those who are privileged with volume/audibility, offering themselves as an amplification platform. An able-bodied/white/masc/wealthy/anthro-centered person may have disproportionate access to volume. Allowing their bodies and voices to be controlled by those with less access could be a form of solidarity. [4]

[1] In this text, the hyperreal coordinates of North and West are measured standing from the Philippines. The hyperreal West is a term I have encountered in Indian academic texts, referring to the idealized West present in the post-colonial imaginarium. The politics of North and South are just as codified into our thinking as those of East and West.

[2] In the Filipino language, the word tribe is conflated with the word *katutubo*. Literally translated, katutubo means something like "of common roots." It is perceived as a dignified and politically desirable form of address (or identity) for indigenous persons. When translating the plural form (*mga* katutubo) to English, the word "tribe" is used in academic writing as well as in popular speech. Since English is not the native language of katutubo, there is little knowledge or preoccupation with the negative history of "tribe" in English.

Filipino is one of two official languages of the Philippines, the other being English. When Filipino was "discovered" by local linguists and named as a national language, it was the object of heated debate in the 1980s and 1990s. Filipino is a lingua franca derived from Tagalog, the most common language spoken in the northern Philippines where Metro Manila—the country's capital, traditionally viewed as the seat of political, economic, and social power—is located. This hybrid language is almost identical to Tagalog, though it contains a more fluid concept of grammatical and syntactical correctness. Certain mistakes in popular use of Tagalog were consistent and persistent. These errors reflected speech and grammar patterns of non-native Tagalog speakers from other regions. These slight distinctions were recognized to have coalesced into an entirely new linguistic form, and thus, Filipino became the language of instruction across the nation's school curriculums.

There was some controversy about why Filipino was chosen as the national language. It is not so ostensibly distinct from Tagalog, which is not the preferred native tongue for the population's majority. Despite its extreme similarity to Tagalog, Filipino is designated as a fully-fledged language, while all other tongues spoken in the country are demoted to mere dialects, despite the vast and rich linguistic differences between them. Demographically speaking, though Bisaya, another "dialect" of central and southern origin, is spoken more extensively by the country's population, it carries some stigma of being unrefined and rural (probinsyano). It is looked down upon quite specifically by the Tagalogs. Global North-South politics of capital access and exclusion are reenacted within the archipelago.

[3] "While the ilustrados* could have been critiqued for an assimilationist approach that glorified the image of the colonial masters, the excerpt from Vicente L. Rafael's book *The Promise of the Foreign* ... articulates how 'mimicry' can simply be a tactic. In this context, the ilustrados possessed an understanding of their own political leanings, one that outwardly seemed to suggest support for the 'civilizing project' promoted by Spanish colonizers but that nevertheless masked another motivation: to place the 'foreign ... outside of oneself.' Consequently, dress, manners, and even food become merely equivocal concessions to Spanish colonial power, not evidence that they shifted their attention away from national and cultural independence."

Sohn, Stephen Hong (2010) 'Los Indios Bravos: The Filipino/American Lyric and the Cosmopoetics of Comparative Indigeneity'. *American Quarterly* 62 (3), 547–68. Accessed August 25, 2020. Via: http://www.jstor.org/stable/40983419

**Ilustrados refers to the well-educated Filipino elite during the Spanish colonial era, many of them of Spanish creole descent. The Philippines was a colony of Spain for 300 years, and after 1898—the year in which both the Philippines and Cuba were liberated from Spanish rule—it became a colony of the United States for half a century.*

[4] Ventriloquism should be employed with care to avoid appropriating resources, extractivism, or speaking for another whom one cannot adequately represent. It is presented as a strategy to reverse power flows, not reinforce them. From their position, the channel should be aware of the danger of those acts as well.

VERTICAL WORD

Laying the letters of words on a vertical rather than horizontal path. The key to the proliferation of this move could be the needs of store owners to advertise at the entrance of their establishment. There is not much space at the entrance of a tropical storefront for the purpose of informing the customer of all the services they offer. Usually, these service listings are placed on vertically oriented placards outside of the store or painted on the column that separates one store front from another. With this design surface, placing letters on a vertical path is visually pleasing and maximizes space. Tropical cottage industry marketing principles (of the Philippine variety, at least) dictate that all goods and services offered by an establishment should be legible to customers from the outside. Patrons are looking for one–stop–shops for their needs, so the more services one is able to advertise, the more likely they will be perceived as professional, skillful, or at the very least practical. Especially in megacities such as Metro Manila, plagued by immense amounts of vehicle traffic, the convenience implied by patronizing just the one print shop is highly valued. Manila's rush hour lasts six hours, from 3 to 9 PM, if you are lucky. In this context, any time saved from a client's commute is a strong selling point. Examples of successful copy shop models, at different scales, might be: a) a convenience store that also does desktop printing and minor graphic design, such as wedding invitations or laminating ID cards; b) a copy shop that microprints (one hardbound, gold–embossed student thesis) and macroprints (tarpaulin billboards).

TROPICO-VERNACULAR

With due thanks to Alexander Provan of Triple Canopy, who coined this glossary term as a title for an essay I wrote and he (and four others) edited.

Here, vernacular is adopted from its meaning in architectural language. In architecture, vernacularity implies structures that are built without professionally certified architects. The term does not subscribe to the idea that someone is not a designer simply because they do not have an academic degree or other formal certifications that ordain them as such. It's more interesting to think of the vernacular designer's advantage being that they do not need to unlearn as many restrictive notions of what is "proper." While conducting field work on vernacular typography in the Philippines, it became clear that "fancy" graphic designers working in air-conditioned design studios often had less technical knowledge of typographic construction than street-based sign painters. It does not follow that a lack of formal training implies less literacy in formalist notions. This gap of access is widening, in some ways. With the encroachment of digital print services on the folk typography trade, sign painters are struggling to stay afloat.

"Vernacular could be understood," said Nathalie Hartjes during a sidewalk conversation outside of Showroom Mama, "as contemporaneity." That which is not just culturally but also temporally specific. Authentically of its time, a snapshot of an evolution in the present state.

In the use of vernacular, there is sometimes a sense of judgment, a moralization of aesthetics, a verdict on whether something is correct or incorrect according to the canon. This judgment is not intrinsic to the word vernacular but is rather the result of a rejection of popular tastes as necessarily without value. It is preferable to use vernacular with more love for the popular contemporary, considering it a site for serious, tender study.

Vernacular is also understood as a language in itself. A (visual) slang. What is spoken in the vernacular by a particular culture, community, subculture, alterworld.

The term tropical is used consciously, as an acknowledgement of the ties between nature and culture that tend to reoccur in fraternal (but not identical) manner across

CARWASH
P80
FREE
WIFI

SIGN
Smart: 0999-868-3291
Globe: 0905-912-7799
PANAFLEX
PLASTIC SIGN
STICKER
T-SHIRT PRINTING
Rubberized, Emboss
Ordinary, Heatpress
SIGN
BILLBOARD

MONEYCHANGER
GIODANIELLE

meteorologically defined regions. This is not an essentialist employment of the word. It refuses colonial and eugenic explanations of how something like geographical temperature (and natural landscape) could affect cultural temperament (or built environment, or social specificity).

The tropical is usually maximalist in either size, scope, or texture. Minimalism can occur, and when it does, it is often (but not always) a sign of limited technical or financial resources on either the supplier or customer end. Minimalism can thus be framed as a lack of capital, in the tropical sense, which is the opposite of its significance in the North/West.

HORROR VACUISM

The phenomenon by which the nature of the designer is to abhor a vacuum. In the tropico-vernacular, empty space is filled with as much information or graphic substance as humanly possible, with as much variety as the designer can muster in terms of font choice, color palette, and graphic additives. The result is a textural layering of signification that could cater to any of the following urgencies or matters of fact:

+++ Insufficient budget for more than a single point of contact with customers. Just the one billboard, signage, poster opportunity. All information must be offered comprehensively. There may never be another opportunity to convey the message.

+++ Small sizes for point-of-sale advertising in sari sari [5] stores or other small establishments. These may include tarpaulin awnings or banners, paper brochures taped to glass display counters or storefront windows, sandwich boards, et cetera.

+++ Billboards placed by major thoroughfares plagued by high density traffic jams, often on the side of narrow buildings. Which means people are stuck in their cars for long periods and have the inclination to read finer print.

+++ The rejection of whiteness as a symbol of (visual) poverty. Emptiness provokes angst. Festive, multicolored, and dense ornamentation are attractive signifiers of monetary wealth, one-stop-shop-ism, or communality (social capital). The more colors, the more tastes are covered " for the whole family," the more services and goods implied, the more popular a service provider is judged to be. Few things are more satisfying to a Filipino customer than the idea of variety folded into the promise of a socially plural experience. Being alone in one's lifestyle choices, as a consuming member of society, provokes fear. Even for the wealthy, exclusivity is still somewhat of a herd experience. They shop in large-scale malls clogged with customers. They live in gated communities, safety in numbers. They vacation in luxury resorts where they enjoy socializing and/or conspicuously displaying status. Wealth is worn prominently on the skin. This, too, is a precolonial trait. The richer the owner, the more decorated the object. In case of economic poverty, ornamentation can be simulated with color or textural variety.

Horror vacuism is linked to best practices in sari-sari retail display. Almost all goods available in an establishment must be visible to the customer from outside of the store. They should also be arranged to convey lysergic diversity rather than Cartesian order. Variations in the juxtaposition of size and color are favored to give the illusion of a tantalizingly complete mix. Variety, ill-perceived as chaos, underlies an intuitive order. It is preferable for items to be displayed in bulging bunches that cover the storefront window--typically, a wire-mesh window with no glass. They must also hang festively from the ceiling, columns, or walls, like ripe breadfruit on a particularly fecund tree. It is not preferable for colors to be arranged in a minimalist fashion (no gradients or by-color organization), as clients would be turned off. They might translate the lack of vibrance in color scheme to a lack of variety in the store's stock, and they might head elsewhere for their one-stop-shop needs.

With due thanks to Pamela Cajilig, a Filipino design researcher, for her investigations in vernacular retail marketing.

[5] Sari sari stores are independently owned convenience stores. It is common to see them occupy small, makeshift structures at sidewalk level, appended to the front of the store owner's house. They are often constructed as an afterthought, taking over what might have been a garage or street-facing room.

ARBITRARY ACRONYM

Filipino institutional speak is plagued by alphabet soup. This love affair with acronyms could be a postcolonial throwback to American military language. It is employed for various motives:

a) To shorten a long name;

b) To codify lengthy information in a more entertaining way;

c) For name recall purposes. During campaign season, politicians vie for the catchiest mnemonic acronym. Elections are won more often by those whose names are familiar to voters, regardless of the content of their political platform. The sea of political acronyms is as vast as it is complex, with letters arbitrarily chosen for abbreviation. DU30 is Pres. Rodrigo Duterte. Pres. Joseph Estrada is ERAP, which, when written backwards (pare), spells abbreviated slang for kumpare (comrade) and means something like " bro " in English. Marikina City ' s vice-mayor in 2013, Jose Fabian Cadiz, used an unorthodox formula:

Cyberwar
Against
Dangerous and
Illegal
DrugZ;

Acronyms are opportunities to be humorous, and the Filipino social framework favors the Joker archetype. Authority figures often depict themselves as jokers to win constituent favor. If they can be laughed at, they are less intimidating, more trustworthy. Many politicians were actually celebrity comedians before entering public service.

JOKER	Type and typography conferences with all-male panels? Never heard of them.	Individualism was a mistake.	I've seen through the political power relations at my university.
I feel guilty about not working enough.	Stress, lack of motivation and exhaustion are welcome topics in my classroom and workspace.	I know Sara De Bondt's 2012 research on gender division in European graphic design.	*JOKER*
I like to let my male colleagues do the care work from time to time.	I don't give a fuck about classifications and presumptions that go along with them.	I think that education should represent society.	I share my job quotes with my peers.

INSTRUCTIONS: Copy the template for the number of participants playing. Each bingo field contains a statement. A moderator reads out the statements on the bingo sheet in a random order. When a player agrees with the statement, they cross it out. The jokers are fields for your own statements, which you can add before the game starts. The game is over as soon as one player has crossed out six statements and called B-I-N-G-O! But that's when the game really starts: share your gossip, fuck-ups and strategies!

B I N G O ! ?

Collective work constellations are thrilling.	I ignore modernist formulas and rules in my design work.	Sometimes I'm lazy for political reasons.	I call friends to ask for advice when insecurity strikes.
Umm, what's genius?	I hardly find myself in design history in the way that it is written, if at all.	*JOKER*	Pitches, go back to the 90s!
I've never been accused of having computer problems for biological	I have heard of a residency that also offers childcare.	I know many emancipatory work models and regularly exchange ideas with	When students go on strike, the university has to shut down. Harr harr.

INSTRUCTIONS: Copy the template for the number of particip playing. Each bingo field contains a statement. A moderator read the statements on the bingo sheet in a random order. When a p agrees with the statement, they cross it out. The jokers are field your own statements, which you can add before the game starts game is over as soon as one player has crossed out six statement called B-I-N-G-O! But that's when the game really starts: share gossip, fuck-ups and strategies!

I try to reflect on my own privileges and become aware of my blind spots.	*JOKER*	I write proposals for colleagues, because we all sell ourselves too cheap most of the time.	Design compendiums with an extra 'Women in Design' chapter are so contemporary.
Decolonial and inclusive examples must be integrated into teaching.	I speak my mind in the classroom.	Everyone has to be paid fairly in the projects I'm involved in.	Assembling an all-female design jury only once doesn't make a difference.
I know bell hooks' definition of feminism.	Objectivity, factuality and neutrality play no role in my design.	*JOKER*	No payment for my talent and commitment? Nah.

INSTRUCTIONS: Copy the template for the number of participants playing. Each bingo field contains a statement. A moderator reads out the statements on the bingo sheet in a random order. When a player agrees with the statement, they cross it out. The jokers are fields for your own statements, which you can add before the game starts. The game is over as soon as one player has crossed out six statements and called B-I-N-G-O! But that's when the game really starts: share your gossip, fuck-ups and strategies!

BINGO!?

Art schools have really good policies for dealing with discriminatory and sexist attacks.	I swap freelancing tricks with my peers.	When my professor throws chairs in class, it's just an expression of male creativity.	I am aware that design (re)produces discrimination.
I've learned to appreciate and endure differences.		For my last pitch, I negotiated the hourly rate together with the other invited designers.	Technical problems with my file? I'd better ask a man.
Citation politics: Like Ramia Mazé, I check my references for their cultural …	I get worked up about design history's patriarchal narrative.	I know more design studios that are run by women than by men.	When it's time to get someone on board for a job, I try to look beyond my own …

INSTRUCTIONS: Copy the template for the number of particip… playing. Each bingo field contains a statement. A moderator read… the statements on the bingo sheet in a random order. When a p… agrees with the statement, they cross it out. The jokers are field… your own statements, which you can add before the game starts. … game is over as soon as one player has crossed out six statement… called B-I-N-G-O! But that's when the game really starts: share … gossip, fuck-ups and strategies!

‘Figures of Solidarity’ is founded on a self-determined search for alliances, cooperation in resistance and strategies for visual offensives. Graphic solidarity is premised on an emancipatory indignation at social conditions and inequalities, or mutual identification of a shared problem, with the knowledge that differences must also be endured and negotiated.

This isn’t about national or institutional solidarity, but solidarity as a political struggle based in social movements. The focus is on our willingness and support of the enforcement of justice—aiming for radical equality hout creating hierarchies of giving help or of sacrifice.[1] t the same time, the call solidarity feels almost an exhausted slogan 2020—a time of battling andemic, when gov- ments offer much more pport to the financial wers of the markets and remind individuals to in solidarity, all while cial inequalities are in- asingly exacerbated. A rent strike would have been ne with solidarity as a collective answer. But despite the reasing vagueness of solidarity as a term, we are still ven by a desire for more relational ways of operating society.

eminism has a lot to do with solidarity, but being equal esn’t necessarily mean the same for everyone. Since 1980s, bell hooks has taught us to recognize the dif- ences within the feminist movement, and that if we nt our movements to be inclusive and solidary, we need make space for negotiation and critique.[2] Intersectional idarity takes into account t heterogeneous and tentially incommensura- struggles intertwine d build on mutual criti- m. Within a group or vement, there are always

1 Bini Adamczak is an author and artist working with political theory, queer-feminist politics and the past future of revolutions. In 2017, she published the volume Beziehungsweise Revolution: 1917, 1968 und kommende. On Aug 5, 2020, @bini_adamczak tweeted “A relational solidarity is not limited to instrumentally perceiving shared interests. It’s as far removed from egoism as it is from altruism. Because #solidarity aims at equality, it shuns the hierarchy of giving help as well as that of sacrifice.”

2 bell hooks is an African American philosopher who advocates for feminist and anti-racist approaches. She has made many feminists aware of their own entanglements in racism, sexism and class domination. hooks, bell (1986) ‘Sisterhood: Political Solidarity between Women’, Feminist Review 23.

wanted@
whose.
agency
SUCHE
Gesell
schaft
WHOSE
BIETE
sales@
whose.
agency
kritik
out side-

erent levels of privilege and, conversely, different and ltiple ways of being affected by power relations and associated discriminations. Social realities are differ- and diverse, and to assume otherwise would make pursuit of solidarity just as corrupt as what it seeks oppose.

ut what kind of images of graphic solidarity can really irect attention economies? What strings for tactical istribution can graphic designers pull? First of all, col- tive criticism should be an occasion for empathic operation and "complicity." Graphic designers with a versity degree do not have to surrender to boring, nteresting and exploitative job offers. The graphic de- ner's tool kit can destabilize invisibilities and fuel tures in hegemonic vision. One of the fanatical habits t could emerge here is the snuggling up to surfaces esistance, without ignoring supposedly conven- nal media.

few years ago, I came across a facsimile of the *Gay a Telephone Directory*. This US American telephone ectory was originally published in 1983 by Gay Interna- nal Inc. In it, eclectic typographic layouts with sophis- ated neon tube typefaces interact with the amateurish ographic settings of the personals and ads. The ings in the *Gay Area Telephone Directory* depict an BTQI+ community that only experienced marginal bility in the 1980s. A phone book with agency? Yes, phone book radically yet casually demands visibility the realities of homosexual and queer lives. It is im- ssive how a phone book became a tool of resistance a community that was excluded, discriminated ainst and stigmatized, particular with the advent AIDS in the USA.

July 2018, I sent about emails to feminist iling lists:

SEEKING: Contributors for feminist classifieds of resistance
OFFERING: Ad space for feminist classifieds of resistance
I'd like to invite you to post a classified ad free of charge. I have set up a project called whose.agency for this purpose. Only networks, political groups, musicians, cultur- al producers and artists from the local and international feminist milieu need apply. With this project, my ambition is to form alliances

and push political, polemical, fictional, emancipatory, or humorous feminist community demands within a setting of commercial exchange. Whether it's salary demands for reproductive work, personal ads, political group mediation, calls for donations to associations ... it's up to you.

In short: Send me brief texts (max. 80 characters) for the categories SEEKING and OFFERING. Selected texts will be designed in a classified ad format, which will then be placed at important commercial hubs within Leipzig's cityscape. Each contributor can decide whether they would like their identity to be visible or anonymized. A form for submitting ads is attached below. Please send seeking ads to wanted@whose.agency and offering ads to offer@whose.agency.

whose.agency will utilize digital poster spaces in the city of Leipzig as a medium; large-format advertising spaces that ture moving images installed on streets densely populated by re stores. These spaces are mainly used for brand presentations by porations such as Parship, H&M, etc. In the visual translation the classified ads, I will be wo ing within a purely formal typographic framework, in order to s into this specific environment and to demand self-determined m ket participation.

In August 2018 and from Decemb to March 2019, the classified a will occupy the digital poster spaces in Leipzig city center f of charge and, in March 2019, al the ads will be shown at the Gf (Leipzig Museum of Contemporary Art). whose.agency is made possi by the INFORM Award 2018. The INFORM Award, an annual prize o 5,000 euros, is awarded by the GfZK for conceptual design at t intersection of graphic design and art.

wanted@
whose.
agency
SUCHE
den
Pfad
gegen
ANTIFASCHISTISCHER FRAUENBLOCK
LEIPZIG
afbl.org
das
Patriarchat
WHOSE AGENCY IS
A FEMINIST AD SPACE

In the preparatory phase, I brooded over the possibiliti for using solidarity as a tactic in graphic design in close cooperation with the GfZK team, and also how our wish for solidarity can be put into practice with the institution support. We talked about which of the spaces in the GfZ have the most public visibility, as well as the museum's outdoor advertising. When Leipzig's municipal governme issued their permission to install digital screens in the city center, the city also negotiated an advertising quot which it gives away free of charge to push local cultural offerings. By using the institution as a trojan horse, I was able to "smuggle" a total of 25 ads from anonymous, local and international feminist individuals and groups onto the commercial screens.

The suspicion that a designer's work is only superficia may be true on some level, as we mostly decorate and illustrate surfaces, plastering them full bleed. Though wh we let these surfaces connect in solidarity, we're not only chipping away at shapes and colors, but also at structures and attention economies.

wanted@
whose.
agency
WANTED
Feminist
design
practices
WHO
WANTED
depatriarchise
design.com
END
of
pat
JCDecaux

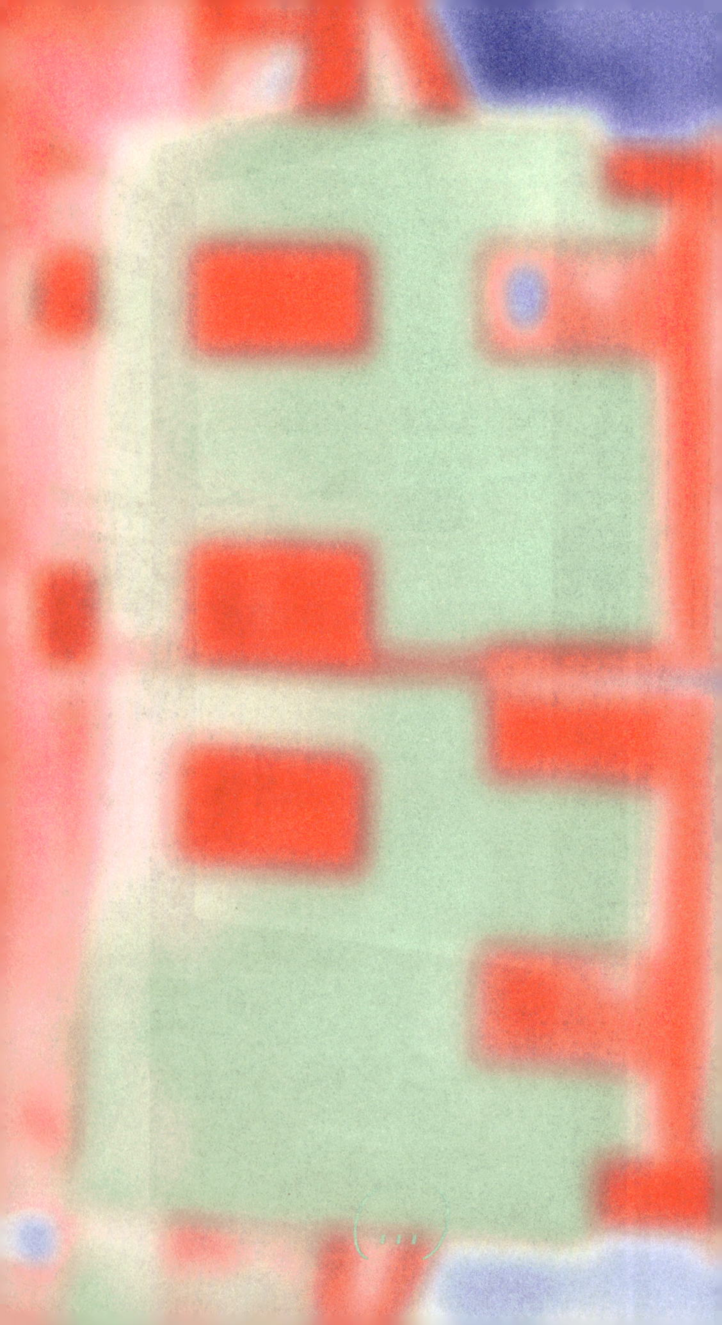

rom for Lessons Hydra

Dear Crea tur es-in-arms,

Welcome to a nasty compromise. The hydra, that many-headed monster, shares her fate with us graphic designers. In a laborious trial, the hydra must overcome a seemingly endless series of ilemmas and conflicts of interest in her design career. If he loses one head in the process, two equally magnificent eads immediately sprout afresh. Any attempt to contain or suppress the phenomenon only creates more problems and calates things further with the possibility of multiplying her heads. But let's briefly explain how we got here:

“Every professional practice operates in a state of schizophrenia, in a situation full of inescapable contradictions,” Jan van Toorn, Dutch designer and critical practitioner, wrote in his 1994 essay ‘Desig and Reflexivity.’ [1] In it, he describes how designers’ professional practices are structured by attempts tc mediate conflicts of interest between the client, the public and the designer’s own concerns. Sadly, thi often leads to a feeble consensus that cements the established order, with all its rabid dualisms an egocentric implications. Usually, designers smooth-out conflicts and their symbolic production legitimizes the current social order, including the patriarchal conditions of domination and production

1 van Toorn, Jan (1994) ‘Design and Reflexivity’, *Visible Language* 28 (4), Blauvelt, Andrew, ed., Providence: Rhode Island School of Design, 319.

riefing | feedback

Designers want to affect the world but, at the same time, their clients and public demand that all goals are comprehensibly represented before they agree the realization of the concept. This glorified plausibility is all too often couched in the language of comfortable ereotypes and so-called "normal" behavior. The designing hydra finds herself in a quandary: she's constantly pected to produce the most legitimate and familiar image possible with the vocabulary of the present in order to ivey a future that seems predictable and "true." Meanwhile, all the parties involved want to dictate this image of ne future. Graphic design and graphic production may feel ke a nasty compromise. But the hydra is used to standing up for herself in the face of multiple stakeholders, without desire for reconciliation, and is entangled in private and public ideologies. The hydra is also particularly good at defending herself against ostensible factuality and smuggling controversial figures of interpretation into her design.

blank page | **old habits**

Being conscious of one's schizophrenic positi
from the outset helps designers to cope
much better than just despondently trudgin
along on predetermined and controlled lines. After
all, the hydra also has a few self-determined heads
waiting to sprout that help her hold her ground agains
consensus, dependencies, correctness and plausibilit
As van Toorn said in *User-Centered Graphic Design*
Mass Communication and Social Change in 1997:
"Designers who do not recognize the insurmountable
conflict of interests in which they work, lose entirel
any possibility of liberating the disciplinary
practice from restrictive institutional character."
Narrative discontinuities, fictitious interventions a
digressions make it possible to intervene in these
legitimized systems with one's own visual tools for
survival. Patriarchal capitalism, too, is often descri
as mutable and many-headed. But shouldn't this be
a reason to confront the system with such a form, too
With every head recalcitrant in opposition? The
hydra disturbs herself and others.

Sincerely,
Another trouble-making head

2 van Toorn, Jan (1997) 'Deschooling and Learning in Design Education', *User-Centered Graphic Design: Mass Communication and Social Change*, *Frascara*, Jorge, et al, eds. London: Taylor & Francis, 128.

In memory of Jan van Toorn (1932–2020).

200 SISTERS SOUVENIRS celebrates the many unknown women depicted in painting and sculpture in the 200-year-history of the independent art institution Badischer Kunstverein (BKV) in Karlsruhe, Germany, as well as the few female artists, the two female directors and the all-female list of secretaries from the past 200 years. This celebration carries with it a dedication to an intersectional feminism. One that understands that cultural patterns of oppression are systemic, interrelated and include race, gender, sexuality, socioeconomic status and ability.

200 SISTERS SOUVENIRS appropriates and (mis)reads the archive of exhibition catalogues of BKV, like the gender-fluid appearances of many portraits from the early 20th century or paintings called *Hausfrau (Housewife)* and *Die Irre (The Madwoman)*. It reshuffles the visibility of all artists, acts, appearances and individuals who, knowingly or unknowingly, disrupted patriarchy within the mental, emotional and physical space of the BKV.

200 SISTERS SOUVENIRS turns archival research into usable objects like tote bags, bookmarks or lanyards: custom-made, woven ribbon consisting of text fragments from the catalogue archive, shrink plastic charms with images also from the archive and graphic elements from *LAVA* magazine (a Karlsruhe women's magazine that published 13 issues from 1989–1994) and a collection of logo-bleached and modified pre-used cotton bags and dress shirts. For the duration of ***200 SISTERS SOUVENIRS***, members of BKV were invited to donate a piece of clothing in exchange for a modified one.

Finally, ***200 SISTERS SOUVENIRS*** circulates the resulting body of work back into the city of Karlsruhe and beyond.

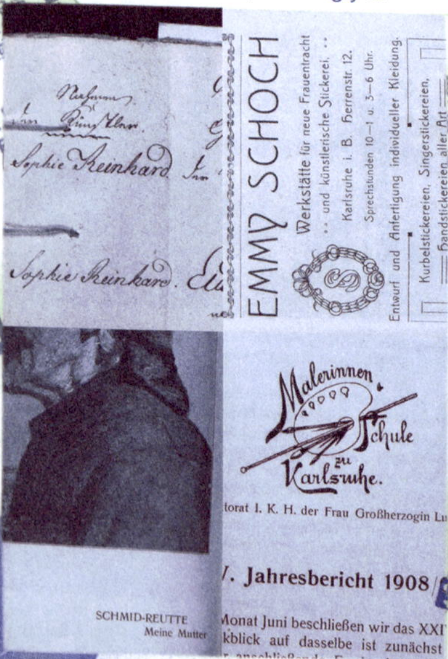

Through objects of desire and daily life, these souvenirs re-appropriate the language of commerce for claims of female empowerment while emancipating a feminist exhibition (mis)reading from moral claims and political correctness.

200 SISTERS SOUVENIRS*—200 years of exhibition catalogues, side notes and slippery images, a feminist exhibition (mis)reading* was part of the 200 Years of Badischer Kunstverein program, presented in the foyer of BKV from May 2018 until April 2019.

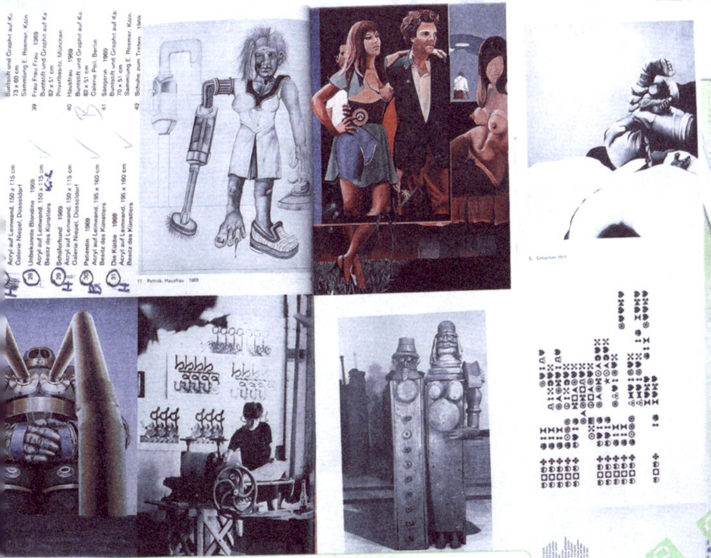

S FOR SLIPPERY IMAGES

Inducing slipperiness—shifting meanings—in questionable material is a strategy of feminist (mis)reading, especially when dealing with archival material. It is also a refreshingly reparative method of disruption, of "affirmative sabotage":* Instead of categorically rejecting problematic depictions and representations from the safety of present-day political correctness, the material of the critique is fully entered into and intimately worked with. The strategy chips away at the surface of dominant and discriminatory narratives inscribed onto images and artifacts in order to see which stories or moods live underneath them. In doing so, images are made slippery and gain agency from derogatory intentions or normativizing perspectives. They shift their forms and meaning from slumbering in the margins into more ambiguous waters in order to overwrite themselves with alternative ways of reading.

In my approach to the BKV catalogue archive for ***200 SISTERS SOUVENIRS***, slipperiness meant actively "failing" to acknowledge visual or textual embodiments of sexism, inequality and marginalization in the catalogue history of the BKV, figuratively as well as structurally. I was dealing with

around 300 publications, brochures and leaflets—mainly exhibition catalogues or monographs about exhibited artists, dating back to 1818. Next to reproductions of art works, portraits of artists, or photos of artists' studios, my (mis) readings extended to captions, biographies, texts, advertisements, photos of openings, events and exhibition views.

200 SISTERS SOUVENIRS includes a publication brochure and an accompanying souvenir collection, which uses industrially woven ribbon with textual (mis) readings from the catalogue archive as its base material.

* "Affirmative sabotage" is a concept introduced by Gayatri C. Spivak: "I used the term ... to gloss on the usual meaning of sabotage: the deliberate ruining of the master's machine from the inside. Affirmative sabotage doesn't just ruin; the idea is of entering the discourse that you are criticizing fully, so that you can

C FOR CRITICAL EMBRACES

'C for Critical Embraces' describes an approach to design research that is aware of one's personal entanglements in the objects and themes of one's critique. Thinking along the idea of reparative instead of paranoid reading, 'critical embraces' allow for criticality to be porous, tender and flawed.

Translating my archival research to usable objects such as tote bags, bookmarks or lanyards has allowed me to work through the agency of '(mis) reading' and the production of alternate slippery visibilities on a material, corporeal and, to a certain degree, commercial level.

200 SISTERS SOUVENIRS was presented as a showroom in the foyer of the BKV, where the merchandize and the publication brochure were offered for sale—spreads from which show images from the archive that are repeatedly interrupted by advertising pages for the merchandize. Staging a showroom in a foyer—and not in an exhibition space—plays with the marketing of feminist cultural production, offering a seemingly low-threshold access to my reading of the archive.

LLIANZEN↗0
00 Sisters So
00 Jahre Auss
andnotizen u
feminist exhi
ebecca Steph

With this setting, I responded to two developments that I had registered in the course of my research: on the one hand, there is the increasing commodification of feminism and, on the other, the growing pressure on cultural institutions to align their programming with commercial prospects. The commercialization of feminism "lite" is emphasized in pop culture and fashion, where it's been made trendy through simplified gestures of "empowerment," which has become quite a profitable business in the last few years (a plain white T-shirt by Dior with the slogan "We Should All Be Feminists," for example, currently sells for $860).

At the same time, cultur stitutions in the Global North under pressure to increase "a sibility" in their event-oriente programming and to cater tc ever-growing audience. It is coincidence that museum sh are growing in size, importar and visibility.

Appropriating and simula gestures of commercializatic and branding in the staging ***200 SISTERS SOUVENIRS*** a "pro-profit" showroom at B Badischer Kunstverein, crea room to expose these mecha nisms and, at the same time, plore their potential—allowir a simultaneity of contradictic including my own, to surrenc into a critical embrace.

B FOR BLEACHING

As a conceptual strategy and feminist editing method, 'B for Bleaching' creates visibility through removal. By erasing dominating information from the literal or figurative surfaces of existing material, it allows for previously hidden or suppressed layers of information to appear. Bleaching can be applied to digital or analog material, images, texts, objects and histories. It is an analogy for uncovering voices, stories and biographies, while exposing those structures of discrimination that generate and sustain under- and misrepresentation.

With ***200 SISTERS SOUVENIRS***, I bleached into the surface of the structural exclusion of women in the history of BKV, while pointing to the many unknown or anonymized women, artists and art workers. Applied as a reverse printing technique to all textile-based souvenirs, the ***200 SISTERS SOUVENIRS*** logo was acid-printed onto pre-owned tote bags and shirts using household bleach, different kinds of stencils and freehand techniques. Instead of adding ink, as any conventional printing process would, the sodium hypochlorite that was used removed pigment from the fabrics and revealed unpredictable kinds of color and logo forms.

The models for ***200 SISTERS SOUVENIRS*** were all members of Badischer Kunstverein.

Tarzan, von Monika, 8 Jahre.

200sisters-blog1.tumblr.com

C for Collective Uncertainties

all experience vulnerabilities and insecurities, both in our private lives l as professionals. Personal issues are part of our everyday realities, but habitually hidden away—or at least smoothed over—in professional ıtexts. Instead of engaging our environment in the uncertainties, (mis-) ɛrpretations and (over-)reactions that make up our lived experience, we :inctively try to cover these traces of our most human character traits. · awareness of who we are and how we function in interaction with our roundings are valuable qualities. In keeping silent about what we experi- :e, we lose a powerful tool: the capacity to take charge of our needs and potential for solidarity with others. 'C for Collective Uncertainties' is attempt to share our vulnerabilities in order to find common emotional und. We want to encourage each other to honestly engage with these lerrepresented parts of our—and each other's—being, to break the di- ɔtomy of good and bad features, of professional and amateurish behav- of so-called strong and weak minds. The projects F for Failing Queerly

P for Professional Amateur

E for Embracing Differences

not only address these topics in a theoretical form, but make them an ential part of their working process. In the spirit of sharing and giving .ce, Hanna Müller and Mio Kojima invited **Juliana Vargas Zapata** l Severin Geißler to talk about personal struggles and professional limits. ɛ following is an excerpt from the conversation, which was held as a ıel at the GUD Symposium.

:'s begin by talking about failure. Severin, your glossary ·m is called 'F for Failing Queerly.' How are these two terms— ling and queerness—connected?

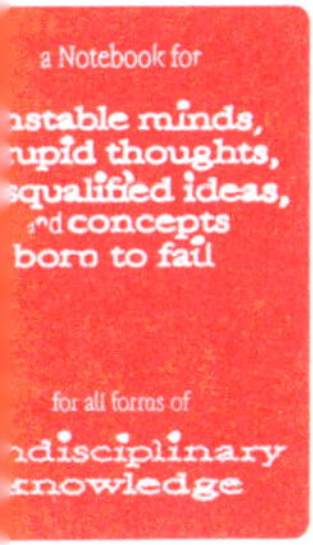

Halberstam, the author of the book *The Queer Art of Failure*, sees the connection in childhood. According to him, childhood is an essentially queer experience, as gender roles are usually not embodied yet—there is no romance, no eroticism. Most of the early learning processes in childhood happen through failing: learning to walk on two feet, for example, a skill learned through constant stumbling and falling. Later in life, the connection lies more in the characteristically queer position as a non-productive part of society. Not getting children and not being married, or, back in the time of the AIDS-crisis, having a high risk of HIV-infection is also strongly associated with failure. In a capitalist society, failing—as the opposite of winning and accumulating wealth—is seen as something bad. It is a condition in which certain, mostly normative, expectations are not fulfilled.

Your initial idea was to transfer the concept of failure to the printing process. Experimenting with your five analog reproduction methods, did you get results that questioned or undermined your initial expectations of failure?

As I was consciously trying to fail, my expectations adapted to what we would generally consider a failed print. If you try to fail deliberately, y might not fail at all—at least not from your own perspective. But what ppened during the process was that I broadened my initial expectations to a much wider field of results.

Also, the moment of surprise played a big role in the process—each print looks a little different, has its own particular irregularities and imperfections. All printed images were designed digitally, which was an important point for me: in graphic design today we are mainly working with digital tools and the design process seems to end once we send our files to the printer. The resulting prints look exactly like the previews on our digital devices. This fact changes the way we produce print media. But why should the characteristics and limits of a display also limit the printing process? The prints in the noteboo I designed might appear strange to the reader, who regards it throug their own expectations. On the one hand, those printing colors produced from plants are weak and unstable. They change their appearan with time and fade quickly. On the other hand, the reproduction tech niques I used, like silkscreen, linocut, stencil and so on, include far fewer details than what we are used to from industrial offset prints. Ir a way, these techniques are born to fail—in other words, to not fulfill our normative expectations of a good print.

In most cases, posters are not designed for durability, and neither are the colors you used. Do you think that the fast pac of the capitalist market makes it possible again to design thin that don't have to last? As, for example, using colors that fade away quickly?

Yes, I think it would be a wonderful vision for the future to include th purpose of a print product more directly into the production process and to choose the colors and materials according to their intended li span.

By using different printing techniques and colors you have already professionalized failure to a certain degree. Is there a difference between professional and amateurish failure for yo

Maybe you can exchange the word professional for conscious, and amateurish for unconscious. You are professional when you know what y are doing, dilettantish when you do not know—you “unknow.” I gue failing unconsciously is not really failing. Failure is always a process of rating or judging—the moment you start rating a project or a behavic this is when the failing happens.

you try to eliminate this moment of rating from your design
ıctice?

I don't want to eliminate it, but rather edit it, change the criteria, add or delete variables and stretch the boundaries. Why don't we print with carrots?

ve already talked a bit about being amateurish and acts of
.ettantism. This is a subject you, Juliana, also dealt with.
ı you tell us what the term dilettantism means to you?

Dilettantism comes from the Latin word "delectare," to enjoy. It is the opposite of being a professional. Somebody who enjoys doing something without having a formal education in it or doing it as a career. Practicing something voluntarily, out of pleasure. I'm interested in doing new things without having much previous knowledge about them. ot taking things so seriously, being naive, letting go of expectations and enjoying the surprises that come with that.

I think, we often forget that tools are made for us to control and not the other way around.

ring your work on the publication, did you feel like an amateur
like an expert of graphic design?

Absolutely like an amateur. At first I didn't know what to do, I was experimenting, talking to myself about what I was doing and the new functions I was discovering. I really didn't have a clear idea. It was all about this "first time" feeling. I didn't put any pressure on myself, I had no expectations—it felt so fresh and authentic. This

project became really emotional for me. It took me to my limits, because I'm a perfectionist and once I knew my experiments were going to be my final project, all of a sudden the expectations came rushing in all at once. It felt like everything changed: suddenly, things could go wrong, I could fail. It was difficult for me, because I was juggling with seven tools at the same time and had to make them all fit into one publication, even though they were all so different. I started to think how to handle all tools: "Should I fake experiments?" "What is the right way to put them together?" "How do I make it 'professional?'" This last question put a lot of pressure on me and I really started to struggle.

ıld you give us some insights into these tools? What kind of
struments did you use and how did it feel to work with them?

OpenOffice Draw was the worst for me. I picked out one function: free drawing on top of a font. I started to work with it, but realized it took me a long time. I was already halfway through, so I decided to finish it. It took me 14 hours in the end. I regret doing it now.

The complete opposite would be OpenOffice Writer: I worked on that for only 20 minutes. I was just discovering all kinds of differe functions. For example, I didn't know how to put a background color, so I highlighted the text. But what about the white frame? How could I fill it? I had to come up with an idea, so I made a fra out of different forms and I loved it. With OpenOffice Impress I tri to play with different layouts. I kind of lost control of the program There are elements in my puplication where I can't understand the logic of what I did anymore. I don't even know if in the final pu cation the pages are in the right order. At some point, I stopped liking my project, because it was too close to me, too emotional. couldn't see it objectively. But when I finished it, I realized that th was the real value of the project. It gave me a hard time, it made me face my self-doubt, my fear of failing, etc. Now I think it is eas to make a sleek object, with everything clear and a sophisticated grid, rather than doing a chaotic publication with lots of formats a papers and printing techniques. They all have to come together ir a "messy pile" and form some kind of link or connection.

You talked about the emotionality of your project and your fear I think this is something that relates well to our project wher we dealt with weaknesses and insecurity. Let's start by trying to find a definition for these terms, too. Hanna, what are wea nesses for you?

Weaknesses are clearly negatively connoted for me. I experience them as something unpleasant: situations tha embarrass me, in which I feel vulnerable. Often these are very emotional moments. Besides, for me, being weak often means not being able to do something that I would

actually like to do or believe I should do. One of the goals of our project was to put the qualities that you perceive as weaknesses in yourself into a different context, or look at them from a different perspective.

Concerning our project, I feel similar in many ways. We wo

change the notion of weakness towards a more positive set of connotations.

As for the term "weakness" in general, for me, weaknesses are parts of my character that I don't know how to deal with, or situations in which I am unable to act differently, even if I want to.

Yes, I think one word that is very important for me in thi context is insecurity. Many insecurities I perceive as weakness. And when I am secure, I feel strong in contras to that.

For me, insecurity also has a lot to do with worrying. Not being sure, but also not feeling comfortable. When I think of weakness, I have the image of something that should hold but, because it is weak, it breaks. It can't hold up, even though it should. So again, it is about expectations that are not met.

ecurity and weakness, not knowing—you can't evaluate these things :ause they are so very subjective.

: first thing that came to my mind when I saw your publication was also in- ırity. That's what your title implies: I don't know. Are you sure?—I'm unsure. said, a weakness is something unpleasant or embarrassing for you. That im- s that there is a standard against which things are judged, similar to failure.

As with failure, it totally depends on what standard you set and in what context a strength or weakness is being considered.

his case, strong is the standard and weak is what doesn't meet the standard. ıaining "strong" means meeting a standardized expectation. If you show .kness, the barrier breaks.

: changing your point of view—this stubbornness has rather negative ınotations for me. Uncertainty is more of a weakness, but it is a strength ;ay that you are not sure.

Yes, that is something we also wanted to transport through the title of the publication.

To accept being weak, the not-knowing, and being able to say that out loud.

And our title also suggests that another person can help us question our perceived "not-knowing," so we might realize that we actually do know after all.

me, there are two sorts of designers. The ones who design very ıitively and the ones who set up rules for themselves. How did you › proceed?

For both of us, dealing with typography was a source of uncertainty when designing the publication. Indeed, there was a point when we very consciously made the decision to deal with this uncertainty and to face it. And I think our publication now shows this very well, because we have selected quite a lot of different fonts and developed a method, or came across one, by which we could turn this uncertainty into a certainty. We started to select fonts no longer primarily according to aesthetic principles. Instead, we looked for other, more political categories that we found important in our context. These are: fonts that were designed in collaborations, fonts that were drawn by women and fonts that were created by our fellow students. With this framework, it was not only easier for us to choose fonts, the work was also more fun, even though we actually restricted ourselves in our freedom.

Were there any frictions when you combined all these different fonts? Intuitiv
you would probably make decisions based on visual criteria. Did your concep-
tual decision lead you to realize "oh, they don't fit together visually," or did
just work out?

Well, when it came to the fonts for the interviews, we both decided from a very subjective point of view. Hanna wanted to use Flefixx because her friend Sun Young Oh designed it and I have been using Luis Junkers' font Edgy quite often before, so it already felt like my voice. During the typesetting we noticed that the two fonts work quite differently in terms of tone and loudness. But rather then seeing it as a technical problem, we came to like the different characteristics and individual voices Since polyphony was an essential part of our project, this was perfect!

We would like to finish our talk with a speed-round of question where each of us has to decide between two absolutely unpleasa options.

Mio and Hanna, would you rather be reduced to your weaknesses or tot overestimated?

I would go for being overestimated. Of course, it increases the fear of being exposed as an impostor that a lot of people seem to have. But I think it can also be very positive or even empowering when people see something in you. If we are shown our potential. I think it can lead to us being more confident in ourselves and taking more risks. If we were repeatedly shown our limits, we would be standing still and would never experience success.

Oh, that's interesting! I would choose to be reduced to my weaknesses because, for me, one of the most uncomfortak situations is to feel exposed to other people's expectatic that I can't fulfill. This causes so much pressure and is actually one of the most stressful aspects of my life the days. So, I would prefer being underestimated to being overestimated.

Severin, would you rather not be able to fail at all or have to fail in everything you do?

I guess I would go for failing as a lifestyle. It is much more surprising and offers so many new perspectives on life. Also, when you always f it becomes a routine and your own criteria adapt to that—then you are only failing in the eyes of others, but you can't fail yourself anym

Juliana, would you rather be surrounded by professionals all the time or onl have amateurish tools to use?

I would love to be a professional amateur. It is hard to learn to always enjoy being naive, being intuitive and discovering new thin I would like to learn how to cherish these things.

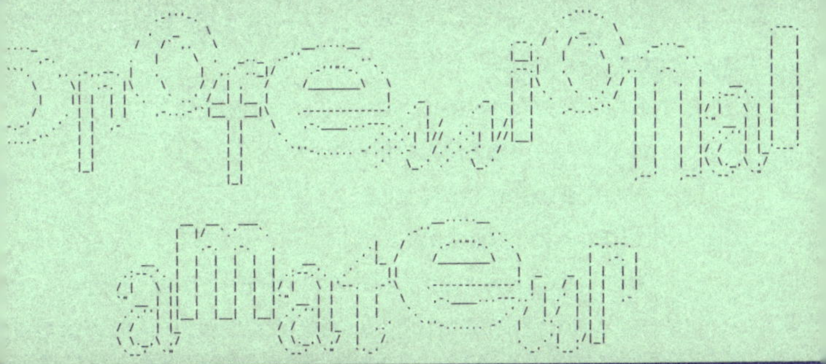

xtEdit File Edit Format View Window Help

:･ﾟ✧ think about ordinary tools ✧ﾟ･:

ORDINARY
we can get them for free
(to use online or download for free)

O ORDINARY
our options will be limited
(yes, indecisive designers, this one is for us ;))

OO ORDINARY
we never even thought of using them

what if we returned to the online painting game we used to play as children?

or the office software we used to make our school assignments?

or the boring text editing software on our computer?

what if we just looked for tools designed for any ✧
rson with access to a computer and the internet? ✧
what if anything is design software in disguise? ✧

Ⓐ Ⓝ Ⓓ Ⓢ Ⓣ Ⓐ Ⓡ Ⓣ

Ⓔ Ⓟ Ⓤ Ⓡ Ⓟ Ⓞ Ⓢ Ⓘ Ⓝ Ⓖ Ⓣ Ⓗ Ⓔ Ⓜ

ng gö öf cänönïc dësïgn söftwärë
älsö mëäns
tïng gö öf ëxpëctätïöns änd rülës:

n dεsIgn orIεnTεd Tools chαllεngε us

TextEdit File Edit Format View Window Help

non design oriented tools challenge e

To have fun with them

To use them for things they were not made for

To come up with solutions for their limitations

To not take them seriously

To push them to their limits

To look for all possible combinations of their few options

To explore the quirky functions designed for their unfamiliar pur

ƗF WĒ ŖĒPŰŖPØSĒ Â ŦØØŁ,

ŦĦĒ ČØNSĒǬŰĒNČĒS ÂŖĒ

SŰŖPŖƗSĒS &

ĒŖŖØŖS

ŦĦƗS ĐƗSÂĐVÂNŦÂG

ČÂN ǬŰƗČKŁ

ƁĒČØMĒ ÂN

ÂĐVÂNŦÂGE

for my mission of ṛëċḳḷëṡṡ ṛëṗüṛṗöṡïṅġ, i experimented with seven different tools and collected the results in a publication c

☆°.*.˳° ☆°.*.˳° °.*.° ☆°.*.˳° ☆°.*.˳° ☆°.*.˳°

god bless helvetica is here... IS THIS HELVET

.˳° °.*.˳° ☆°.*.˳° ☆°.*° .*.˳° ☆°.*.˳° °☆°.*☆°

here are some of the experiments that i did (/¯◡ ‿ ◡)/¯

ttttttttttttttttttttttttttthis was made with cloudpaintttttttttttttttttt

xtEdit File Edit Format View Window Help

re i could work with patterns and textures in black and white
stead of colors. i didn't find this feature anywhere else :/
re are many fonts (idk why but most of them are named
ter cities) / font sizes / effects.

tttttttttttttttttttttttttthis was made with JS painttttttttttttttttttttttttttttttt

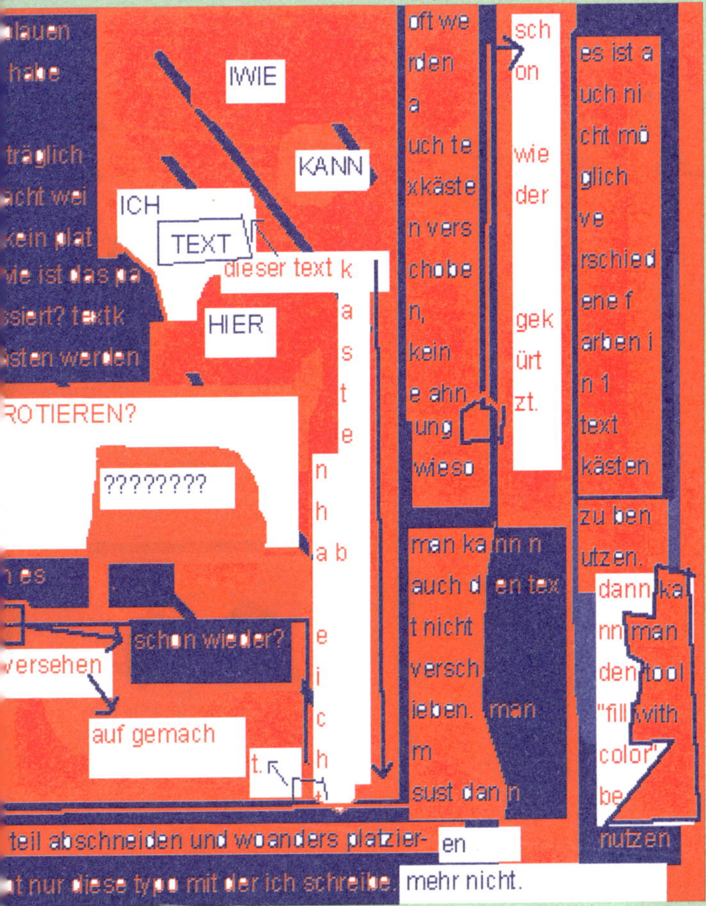

re is just one single font with a single font size, butttt this
nitation felt very liberating to me :-) because i could select the
text and then extend or shrink its form, it became distorted
and even more pixelated

 TextEdit File Edit Format View Window Help

and even more pixelated.

➠ the "fill with color" option either does what you want it to do
complete opposite ¯\(°_o)/¯

➠ it is impossible to move something once it has been positior
my solution was to cut up objects in order to move them, b
then the cuts left blank gaps in the image that i would hav
to fill again. i can live with that.

tttttttttttttttttttttttthis was made with OpenOffice Drawwwwwww

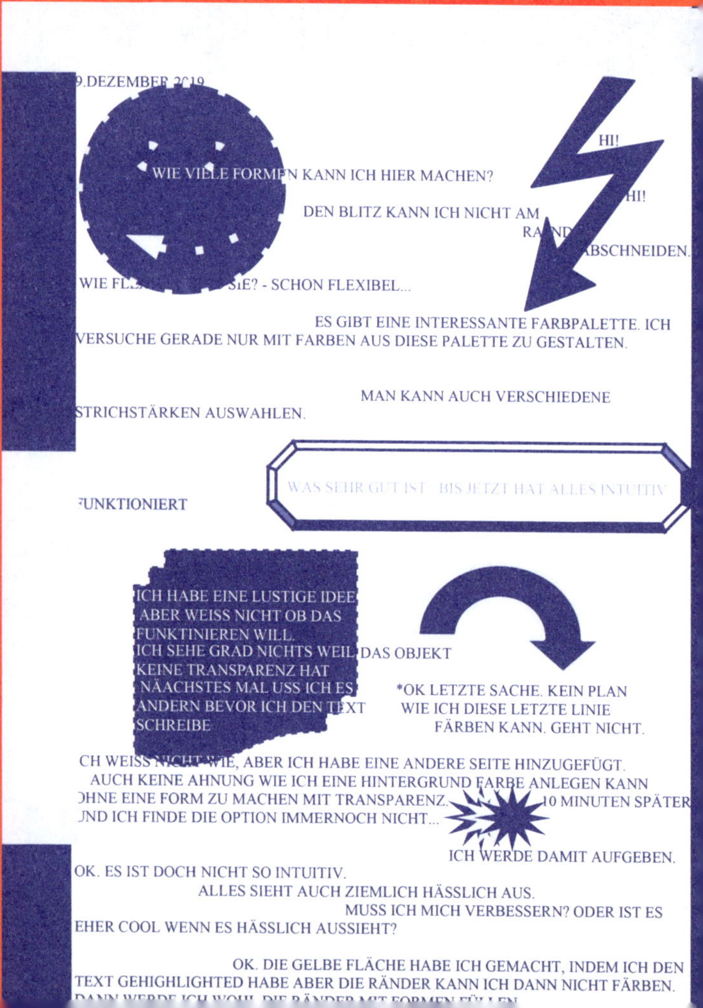

xtEdit File Edit Format View Window Help

DANN WERDE ICH WOHL DIE RÄNDER MIT FORMEN FÜLLEN.

BIS DANN*

re are many different forms, transparencies and outlines.
re is a very funny, interesting color palette.
uldn't select a background color so i had to highlight the
ooole text in order to create a background, but then i couldn't
olor the frame of the document :0
solution was to make quirky frames out of different forms and
urned out pretty cool (ﾉ◕ヮ◕)ﾉ*:･ﾟ✧

tttttttttttttttttthis was made with kimdmons painttttttttttttttttttttttttt

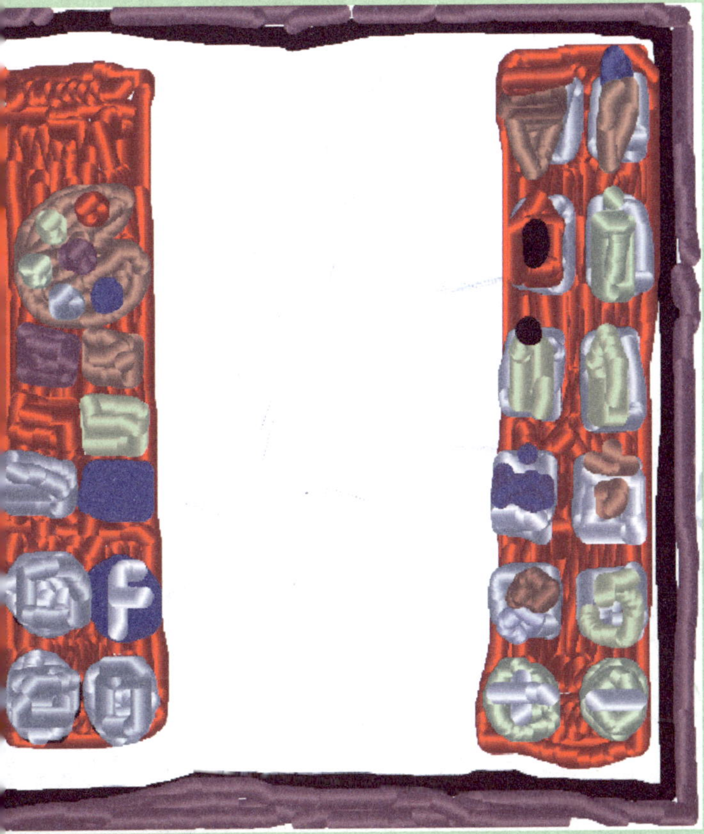

possible to make up your own color palette.
re is no writing tool, because the program was made for kids

TextEdit File Edit Format View Window Help

⇝ there is no writing tool because the program was made for
i thought this was cool because it forced me to focus on ju
experimenting with all painting tools and äṅd ï ḧäd ä ḷöt c

⇝ the materiality of the painting tools is very similar to IRL per
crayons, even erasers! the eraser tool is soo weird, it make
canvas kinda “dirty” when you erase something with it o.

ttttttttttttttttttttttttttttttttttthis was made with pixlrrrrrrrrrrrrrrrrrr

➲ it is not possible to put pictures on the canvas: pictures can be drawn with the pencil tool.

➲ (╥﹏╥) something went wrong with the download! in order to
my experiment, i had to make a screenshot of the thumbna
now it looks so pixelated that I can’t even read what it
says, but i think it has a lot of character <:-)

↘THESE ARE THE TOOLS I WORKED WITH
➪ cloudpaint.com ➠ jspaint.app ➼ OpenOffice Write
⇝ kidmons.com/game/paint-online ➲ pixlr.com
➻ OpenOffice Draw → OpenOffice Impress ➧

ḅüẗ ẗḧëṛë äṛë ëṅdḷëṡṡ ẗööḷṡ öüẗ ẗḧëṛë

*:･ﾟ✧ ḊäṚë ẗÖ ḦäṾë ḞüṄ ẅiṪḧ ṪḧëṀ!✧

S for STYLE DEFENSE

I'M WAY TOO COLD,
I SAY, "BURR!"
HENNESSY ON ICE, BRO,
BURR, BURR, BURR
YOU'VE ALREADY HEARD OF ME
FOR SURE
YOU SEE ME ON THE STREET
AND YOUR MOM SAYS, "BURR!" *one*

I SAY CATASTROPHE
IS AN ANSWER
BECAUSE I BELIEVE CLICHÉ IS A
QUESTION *two*

Calling a design work "too trendy" or "too stylish" is a classic knockout argument in any discussion about "good design." Words like style are used as defensive curse words to express that one finds a certain design superficial, unintelligent, empty, self-indulgent or simply illegible, it reveals itself to be a rather spurious point.

Our warriors of style have a nose for the zeitgeist. They wrestle with unfamiliar tools and technologies as they respond to circulating aesthetics, imagery, connotations and vibes, before things can be named, placed or rationalized.

1 ◐ Haiyti (2020) …rr', *Influencer*, Warner.

…r ist viel zu kalt, … sage: ‚*Burr*!' / …nessy auf Eis, …ka, *burr, burr*, …r / Sei dir sicher, … hast schon von … gehört / Du siehst …h auf der Street … deine Mum sagt: ‚*Burr*!'"

…O Carson, Anne …13) 'Variations on … Right to Remain …nt', *Nay Rather*, …ier 21. London: …lph Editions, 10.

…e resort to cliché …ause it's easier …n trying to make … something new. …licit in it is the …stion, Don't we …ady know what … think about this? …n't we have a …nula we use for …? Can't I just send …tandard greeting …t or paste in a …nshot of what it … like rather than …ng to come up with …original drawing?" — Ann Carson

We need
army of
sticky
stuffed
multi-
catastrop
trends a

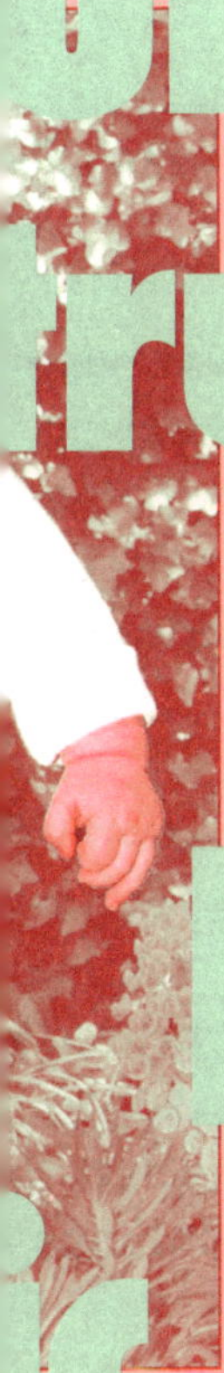

tender
unstable,
rudeling,
burr!
headed,
ic, emo,
styles.

Gazing at uncomfortably charged surfaces, the steadfast critic of style clears his throat, irritated, threatened perhaps, and delivers another punch: "This is lacking any depth" or "Where is the criticality?" He frowns upon works that don't follow the prescribed rules for criticality, maybe because they flirt with corporate or vernacular aesthetics, or, even worse, dare to remain slippery between subjectivity, assimilation, homage and critique.

Yet no style development takes place in a vacuum. We cannot separate visual languages from their situatedness within society, culture and its socio-political circumstances. Riding on styles—designing with non-linear tactics—can be a pungent tool for commentary and critical reflection.

We need to insist on a richer vocabulary to reflect and discuss, a language for design that goes beyond our metrical vocabulary, paranoid readings or armchair criticism. We need more text production on contemporary aesthetics in relation to design practices and we always need more designers to write about their observations, crushes, methods and choices.

S for STYLE DEFENSE

und Engagement
BÜRGERBÜR
AMBIGUOUS STRATEGIES
AND UNSICHERE
INDIFFERENCE:
SELF-ABOLISHED VISUAL
ARTEFACTS
AND POST-AUTHENTIC
AVATARS
ENTZIFFERN AND
KONTHEXTUALISIEREN
UMARMEND
IHRE
COGNITIVE
DISSONANCE
97

STOP BEING DESPERATE
CORPO
RATE
BODY
YOUR BODY IS A HOME OFFICE
SMART
Connecting to
ImagiNation...
CU @ 127.0.0.1

a book about algorithms and sociology that humans
project a lot of magical thinking onto
computational systems, "because we
have a physical need for miracles
and poetry?", they wonder. The
author of the book argues that
we treat our digital devices like
oracles, we trust and believe so
much in their assumed objectivity
and perfection that we even want
them to tell us what to do. Appar-
ently, we put computation on a
pedestal and create a religious
experience around it in order
to distract us from the
2

hope

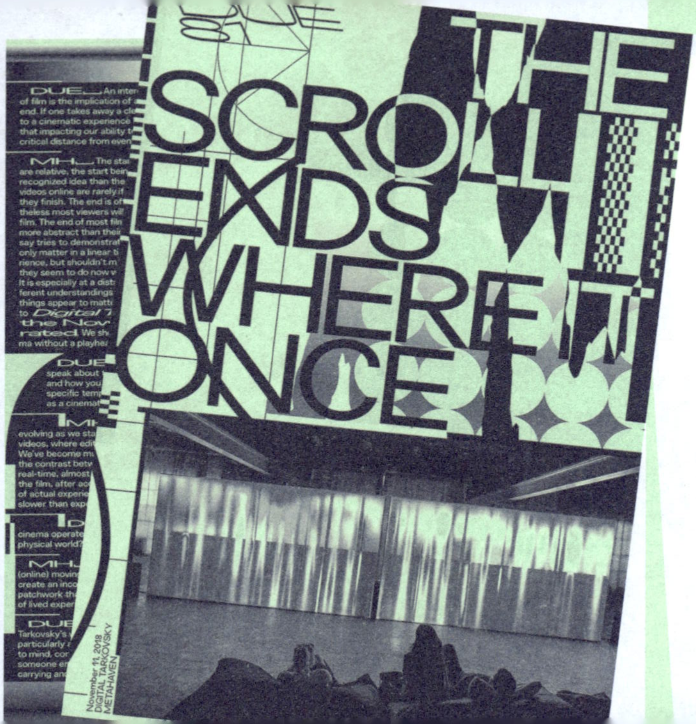
THE SCROLL ENDS WHERE IT ONCE
November 11, 2018
DIGITAL TARKOVSKY
METAHAVEN

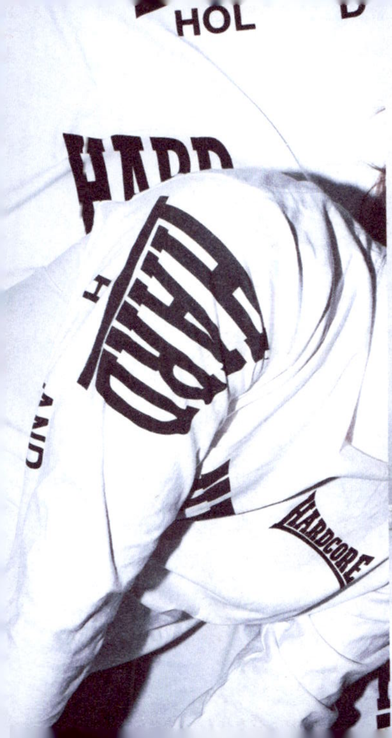
HOL
HARD
HARDCORE

PROSTHETIC
IMAGINARIES
IS THERE A
HAMMER?
IT ALL
DOWN
UNDISCIPLINED
TOOLKIT

B for Being Many

CLARA BALAGUER

(Makati City, Pisces Metal Monkey) is a cultural worker. From 2010 to 2018, she articulated cultural programming with rural and underserved communities in the Philippines through the Office of Culture and Design, a residency space and social practice platform. In 2015, Balaguer co-founded Hardworking Goodlooking, a cottage industry publishing hauz interested in horror vacui, thickening research on the post- (or de-)colonial vernacular, collectivizing authorship, and the value of the error. Currently, she coordinates the Social Practices course at Willem de Kooning Academy and teaches Experimental Publishing at Piet Zwart Institute in Rotterdam, Netherlands. Frequently, she operates under collective or individual aliases that intimate her service in a given project, the latest of which is *To Be Determined*.

ECE CANLI

is a design researcher, artist and musician, born and raised in Turkey and based in Portugal. She holds a PhD from Design at University of Porto, Portugal, and an MFA in Experience Design from Konstfack University College of Arts, Crafts and Design, Sweden. Canlı's tools of investigation include texts, voice, sound and artifacts. Her academic work sits at the intersection of decolonial queer feminist epistemologies, material regimes and body politics; more specifically, socio-spatio-material constitutions of gender, sexuality, race and other identity categories. She is a founding member of the research collective Decolonising Design Group and currently a researcher in CECS (The Communication and Society Research Centre) at University of Minho, Portugal. In her artistic and vocal practice, she explores counterfactual narrativity, corporal and mental delinking, and extralinguistic expressions through extended vocal techniques. Canlı currently composes and performs in music collectives including NOOITO and COBRA'CORAL, as well as in her solo project VOX FLORA, VOX FAUNA, while continuing to create and perform as a soloist.

MIRIAM CAHN

is an artist whose career has spanned more than five decades. Born in 1948, in Basel, Switzerland, she was influenced by performance art and the feminist movement of the 1960s and 1970s. Cahn developed her work in the 1980s, incorporating large black drawings of televisions, fighter jets and other seemingly male-dominated vernacular. From her early works, which were strongly influenced by feminism, to her later creations, the subject of her paintings has been the body. Her focus ranges from the initial development of new portrayals of the body to the disclosure of the current entanglement of people in the web of economic and ideological contexts. Recurring themes in her work are complex interpersonal relationships, family constellations, women in society, as well as refuge, war and violence. By countering the traditional representation of female and gender-specific roles, Cahn's pictorial worlds push to abolish social norms.

STUDENTS OF THE ACADEMY OF FINE ARTS LEIPZIG AND MARKUS DRESSEN

Markus Dreßen graduated from the Academy of Fine Arts Leipzig, Germany, in 1999. Together with Anne König and Jan Wenzel, he founded the collaborative project Spector and was co-editor of *Spector cut+paste*. The publishing house Spector Books was founded in 2008.

Since 2006, Dreßen has been Senior Lecturer for graphic design students at the Academy of Fine Arts Leipzig. He has received numerous awards for his design work, such as the Golden Letter in the 2004 competition for Best Book Design From All Over The World. In 2013, Dreßen was awarded the Ladislav Sutnar Prize by the University of West Bohemia in Plzeň, Czech Republic, for his contribution to the field of graphic design, his pedagogical work at the Academy of Fine Arts Leipzig and for his publishing activities.

Dreßen's contribution for the *GUD* was developed together with participants of the Academy of Fine Arts Leipzig, winter semester 2019/2020: Hanns Bahra, Hannah Flügler, Nina Gohlke, Rami Hariri, Yeongseon Jeong, Gwendolin Karré, Leander Kreißl, Frédéric Maier, Frédérick Manstein, Lion Mayer, Ossama Morad, Sören Sandbothe, Milad Shahmoradi, Helena Silva, Helene von Schirach, Meta Witte, Valentin Wühr and Jolanda Zürcher.

STUDENTS OF BURG GIEBICHENSTEIN UNIVERSITY OF ART AND DESIGN HALLE

In December 2019, as part of the *GUD* project, Anja Kaiser and Rebecca Stephany taught a workshop at Burg Giebichenstein University of Art and Design Halle, Germany. During this one-week workshop, the 26 participating students were introduced to educators, theorists, activists, designers (and symbols) from past and present, whose work is relevant to a broader feminist discourse around graphic design, which included all contributors to the *GUD Symposium*.

With the aim of encouraging a critical reflection on the gaps and blind spots in graphic design history, the students conceived of speculative encounters between Sheila Levrant de Bretteville and Ada Lovelace, Ece Canlı and the Venus symbol or Hackers & Designers and Muriel Cooper. Corresponding PR materials were on unstable view in the foyer of GfZK during the symposium as a parallel program of fictional announcements.

With Anna Baydak, Hyunhye Byun, Karen Czock, Hannah Englisch, Jule Eretier, Timm Hergert, Lore Janssens, Jo-Fabius Kossack, Nils Krüger, Mingren Li, Lilo Johanna Müller, Pepe Nitz, Helene Otto, Jonas Otto, Katharina Peters, Jakob Petersen, Maria Plasczymonka, Bianca Poppe, Janna Radlow, Maja Redlin, Barbora Satranská, Esben Terje Sonne, Lucie Weiße, Paul Werner, Jasmin Zehe and Verena Zimmermann.

GFZK (LEIPZIG MUSEUM OF CONTEMPORARY ART)

is an exhibition space for contemporary art and a museum for art post 1945. GfZK promotes and imparts international positions on its own premises and in public spaces, it initiates cooperations and carries out research-based artistic projects.

Since the inception of GfZK, addressing local themes in connection with global developments are of particular importance, with a specific focus on participation and the social agency of art. In this sense, the work of the GfZK focuses less on defining a canon of values than on exploring the potentials of artistic and curatorial work and of art mediation, with the aim of fostering criticality through collaborative processes.

GfZK has an interdisciplinary approach and explores the mutual influences between modes of contemporary cultural production. Since 2007, the GfZK has awarded the INFORM Prize to conceptual design for contemporary practices at the intersection of graphic design and art—Anja Kaiser was the awardee in 2017, Rebecca Stephany in 2009.

HACKERS & DESIGNERS

is a collective experimenting, esearching and developing tools nd learning processes with designrs, artists, software developers, esearchers, scientists and theoreicians in the Netherlands and broad. Hackers & Designers began s a cross-disciplinary meet-up ommunity in 2013 and has estabshed a far-reaching global netvork that has grown out of workhops, talks and lectures abroad and y bringing international talent to he Netherlands via the Hackers &)esigners Summer Academy, exhibitions and ublic programs.

Traditionally, Hackers & Designers' activities onsist of hands-on workshops and deal with ɔpics such as web technologies, Peer 2 Peer netvorks, cryptocurrencies, typography, conditional esign, web and interface design, printmaking and imple hardware constructions. Hackers &)esigners uses and contributes to open-source oftware and design and is herefore invested in the ocumentation, distribution nd publishing of projects, vorkshop content, learning xperiences and code.

ANNA HAIFISCH

is a Leipzig-based comic artist and illustrator. She studied at the Academy of Fine Arts Leipzig, Germany, and has worked as a screenprinter for Kayrock Screenprinting in Brooklyn, New York, US. Haifisch has drawn and published multiple books, such as *Von Spatz*, *The Artist* and *Residenz Fahrenbühl*. In 2013, she co-founded Comics and Graphics Festival *The Millionaires Club*. In 2020, Haifisch was awarded the Max and Moritz Prize for best German Comic Artist and an artist-in-residence fellowship at Villa Aurora, Los Angeles, US, commencing 2022.

SARA KAAMAN

is a graphic designer and teacher interested in the intersections of publishing technologies, bodies, politics and poetry. Since 2012, she is the graphic designer and co-editor of *Girls Like Us*, a magazine featuring art, writing, politics and pleasure "more or less female." With Maryam Fanni and Matilda Flodmark she forms the research collective MMS, focusing on investigating labor histories of graphic design via feminist theory and practice. Their book, *Natural Enemies of Books: A Messy History of Women in Printing and Typography* (Occasional Papers), was published in 2020. Since 2016, Kaaman is Senior Lecturer in Graphic Design at Konstfack University of Art, Crafts and Design in Stockholm, Sweden, where she is also Head of the BA program in Graphic Design & Illustration with Catherine Anyango Grünewald. As of fall 2020, she teaches on the MA program in Graphic Design at the Estonian Academy of Art in Tallinn, Estonia. Kaaman also grows plants and relationships.

ANJA KAISER

is active in social-political ontexts and club culture cenes, where she seeks to mplify spaces for resisance through collective vork and design. Since :013, Kaiser runs her own tudio in Leipzig, Germany, vhich works at the junction f graphic design, art and esearch. She incorporates nalog and digital tactics with a feminist urge to destabilize invisibilities. Her research-based ractice investigates the human body as an inevitable object of projection for biologically ɔunded determinism and as a site for deconstruction in a capitalist presence. Kaiser holds an MFA in Graphic Design from the Sandberg Institute, Amsterdam, Netherlands. She has collaborated with a number of accomplices and produced work for cultural institutions and exhibitions such as the GfZK (Leipzig Museum for Contemporary Art) and Le Signe — National Centre for Graphic Design in Chaumont, France. From 2021–2023, Kaiser held an interim professorship for typography at the Academy of Fine Arts Leipzig and is regularly invited to give lectures and workshops in Germany and abroad. In 2017, she was awarded the INFORM Prize for Conceptual Design at GfZK. Kaiser is thrilled to entangle typography, dissent, and agency.

STUDENTS OF KARLSRUHE UNIVERSITY OF ART AND DESIGN (HFG KARLSRUHE)

As part of opening the *Glossary of Undisciplined Design* to a collective editorial process, Anja Kaiser and Rebecca Stephany taught an ongoing seminar at the Karlsruhe University of Arts and Design (HfG Karlsruhe) from October 2019—February 2020. The participating students developed contributions to the symposium that took many forms, from publications to video essays, workstations to sound performances.

Each student contribution included an inquiry. Severin Geißler asked: How can industrialized printing processes be destabilized with a queer approach to failure? Teresa Häußler: How can aspects of care and caring be addressed in design work? Diane Hillebrand: How can the wandering eye be nurtured during a day full of lectures? Florian Knöbl: How can safety measures be applied to digital labor? Mio Kojima and Hanna Müller: What are our propositions for collaborative work that honor our differences? Kathrin Rüll: How can a presence on Instagram navigate between what is professional, self-representation and research? Arno Schlipf: What would a layout tool look like that only provided wobbly grids? Juliane Schmitt: What is the sound of procrastination and deadline angst? And Juliana Vargas Zapata asked: What if, from now on, we only designed using free online design tools?

Furthermore, the students collaborated on different projects for the symposium, participatory interventions, evening programming and workshops, such as a food bar with edible glossary terms and encouraging movement by drifting during the breaks between speakers.

JUNGMYUNG LEE

is a graphic and type designer based in Amsterdam, Netherlands, from where she runs the independent type foundry J-LTF (Jung-Lee Type Foundry). Through J-LTF, Lee's primary focus is telling stories and exploring the life of typefaces and their emotions—as she manifest typefaces have their own course of life and Lee has them explore their imaginary life in various media: her typefaces have conversations on exhibition walls, act as distinct subtitles in type specimens-gone-rap music videos, or are used by artists and writers in the experimental journal *Real-Time-Realist*, which uses writing to explore a spectrum of emotions. Published under J-LTF PRESS, the second and current issue of *Real-Time-Realist* explores ecstasy, joy, serenity and love.

SHEILA LEVRANT DE BRETTEVILLE

is a first-generation American graphic designer, public artist and educator whose professional practice reflects her engagement with feminist dialogue and audience participation in graphic design processes and projects, while stretching the design discipline to reform the public sphere. Shaped by participating in political activism and women's movements of the late 1960s and 1970s in the US, de Bretteville initiated the first Women's Design program in 1971 at California Institute of the Arts. Together with Judy Chicago and Arlene Raven, de Bretteville founded the Woman's Building in Los Angeles, where she ran the Women's Graphic Center. In 1981, she set up a Visual Communication and Illustration Department at Otis Art Institute in Los Angeles to match their new partner, the Parsons program, in New York. When "percent for art" ordinances were enacted in American cities, de Bretteville began reorienting her practice within the social space of lived experience. In 1990, she became the first woman with a lifetime professorship at Yale University's School of Art as Director of Graphic Design, a position which she still heads today.

BRYONY QUINN

is a writer, editor and lecturer based in omerset, UK. She writes in the intersection of visual cul- ıre and literature, with a focus on obliquity—things that ·an, diagonals, digressions—writing patterns, women in esign education and cultural etymologies. Quinn has been ublished by *Bricks from the Kiln* (*BFTK*), Reaktion ooks, *Failed States*, and *Riposte*, and presented her writ- ıg at Turner Contemporary, Frieze Art Fair, Royal College f Art (RCA) and Turf Projects (in collaboration with Peter encini). She is co-editor of *BFTK #4* and founded the esign journal *A Line Which Forms A Volume*. Quinn is an ssociate Lecturer teaching on MA Graphic Media Design, ondon College of Communication, Visiting Lecturer at ıe RCA, and Senior Lecturer and Module Leader of Con- extual Studies at the University of East London. Previously, ıe has worked for art and literary institutions including itzcarraldo Editions, Artangel, Liverpool Biennial, and Bar- ican Gallery. Quinn holds an MA in Critical Writing in rt & Design from the RCA, where she was recipient of the ınnual Critical Writing Prize, editor of *Arc* and co-organizer f a conference on the life and work of John Berger.

VINCENT SCHIER

is a curator and art historian living and working in Berlin, Germany, and elsewhere. He is the Artistic Director at Kunstverein Göttingen and has been working at the Kunsthaus Dresden and at the art association nGbK in Berlin. Schier works in institutions and as a freelancer, appre- ciating both. In his curatorial work he is interested in collaborative and collective working methods, which is why he keeps returning to working in groups. He is a member of the curatorial collective RealismusStudio and of other groups, which sometimes don't even have a name.

Also, in his exhibition making practice, Schier's main focus lies on the individual in relation to societ(ies) and space—physical space as well as social space. In doing so, he hopes to be able to question prescribed roles and hierarchies, particularly in exhibition making practices, at least sometimes.

Schier holds an MA in Art History from the Free University of Berlin, and an MA in the extra-occupa- tional studies Cultures of the Curatorial at the Academy of Fine Arts Leipzig.

He is also a fan of graphic design.

REBECCA STEPHANY

is based in Berlin, Germany, and works at the inter- ection of design, art, research and education. Her poly- honic cultural practice navigates the increasing dissolution etween the autonomous and the applied, the organic nd the technological or the individual and the collective, vhile investigating the designer's body as a site for self- xploitation and identity production. Feminist ocial critique increasingly fuels Stephany's ndisciplined tools for research and visual rticulation. Recent projects and exhibitions ıclude *200 SISTERS SOUVENIRS* at adischer Kunstverein, Germany, and *Life tense* at Nida Art Colony, Lithuania.

Stephany studied graphic design at the errit Rietveld Academie, Amsterdam, etherlands, and obtained her MFA in Criti- al Studies at the Sandberg Institute, msterdam. In 2009, she was awarded the NFORM Prize for Conceptual Design t GfZK (Leipzig Museum of Contemporary rt). In 2010 and 2011, Stephany was rtist-in-residence at the Rijksakademie, msterdam. From 2007–2016, Stephany ıught in the graphic design department f Gerrit Rietveld Academie. From 2016– 021, Stephany was professor for Visual ommunication at the Karlsruhe University f Arts and Design (HfG Karlsruhe), 2021 she was appointed professor for raphic Design at Kunsthochschule Kassel.

FRANCISKA ZÓLYOM

works as a curator and is the Director of GfZK (Leipzig Museum of Contemporary Art). In collaboration with artists, researchers and experts of everyday life, GfZK investi- gates processes of social transformation and explores transcultural phenomena: How does artistic work resonate with the cultural, political and economic context in which it takes place? How do methods of aesthetic research and critical analysis inform individual and collective agency? Many of the curato- rial projects by Zólyom, such as *Experi- mental Jetset: Provo Station*, *Little Warsaw: The Battle of the Inner Truth*, *Natascha Süder Happelmann: Ankersentrum*, start out from these questions and unfold in the course of interdisciplinary and collaborative processes. At the same time, these projects and processes are crucial in shaping the institution and the relations that GfZK establishes.

A NOTE ON TYPE

This is a book with many faces.

Individual contributors, who have autonomously designed their glossary terms, have acquired or obtained the appropriate rights of use for the fonts that they have worked with.

We (Anja and Rebecca) have also used a variety of typefaces and would like to explicitly thank the type designers who provided us with their fonts free of charge:

Jungmyung Lee (Jung-Lee Type Foundry) for Pirelli. Moritz Appich for G2 Erika Mono; Dinamo for Monument Grotesk and Monument Grotesk Mono; Katharina Köhler for Rosart; Clemens Piontek for Vevey Positive; Gaile Pranckunaite for ANG-1, Figures and MC Round; Charlotte Rohde for Valkyrie; Andrea Tinnes for Allgemein Grotesk and Allgemein Grotesk Mono.

In addition, we have used the typefaces Cairo by Susan Kare (remastered by Haley Fiege), Joseleen by Jungmyung Lee, Citizen by Zuzana Licko, Times Dot by Laurel Schwulst, Review Mono by Sophie Wietlisbach and many more.

We also wish to make special note of Badass Libre Fonts by Womxn (Loraine Furter), design-research.be/by-womxn; we have used the fonts Authentic Sans by Christina Janus and Desmond Wong, Cirrus Cumulus by Clara Sambot, TorreFarfan by Estefanía González Sánchez.

IMAGE CREDIT

B for Blanketing

105 *B for Blanketing* by Juliane Schmitt and Juliana Vargas Zapata, mockup, 2020

106–107 *B for Blanketing* by Juliane Schmitt and Juliana Vargas Zapata, scan, 2020

106, 107, 108 *B for Blanketing* by Juliane Schmitt and Juliana Vargas Zapata, participatory installation, GfZK, 2020 © Jana Hofmann

B for Bleaching, C for Critical Embraces, S for Slippery Images

253, 256–257, 260 *200 Sisters Souvenirs* by Rebecca Stephany, 2018 © Robert Hamacher

254–255 *200 Sisters Souvenirs* by Rebecca Stephany, scan of Karlsruhe Women's Magazine *LAVA* (1989–1994), 2018

254, 255, 256, 260 *200 Sisters Souvenirs* by Rebecca Stephany, publication spreads, 2018 © Evi Künstle

258–259 *200 Sisters Souvenirs* by Rebecca Stephany, installation at Badischer Kunstverein, 2018 © Felix Grünschloß

258–259 *200 Sisters Souvenirs* by Rebecca Stephany, merchandise scan, 2018

C for Care Advice

169, 170 *C for Care Advice* by Teresa Häußler, participatory workstation, GfZK, 2020 © Jana Hofmann, Cécile Kobel

171, 172, 173 left *C for Care Advice* by Teresa Häußler, participatory workstation, GfZK, 2020 © Alexandra Ivanciu

173 right, 174 *C for Care Advice* by Teresa Häußler, close-ups, 2020 © Jana Hofmann, Cécile Kobel

C for Collective Uncertainties

53 *a Notebook for unstable minds, stupid thoughts, disqualified ideas and concepts born to fail* by Severin Geißler, publication, 2020

55 *Professional Amateur* by Juliana Vargas Zapata, publication, 2020

56 *I don't know. Are you sure?* by Mio Kojima and Hanna Müller, booklet, 2020

C for Comfort Your Work(un)flow

213, 214, 215 *C for Comfort Your Work(un)flow* by Juliane Schmitt, performance and costumes, GfZK, 2020 © Jana Hofmann

217, 218 *C for Comfort Your Work(un)flow* by Juliane Schmitt, performance and costumes, GfZK, 2020 © Jana Hofmann, Cécile Kobel

CI for Corporeal Identities

195 *Please Divide in Groups of Two or Three* by Anja Kaiser and Simone C. Niquille, digital mascot mock-ups, 2019

196 *Please Divide in Groups of Two or Three* by Anja Kaiser and Simone C. Niquille, title graphic, 2019

198, 200 *Please Divide in Groups of Two or Three* by Anja Kaiser and Simone C. Niquille, video stills, Leipzig, 2019

199 *Please Divide in Groups of Two or Three* by Anja Kaiser and Simone C. Niquille, spatial

175, 178 *D for Drifting* by Severin Geißler, Kathrin Rüll and Arno Schlipf, scan, 2020

176, 177 *D for Drifting* by Severin Geißler, Kathrin Rüll and Arno Schlipf, participatory intervention, GfZK, 2020 © Jana Hofmann, Cécile Kobel

F for Failing Queerly

36, 37, 38, 39, 40 Severin Geißler, prints, 2020

F for Figures of Solidarity

242, 245 *whose.agency* by Anja Kaiser, moving poster still, 2019

244, 247 *whose.agency* by Anja Kaiser, moving poster still in public, Leipzig, 2019

246 *whose.agency* by Anja Kaiser, installation at GfZK, 2019 © Alexandra Ivanciu

G for GUD Symposium

295 *U for Unfaithful Contexts* by Diane Hillebrand, spatial intervention, GfZK, 2020 © Alexandra Ivanciu

296 *GUD Symposium*, Academy of Fine Arts Leipzig, 2020 © Alexandra Ivanciu

297, 298, 300 top, 301, 302, 305, 306 top, 307, 309, 310 top, 311 bottom, 312 *GUD Symposium*, GfZK, 2020 © Alexandra Ivanciu

299 *F for Failing Queerly* by Severin Geißler, installation and notebooks, GfZK, 2020 © Alexandra Ivanciu

300 bottom *D for Drifting* by Severin Geißler, Kathrin Rüll and Arno Schlipf, participatory intervention, GfZK, 2020 © Jana Hofmann, Cécile Kobel

Diane Hillebrand and Florian Knöbl, conference scenography, GfZK, 2020 © Alexandra Ivanciu

306 bottom *C for Comfort Your Work(un)flow* by Juliane Schmitt, performance, GfZK, 2020 © Alexandra Ivanciu

308 *C for Care Advice* by Teresa Häußler, participatory workstation, GfZK, 2020 © Alexandra Ivanciu

310 bottom *S for Strudeling* by Severin Geißler, Hanna Müller, Kathrin Rüll and Juliane Schmitt, workshop, GfZK, 2020 © Alexandra Ivanciu

311 top *M for Metabolic Learning* by Severin Geißler and Kathrin Rüll, food bar, GfZK, 2020 © Alexandra Ivanciu

L for Lessons from Hydra

250, 251, 252 *Hercules Slaying the Hydra* by Hans Sebald Beham, engraving, 1545

M for Mad-Mad-Mad PR

143 *Mad-Mad-Mad PR*, installation, GfZK, 2020 © Alexandra Ivanciu

145 *Patchwork not Leaders* by Lucie Weiße, flag, 2019

146 *Beyond the Canon* by Hyunhye Byun, newspaper, 2019

147 *Free the symbol* by Anna Baydak, paper towels, 2019 © Alexandra Ivanciu

148 *Tender Tools* by Hannah Englisch, Timm Hergert and Jakob Petersen, inflatable, 2019, © top and bottom right Alexandra Ivanciu; bottom left Jana Hofmann, Cécile Kobel

149 *Dirty Deeds Done Dirty Cheap* by Jo-Fabius Kossack and Esben Terje Sonne, sticker sheet, 2019

Dilettantes by Karen Czock and Helene Otto, boxing gloves, 2019 © Jana Hofmann, Cécile Kobel

M for Male Monikers

89 *Kento*, internet meme, 2016

90 *Arthur*, internet meme, 2016

M for Messy Histories

179, 180–181, 182–183, 184 *Reality. Not Necessarily a Book.* by Stefanie Leinhos, a scan of a folded sheet of A4 paper that has been blown up to four times its size, color print on 120 gsm paper, 84 × 118 cm, published by studiolent, 2016

M for Metabolic Learning

97 *M for Metabolic Learning* by Severin Geißler and Kathrin Rüll, scan, 2020

98 *M for Metabolic Learning* by Severin Geißler and Kathrin Rüll, food bar, GfZK, 2020 © Cécile Kobel

O for Once Upon a Time

22 left bottom *Codex Seraphinianus* by Luigi Serafini, page from book, 1981

23 left, 2nd from top *Systema Naturae* by Carl von Linné, page from book, 1735

23 left, 3rd from top 'The Country's Races', photographs displayed in a showcase by the Swedish State Institute for Racial Biology at the Stockholm Exhibition, Stockholm, 1930

24 right, 2nd from top @designershumor, internet meme, 2020

27 left bottom Members of Women's Typographic Association, 1925

28 left *Bookmaking on the Distaff Side* by Distaff Side, spread from book, 1937
28 right bottom *Murdoch's New Technology: The Sack*. by A Morning Star Poster, poster, 1986

P for Playing Fast and Loose with Tools
94–95 *Does It Make Sense?* by April Greiman, offset print, 1986

P for Professional Amateur
268, 269, 270, 271, 272 Juliana Vargas Zapata, digital layouts, 2020

R for Relationality
100 *The Special Edition of Aspen Times* by Sheila Levrant de Bretteville, newspaper, 1971
101 left *Design and Human Bodies*, intervention by Class Action Collective at the International Design Conference in Aspen, 1994, classactioncollective.org
101 right *Design and Human Bodies* by Ivan Chermayeff, booklet design for the International Design Conference in Aspen, 1994
102 *A Reexamination of Some Aspects of the Design Arts from the Perspective of a Woman Designer* by Sheila Levrant de Bretteville, pages from *Arts in Society: Women and the Arts*, 1974

R for Reseating
201, 202 Arno Schlipf, drawings, 2020

R for Role Play
31, 32, 33, 34 Relief of a seated poet (Menander) with masks of New Comedy, 1st century BC—early first century AD. Princeton University Art Museum

S for Social Media Surrender
221, 222, 223, 224, 225 Kathrin Rüll, video stills, 2020

S for Strudeling
207, 208, 209, 210 Anna Haifisch, drawings, 2021

S for Strudeling
86, 87 *S for Strudeling* by Severin Geißler, Hanna Müller, Kathrin Rüll and Juliane Schmitt, workshop, GfZK, 2020 © Jana Hofmann, Cécile Kobel

S for Style Defense
274–275 *Working Title, Working Clothes (Adore)* by Rebecca Stephany, campaign, 2015
277 *In Defense of Style* by students of HfG Karlsruhe and Rebecca Stephany, magazine, 2019
278 *Sexed Realities—To Whom Do I Owe My Body?* by Anja Kaiser, beach towel line, 2014 © Laura Jost
279 *My So-Calleds* by Rebecca Stephany with Mathias Lempart, mixed media, 2019
280 *DUE #81, #77* by Anja Kaiser, riso prints, 2019
281 *Working Title, Working Clothes (Wretch Log Oinks (this series of errors and recoveries))* by Rebecca Stephany, mixed media, 2015

282 *If I Had a Hammer* by Anja Kaiser, screen print edition, 2020 © Marc Domage

T for Theory Parody
219, 220 *T for Theory Parody* by Severin Geißler, Hanna Müller and Kathrin Rüll, scans, 2020
220 *T for Theory Parody* by Severin Geißler, Hanna Müller and Kathrin Rüll, game, GfZK, 2020 © Jana Hofmann

T for Tropico-Vernacular Glossary
233 Field research images from Metro Manila, Laguna, Bohol, Philippines 2015–2017 © Clara Balaguer

U for Unfaithful Contexts
45 top and bottom left, 48, 50 *U for Unfaithful Contexts* by Diane Hillebrand, spatial intervention, GfZK, 2020 © Alexandra Ivanciu
45 bottom right, 46, 47, 49 *U for Unfaithful Contexts* by Diane Hillebrand, spatial intervention, GfZK, 2020 © Jana Hofmann, Cécile Kobel

U for Unstable Signs
203, 204, 205, 206 *U for Unstable Signs* by students of the Academy of Fine Arts Leipzig and Markus Dreßen, Academy of Fine Arts Leipzig, 2020 © Nina Gohlke, Lion Mayer, Helene von Schirach, Milad Shahmoradi

U for Unstable Signs
65 *Women in Design: The Next Decade* by Sheila Levrant de Bretteville, poster design,

Thank You

OUR CONTRIBUTORS

For their generosity and commitment: Clara Balaguer, Ece Canlı, Hackers & Designers, Markus Dreßen, Sara Kaaman, Jungmyung Lee, Sheila Levrant de Bretteville, Vincent Schier, Franciska Zólyom, as well as students of Karlsruhe University of Arts and Design (HfG Karlsruhe) and Burg Giebichenstein University of Art and Design Halle (BURG).

PROJECT COORDINATION

For his enormous support with the entire *GUD* project, from symposium to handbook, with versatility and care: Vincent Schier.

GUD SYMPOSIUM (FEBRUARY 20–23, 2020)

For hosting and co-organizing the *GUD Symposium* at GfZK (Leipzig Museum of Contemporary Art): Franciska Zólyom, without her generosity and persistence this project would not have been possible.

For their patience and support: Beatrice Di Buduo, Annett Koch, Domenik Pasemann, Martin Reich and the whole team at GfZK. For hosting the symposium kick-off: Academy of Fine Arts Leipzig (HGB Leipzig). For taking such wonderful pictures throughout the symposium: Alexandra Ivanciu. For their photographic support: Jana Hofmann and Cécile Kobel. For their assistance in design and production: Nor Akelei. For coding the *GUD* website: Arno Schlipf. For their baking support: Backstein—Bäckerei für Zeitgenössisches Brot. For hosting the *GUD* Welcome Bar: Markus Dreßen and students of the Book Design/Graphic Design Foundational course of HGB Leipzig. Thanks, also, to the amazing student line-up from all over Europe who DJed at our closing party.

For embarking on the adventure of copyediting so many different kinds of texts with precision and humor: Bryony Quinn. DZA Druckerei zu Altenburg, especially Laura Nierth for her support and patience. For image editing and assisting us with our custom spot color profile: Lucie Marsmann and Christian Andreas. For copy editing the contributions of students of HfG Karlsruhe with clarity and care: Johanna Schäfer. For their valuable text feedback: Julia Meer, Anne König, Jan Wenzel and Oliver Klimpel. For letting us reproduce their words and work: Class Action Collective, Miriam Cahn, April Greiman, Anna Haifisch and Sheila Levrant de Bretteville. For granting permission to reprint pages from Miriam Cahn's *Writing in Rage*: Hatje Cantz Publishing. For arranging our work retreats at GfZK: Domenik Pasemann.

ANJA AND REBECCA WOULD LIKE TO THANK

Our allies in design education near and far, for your support, trust and honesty. Everyone we have ever had the pleasure to share a classroom with—we have learned so much from you. All our funding partners for their financial support and genuine interest in *GUD*. GfZK Leipzig, BURG, Captcha Festival Mannheim, Berlin Format Club and HfG Karlsruhe for giving us the opportunity to refine and rehearse the *GUD* lecture. Prof. Andrea Tinnes, for inviting us to teach a workshop at BURG. *Missy Magazine* and *A Line Which Forms a Volume* (MA Graphic Media Design, London College of Communication), for featuring *GUD* in-process. Depatriarchise Design and Gerda Breuer (*Women in Graphic Design 1890–2012*), for joining our roundtable discussion about feminism and design in October 2018 at Badischer Kunstverein, one of many beginnings of *GUD*. Director Anja Casser, for hosting the evening.

ANJA WOULD LIKE TO THANK

Anna Haifisch, who helped steer my work through nights and laughter; Franziska Leiste, Stefanie Leinhos and Janett Bielau, for dear moments in the studio. Prof. Anna Berkenbusch and Prof. Andrea Tinnes, who taught me what I know about graphic design with generosity. Anna Jehle and Juliane Schickedanz, for supporting my practice from the start. Simone C. Niquille, for collaborating and sharing her sharp thoughts. A heartfelt thanks to Kerstin and Peter Kaiser.

REBECCA WOULD LIKE TO THANK

My family and friends, you are the twinkle in my eyes. Linda van Deursen, whose presence and generosity made me fall in love with design education. Sereina Rothenberger, for being such a dream colleague and all-time ally. The Communication Design team at HfG Karlsruhe: Juliane Hohlbaum, James Langdon, Michael Kryenbühl, Anton Stuckardt and Ivan Weiss, as well as Chancellor Christiane Linsel, for their amicable and generous support.

OUR PROJECT PARTNERS

GfZK (Leipzig Museum of Contemporary Art) and Karlsruhe University of Arts and Design (HfG Karlsruhe).

gfzk Museum of Contemporary Art Leipzig

Staatliche Hochschule für Gestaltung Karlsruhe

OUR FUNDING PARTNERS

Creative Industries Fund NL, Kingdom of the Netherlands—Berlin Embassy, Cultural Foundation of the Free State Saxony, VG Bild-Kunst, Fördergesellschaft ZKM/HfG, Stadt Leipzig Kulturamt, Rudolf Augstein Foundation, Stiftung Landesbank Baden-Württemberg, Swedish Arts Grants Committee's International Program (IASPIS)

creative industries fund NL

Königreich der Niederlande

Kulturstiftung des Freistaates Sachsen

SACHSEN

Funded by the Cultural Foundation of the Free State of Saxony. This measure is co-financed by tax funds on the basis of the budget passed by the Saxon state parliament.

Bild Kunst

FÖRDER GESELL SCHAFT ZKM/HfG

RUDOLF AUGSTEIN STIFTUNG

Stadt Leipzig Kulturamt

LBBW Stiftung Landesbank Baden-Württemberg

KONSTNÄRSNÄMNDEN

COLOPHON

Concept and Editing
Anja Kaiser and Rebecca Stephany

Contributions
Clara Balaguer, Ece Canlı, Hackers & Designers, Markus Dreßen, Sara Kaaman, Anja Kaiser, Jungmyung Lee, Sheila Levrant de Bretteville, Vincent Schier, Rebecca Stephany, Franciska Zólyom, students of Karlsruhe University of Arts and Design, students of Burg Giebichenstein University of Art and Design Halle, students of Academy of Fine Arts Leipzig

Published by
Spector Books
Harkortstraße 10
04107 Leipzig
www.spectorbooks.com

Supported by
e.g. books Foundation

Third edition, 2026
Printed in Germany
ISBN 978-3-95905-446-1

Coordination
Vincent Schier

Copyediting
Bryony Quinn, Johanna Schäfer

Proofreading
Bryony Quinn, Vincent Schier, Spector Books

Translation
Good and Cheap Translators

Lithography
Christian Andreas, Lucie Marsmann

Color Profile
Pantone 809, Warm Red, 2735
Color Library
www.colorlibrary.ch

Design
Anja Kaiser, Rebecca Stephany
and contributors

Printing
Gutenberg Beuys Feindruckerei, Germany

DISTRIBUTION

Germany, Austria
GVA, Gemeinsame Verlagsauslieferung
Göttingen GmbH&Co. KG
www.gva-verlage.de

Switzerland
AVA Verlagsauslieferung AG
www.ava.ch

France, Belgium
Interart Paris
www.interart.fr

UK
Central Books Ltd
www.centralbooks.com

USA, Canada, Central and
South America, Africa
ARTBOOK/ D.A.P.
www.artbook.com

South Korea
The Book Society
www.thebooksociety.org

Japan
twelvebooks
www.twelve-books.com

Australia, New Zealand
Perimeter Distribution
www.perimeterdistribution.com

G for *GUD Symposium*, Day 1 *GUD Symposium* Kick-Off Top: 'How to *GUD*' by Anja Kaiser and Rebecca Stephany, introduction and lecture. Bottom: 'Looking Back, Looking Forward or What's Design Got to Do with Undisciplinarity?' by Sheila Levrant de Bretteville, lecture.

G for *GUD Symposium*, Day 2 Compiling the Vocabulary of *GUD* with Lectures and Presentations Top: symposium welcome, with scenography by Diane Hillebrand, Teresa Häußler and Florian Knöbl. Bottom: 'Master's Tools vs. Monster's Tools—Reflections and Strategies on Designing as (B)Othering' by Ece Canlı, lecture.

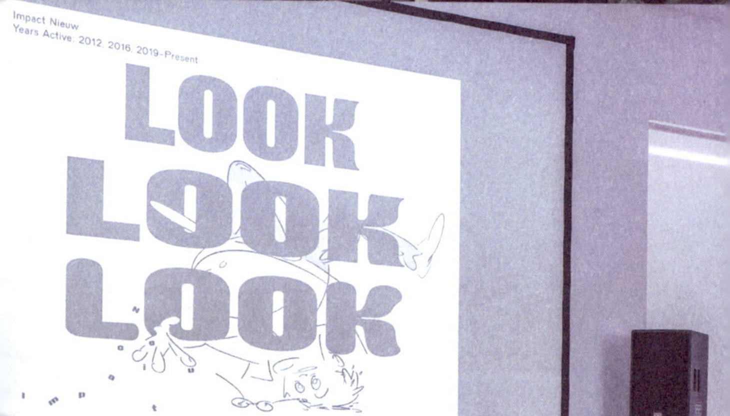

G for *GUD Symposium*, Day 2   Top: 'C for Collective Uncertainties' by Hanna Müller and Mio Kojima with Juliana Vargas Zapata and Severin Geißler. Bottom: 'The Power of Written Language Seen and Felt Through Typefaces' by Jungmyung Lee, lecture. Right: 'F for Failing Queerly' by Severin Geißler, installation and notebooks.

practice more failure
use a tracing guide!
how to draw in the dark?
Failure, of course, goes hand in hand with capitalism ...capitalism... requires that everyone live in a system that equates success with profit and links failure to the inability to accumulate wealth.
(Scott Sandage)
resistance through failure

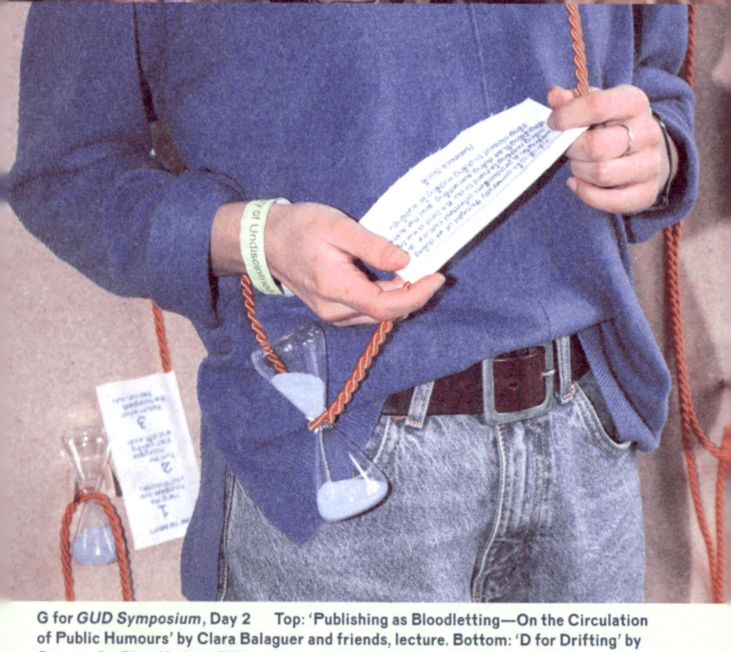

G for *GUD Symposium*, Day 2 Top: 'Publishing as Bloodletting—On the Circulation of Public Humours' by Clara Balaguer and friends, lecture. Bottom: 'D for Drifting' by Severin Geißler, Kathrin Rüll and Arno Schlipf, participatory intervention.

G for *GUD Symposium*, Day 2 Top: 'Challenging Collective Practice—Technical and Collaborative Workings of the H&D Network' by Hackers & Designers (Anja Groten, Juliette Lizotte), lecture. Bottom: '17 Personal Questions Posed to a Set of Rooms, Movements and Machines' by Sara Kaaman, lecture.

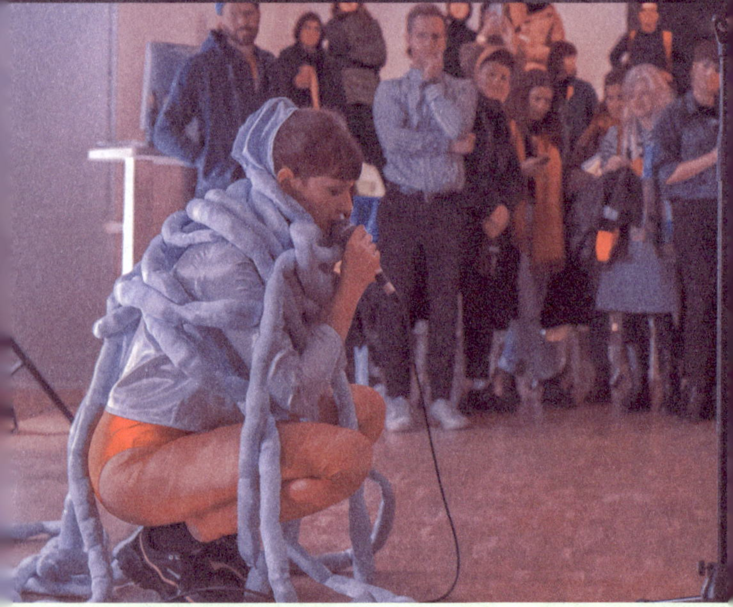

G for *GUD Symposium*, Day 2 Top: 'C for Connecting the Dots' panel with all speakers. Bottom: 'E for Evening Program' with edutainment by students of HfG Karlsruhe and a performance by Juliane Schmitt.

G for *GUD Symposium*, Day 3 Rehearsing the Vocabulary of *GUD* with Workshops and Guided Tours Top: guided tour by students of HfG Karlsruhe and BURG. Bottom: 'Black Box Feedback Loop' workshop with Clara Balaguer.

ONGOING
CARE

G for *GUD Symposium*, Day 3 Top: 'Act of the Role of Typefaces' workshop with Jungmyung Lee. Bottom: 'Imaginary Networks' workshop with Hackers & Designers (Anja Groten, Juliette Lizotte). Left: 'C for Care Advice' by Teresa Häußler, participatory workstation.

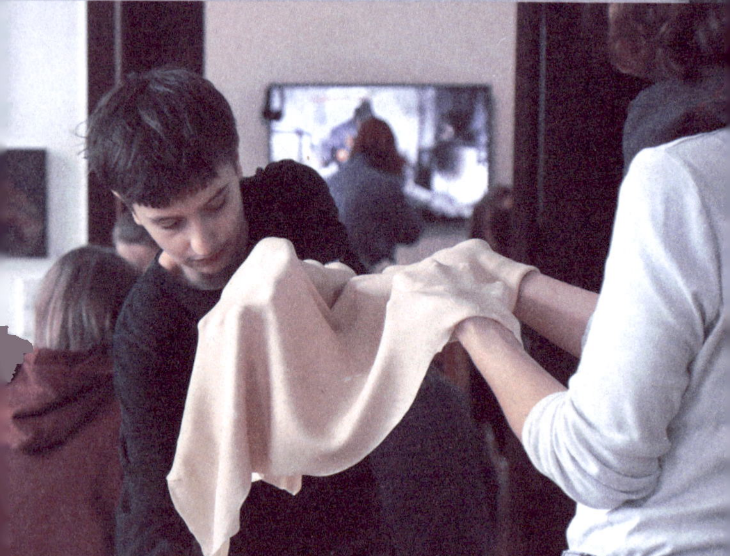

G for *GUD Symposium*, Day 3 Top: 'Soft Logics' workshop with Sara Kaaman. Bottom: 'S for Strudeling' workshop with Severin Geißler, Hanna Müller, Kathrin Rüll and Juliane Schmitt.

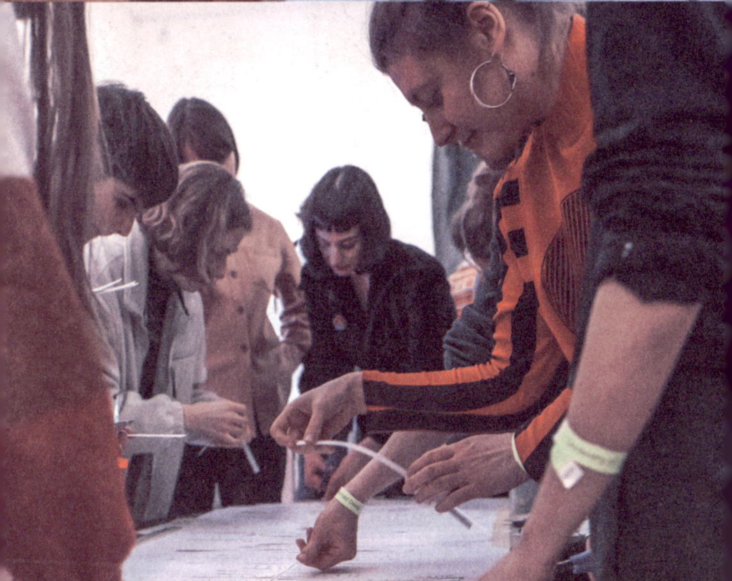

G for *GUD Symposium*, Day 3 Top: 'M for Metabolic Learning' Severin Geißler and Kathrin Rüll, food bar. Bottom: 'Liminal Neologies' workshop with Ece Canlı.